W9-AZP-235

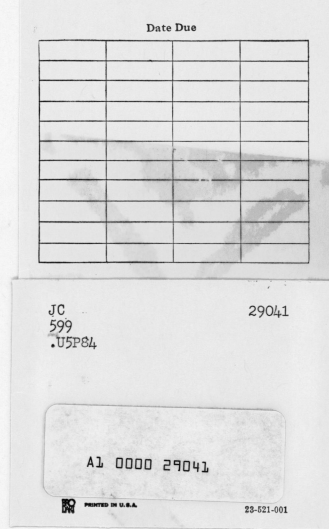

Date Due

JC 599 .U5P84   29041

A1 0000 29041

BRO DART   PRINTED IN U.S.A.   23-521-001

THE PULSE
OF FREEDOM

JC
599
.U5
P8H

Also by Alan Reitman

The Election Process: Voting Laws and Procedures
(with Robert B. Davidson)

The Price of Liberty
(Editor)

290-11

Edited by ALAN REITMAN

THE PULSE
OF FREEDOM

AMERICAN LIBERTIES: 1920–1970s

Foreword by RAMSEY CLARK

W·W·NORTON & COMPANY·INC·

NEW YORK

Copyright © 1975 by W. W. Norton & Company, Inc.
FIRST EDITION
Library of Congress Cataloging in Publication Data
Main entry under title:
The pulse of freedom; American liberties: 1920–1970s.
   Includes bibliographical references.
   1. Civil rights—United States—Addresses, essays,
lectures. 2. United States—Politics and government—
20th century—Addresses, essays, lectures. I. Reitman,
Alan, ed. II. Title.
JC599.U5P84   323.4'0973   74–14613
ISBN 0 393 05527 2

ALL RIGHTS RESERVED
Published simultaneously in Canada
by George J. McLeod Limited, Toronto
PRINTED IN THE UNITED STATES OF AMERICA

1 2 3 4 5 6 7 8 9 0

Contents

Preface

We are living through a period when respect for accumulated knowledge does not occupy the high station it once did. The existentialist emphasis on the current "happening," in the lives of people and of nations, all too frequently downgrades the importance of history, and elevates today's events to the pinnacle of the "real truth." Yet, as knowledge and information are prime requisites in the struggle to achieve and exercise freedom, the past record of personal experience and historical incident is essential. Only if we know the ingredients of the struggle, its depth and breadth, its glories and failures, its human and inhuman elements, can we understand the full meaning of freedom, how it can be won, preserved, and extended.

This maxim applies particularly to the story of civil liberties, a continuing saga throughout history of the individual's never-ceasing effort to attain those "natural rights" which inhere to man despite centuries of subjection to tyrannical rule and oppression. Though it seems, in the torrid pace and proliferating pressures of modern life, a mere wisp in history's memory, the rudiments of due process wrested from King John by England's barons in Magna Carta, or the publishing freedom secured by the end of royal licensing of books, are not too far distant from the here-and-now battles to widen the bounds of fair trial and preserve freedom of the press. Similarly, in our own country, Jefferson's rejection of the Alien and Sedition Acts as violations of free speech and association, and John Brown and the abolitionists' fiery abhorrence of slavery, were

9

the connecting links to the later fight against McCarthyism and to Martin Luther King's moral crusade against racism.

The account of liberty related in these pages does not roam as far back as centuries-old English history. Nor does it describe how, from 1788 through 1790, the seeds of personal rights were implanted in the American Constitution by insistent demands for a Bill of Rights; nor how that tree of liberty flowered in America's dramatic growth and change in less than two hundred years. This book deals with the civil liberties history of the past five decades, a period chosen because it coincided with the fifty-year history of the American Civil Liberties Union when that organization celebrated its half-century birthday in 1970.

Although the idea was conceived then, the book was not prepared, nor should it be taken, as an authorized history of the nation's leading civil liberties organization. The Union's own reports, publications, and activity are testimony to its views of how the rights of people have fared since defense of liberty was put on a full-time organizational basis in 1920. But what the ACLU has done in the past five decades is such an integral part of civil liberties history that any general review must necessarily reflect the organization's actions and opinions. In truth, to tell the story without taking note of the Union's participation, whether praiseworthy or blameworthy, would present the shell without its inner core. This is especially so for the first few decades, when the Union had a near-monopoly in the business of defending rights, and its involvements and leaders were instrumental in shaping the direction and content of civil liberties challenges.

History is not, however, the province of one person or one organization. Neither are its episodes spun separately as loose threads that wind haphazardly on the spool of time. Not only is there an interconnection between past and present events; there is a relationship between these events and what happens to the lives of people, to the strength of nations and the growth or decline of their institutions. From this perspective the recounting of five decades of civil liberties history is best done by historians who not only strongly believe in the cause of human rights, but also possess the sensitivity and objectivity required to connect the unfolding experiences of the half-century struggle for liberty with the imprints these occurrences left on the mind and soul of the nation. With this combination of episodic reporting and resulting impact on the social development of the United States as the criterion, a decade-by-decade division seemed most desirable.

I was fortunate to find five eminent scholar-historians to piece together events and the marks they left, persons generally knowledgeable about civil liberties and well-informed about the particular decade assigned. Professor Paul L. Murphy of the University of Minnesota has written extensively on the development of civil liberties in the World War I and post-war period. Professor Jerald S. Auerbach of Wellesley College analyzed deeply the civil liberties aspects of the thirties for his well-respected *Labor and Liberty: the La Follette Committee and the New Deal.* Professor William Preston, Jr., currently chairman of the Department of History, John Jay College of Criminal Justice, and formerly of Denison University, has contributed numerous articles to professional journals on the meaning of dissent, a subject of keen interest in the war-influenced forties. Professor Emeritus John W. Caughey of the University of California (Los Angeles) is the author of more than twenty books on a variety of civil liberties subjects, most notably loyalty-security and racial desegregation, matters which highlighted the fifties. And professor Milton R. Konvitz of Cornell University, author of *Fundamental Liberties of a Free People* and *Expanding Liberties,* is an internationally recognized scholar. His overview of the sixties is based on long study of constitutional rights and history.

Alan Reitman, editor of this book, is the author and editor of numerous magazine articles and books on civil liberties. Associated with the ACLU for more than twenty-five years, the last seventeen as associate executive director, his intimate knowledge of the spectrum of civil liberties encounters and social struggle provides the basis for interpreting the half-century story of liberty.

In keeping with the civil liberties tradition represented in this book, the authors were free to tell the story as they saw it, with no predetermined editorial conditions or directions. No censorship blinders were placed over them. Their statements, including personal opinions and interpretations, are entirely their own, and should not be taken as representing the position of the ACLU or of the editor. By the same token, the editor's personal views, as expressed in the final chapter, should not be attributed to the Union.

A word on style: the authors' freedom to express themselves as they see fit includes the way in which their material is presented. Some portions dwell heavily on court cases and legal decisions, others stress personalities and institutions, still others concentrate on emerging social movements. To preserve the authors' individual approach to their material, the temptation to unify the chapters by large-scale editing was resisted. The result is a variety of editorial styles and emphases which some readers may find jarring and others refreshing. Whichever is the case, remember that editorial diversity, like other dissimilarities, is the antithesis of conformity and is the touchstone of civil liberties.

No book is ever the final product of a single individual. The loneliest author relies on life experiences, personal relationships—whether fleeting or lasting—and contact with other people to shape the thinking and feeling which eventually emerge as a book.

The Pulse of Freedom was developed in just this manner. Many, many people, some wittingly, some unwittingly, had a hand in its slow but steady development over three years. Thanks first must be expressed to the five authors who gave so fully of their time, not only in the preparation of their own chapters and the necessary revisions, all done by long-distance telephone and the mails in the midst of busy academic schedules, but in general editorial consultation.

My colleagues in the ACLU gave not only encouragement but sound advice and constructive criticism, especially in comments on the final chapter. The list is an illustrious one, comprising all who deeply understand the meaning of liberty and ways of defending it; and including many who were, and still are, jewels in the civil liberties diadem of the five decades: Roger Baldwin, Osmond K. Fraenkel, Aryeh Neier, Norman Dorsen, Alan Westin, Hazel Erskine, Dean Kelley, Joseph Robison, and Arlie Schardt. I especially want to thank Brian Heffernan, who accepted major research assignments with a positive, cheerful, and zestful manner that matched the excellent quality of the valuable data he discovered. Outside the ACLU, the editorial suggestions of Charles Lam Markmann and Emily Garlin were most helpful.

For the long, arduous hours of typing the manuscript, from its inception to the end, much thanks is due several people: Marion Mitchell, Adrian Glass, Chris McDonald, Dorothy Doughty, and Timothy Tyson. Similar gratitude must be expressed to my secretary-assistant, Teddy Neiblum, for assistance in shepherding the manuscript through many rocky organizational shoals, deadline reminders, Xeroxing, and proofing.

Those most close to the person at the center of the editorial project necessarily contribute and also share in the satisfactions and the pains. My family did just that, and grateful appreciation is due them all: my mother, Celia Reitman, whose own strong belief and action in pursuit of social justice certainly was a key factor in leading me to the civil liberties movement, and eventually this book; my brothers and sisters-in-law, Sidney, Norman, Marian, and Syril Reitman, who gave continuous encouragement; and most of all, my wife, Miriam, whose interest, support, patience, and incisive editorial comments not only helped to sustain me but improved the final product; and my daughter, Janet, who understood the absence of her father on "lost weekends" and whose budding appreciation of personal rights and responsibilities provided new insights and invigoration.

Finally, to all those involved in their own quest for liberty, friend and foe alike, people in and outside the American Civil Liberties Union, with whom I have shared common endeavors over the years, my thanks for constantly identifying, refreshing, and shaping the struggle for freedom.

ALAN REITMAN

New York City
March, 1974

Foreword

RAMSEY CLARK

At the outset, I must warn the reader of my bias. Freedom to me is the essential condition for the realization of human potential. The product of a coerced hand or mind, however finely sculpted or skillfully articulated, cannot convey the full unfettered dignity and truth of humanity.

This book is about a spirit common to millions of people who have cared enough to stand up for freedom. It is the spirit of liberty. The history begins in 1920 at the birth of the Union that saved the Union. For better than half a century now the American Civil Liberties Union has provided a main vehicle through which our people have made their individual contributions toward liberation from the repressions of government and society.

The variety of assaults on liberty are seen in these pages to be endless, the techniques of tyranny tailored to the peculiarities and personalities of each epoch. But the threat to freedom has been constant—and never greater than now. The struggle is seen to be not an easy one, the direction often lost.

Our baser instincts tell us to fear freedom because it is uncertain and conducive to change; because it directly exposes truth and disenthralls the spirit of man. For the powerful and the comfortable as well as the frightened and the covetous these are conditions to be avoided. So, down with freedom. And there the struggle begins.

Six eminent scholars and civil liberties experts describe the principal contests of these times between force and freedom. From A. Mitchell Palmer through John N. Mitchell, we witness the uses and abuses of power high and low, the subversion of law to will.

Solid research and meticulously annotated documentation make this volume an essential part of any library that would offer the story of America's pursuit of freedom. Among the *intricacies,* the *complexities,* and the incredible resiliencies of repression in a country which loudly proclaims its devotion to liberty, the broad outline of the nature and substance of that most precious condition can be gleaned. Midst the nitty-gritty of the daily struggle against petty tyrannies and mean coercions, we see finally that freedom has to do with the human spirit.

When Shaw's Devil cynically assures Don Juan, in Hell, ". . . Englishmen never will be slaves: they are free to do whatever the Government and public opinion allow them to do," he really defines tyranny, for the individual can do nothing others do not permit. The illusion of freedom the Devil describes is precisely that most favored by despots.

When Janis Joplin, abandoned by Bobby McGee, cries, "Freedom's just another word for nothing left to lose," she exposes a despair that cannot see its own captivity. Losing sight of the precious worth, the essential human need of personal freedom, we hand our destiny to another. Then we suffer the inner repression of the lost spirit of liberty, a pervasive repression crueler and more stifling than any from without.

Tracing the years of endless struggle, we find that embattled freedom was never more fragile than now. We seek to escape through illusion, or despair. The enormous growth of population seems to destroy the chance for individual worth. Technology proliferates out of control, beyond our capacity to comprehend. The mind boggles at the sheer numbers of our lives. The sweeping, swirling incoherence of change creates yet more turbulence. All give rise to fear. Fear is the ultimate despot.

The vastness of government with its too often insensitive bureaucracies makes due process exceedingly difficult. The sameness of mass media created by a handful, yet the major source of vital information and social mores of tens of millions, threatens the diversity that is the real wealth of humanity.

Technology capable of invasions, even control, of privacy undreamt of by the authors of the Bill of Rights numbs us to the worth of self. Can we understand the catholic, not quaint, wisdom of Emily Dickinson?

> The Soul selects her own Society,
> Then shuts the Door;
> On her divine Majority
> Obtrude no more.

Through all the complexity and confusion, the truth becomes ever harder to find. Unable to find the truth, afraid of it as well, we turn to force. Brute force becomes sovereign. That sovereign employs its dual sanctions, violence and segregation, imperiling survival, destroying freedom and dignity.

The drift toward military government seems barely to concern us. An enormous standing army gives a greater sense of safety. Military surveillance of civilians scarcely outrages us. The assuming of key civilian positions in the Pentagon and White House by military officers is favored as the just desert of heroes. Finally, General Haig, calling the acting attorney general of the United States with instructions from the president to dismiss Special Prosecutor Archibald Cox, a man of law, says, "Your commander in chief orders you." Commander in chief indeed! In a constitutional government, you cannot bend the rule of law with a military command. We have felt the hot breath of tyranny. Did it warm, or chill?

We doubt the capacity of democratic institutions which strive to preserve fundamental human rights to the people. We seek authoritarian solutions. We concentrate power in the presidency. We want decisive, arbitrary action. Freedom becomes the enemy. Do as we say! There appears to be this enormous contest between safety and freedom. We crave safety. Freedom, now called permissiveness, is evil. Our lips curl as we speak the word.

Nothing insures freedom to a place or people. If we are to have it, our major and constant effort must be in creating new means of first preserving, then enlarging the little liberty that remains.

Freedom is the way to find the truth. Change is the fundamental fact of our time. Institutions and individual attitudes must adapt quickly and sensitively to new reality caused by change. Exposure to the truth is the only conditioner that can transform attitudes and institutions through which we can cope with change. Irresistible, inevitable, desirable—perhaps we may see change as the chance for something better and no longer be afraid. The truth can be found only in a state of freedom. Unfettered, curious, skeptical, even heretical inquiry, "wide open, robust, uninhibited," in Justice Brennan's words, can find the truth in time.

We have seen that fulfillment is the flower of freedom and freedom the child of courage. We know courage has been the principal quality we have relied on to secure fredom. But have we understood that courage can only carry the battle, that to overcome we must love?

No inner discipline, however fiercely committed to its concept of freedom, will long preserve liberty for the hated and the feared. Freedom is right because people are inherently good. We have not met an enemy that is us. There is no enemy, there is only us. It is the idea of the enemy, the bad man, the sinister force that we use to deny freedom. Until we overcome our need for enemies, we will fear freedom, and through fear, deny it. The recognition of our common humanity, the equal worth of each person, the love of people is the source of freedom.

This important history illuminates the inadequacy of mere eternal vigilance as the price of liberty. A passionate commitment, constant concern, and steel tradition all premised on a profound understanding of the meaning of freedom are required. But even these will not suffice. Freedom arises from love. Charity in its broadest sense is the essential element.

Freedom is the ultimate gift because it is the chance for fulfillment. It is only a chance, but chance, as Melville tells us, rules both necessity and free will and "has the last featuring blow at events." Given the chance, then, with or without the necessity of circumstance or the will of the driven, fulfillment may be found. Without that chance, neither necessity nor free will can fulfill.

The gift will not be given without love. In its absence, greed, hatred, fear, segregation, and violence, the enemies of freedom, will continue their way of repression. The individual who does not love will not be free of his lesser angels and the society that does not love will deny freedom to the weak, the feared, and the despised.

There is no nobler purpose than the liberation of the human spirit. We should rejoice in the effort and its fond recollection.

But I should not detain you. On with the story of the quest for freedom.

RAMSEY CLARK

New York City
February 1, 1974

THE PULSE
OF FREEDOM

COMMUNITIES
IN CONFLICT

PAUL L. MURPHY

Voluntary bodies devoted to the protection of human rights and human dignity have an honorable history in America, extending well back into colonial times. Nineteenth-century Americans particularly embraced collective, paternalistic efforts in behalf of groups as divergent as the pre–Civil War slave, the disenfranchised woman, and the exploited child. Such programs were extended in the early twentieth century through the Anti-Imperialist League, the American Birth Control League, the National Association for the Advancement of Colored People, and the American Jewish Congress.

The emergence of a national movement to achieve civil liberties for all Americans had to await World War I. A Free Speech League had been organized a few years earlier, but its founder, Theodore Schroeder, had been principally opposed to censorship and divergent restrictions on individual freedom. He particularly opposed laws governing beachwear and prohibiting Sunday music concerts, and set out to abolish licensing provisions for certain trades and professions. And while a handful of Americans did indeed find such restrictions oppressive, the failure of the League to win either significant legal battles or a significant following is indicative of its greater failure to come to terms with the real threats to Bill of Rights freedom which existed at that time.[1]

World War I repression drew together a number of concerned Americans who feared both it and its consequences, and who were prepared to act collectively to oppose both. Both, they correctly felt, were unprecedented. Prior to the Wilson administration's massive war-time program of conscription, espionage legislation, sedition laws, censorship and deliberate surveillance of the mails, and frequent repression of critics of the government,[2] federal authorities, reading the Bill of Rights fairly literally, had not passed laws restricting freedom of speech, press, assembly, or religion. Rather, with the exception of the early, unpopular, and generally repudiated Alien and Sedition Acts, and the federal Comstock Law, banning obscenity from the mails, they had left social control of deviant activities in the hands of the states and local communities. Federal power had been used to curtail labor unrest in the strikes of the late nineteenth century, and federal troops had been sent in to preserve law and order when local authorities seemed incapable of containing an explosive situation. But both circumstances involved principally cooperative law enforcement and not the development of federal programs restricting individual freedom.

World War I brought the specter of something new. Not only did the federal government extend its law-enforcement

[1] For a revealing contrast between the civil liberties views of Schroeder and Roger N. Baldwin, especially during the war period, see the correspondence between the two in the American Civil Liberties Union papers (Reel 1, November 27 and December 7, 1917), New York Public Library.

[2] On the Wilson administration's civil liberties record see: Joan Jensen, *The Price of Vigilance* (Chicago, 1968); William Preston, *Aliens and Dissenters* (Cambridge, Mass., 1963); Horace C. Peterson and Gilbert C. Fite, *Opponents of War, 1917–1918* (Madison, Wis., 1957); and Harry N. Scheiber, *The Wilson Administration and Civil Liberties, 1917–1921* (Ithaca, N.Y., 1960).

machinery into suppressing local actions deemed hostile to the war effort, but the body of legislation enacted to extend such federal authority seemed to imply, as one of its congressional critics commented, "not only a distrust of the people but a resort to methods of the very nations against which the war was being conducted." [3] Referring to the Espionage Act, another stated the position of a significant body of opposition by contending that "a more autocratic, more Prussian measure could not be found in Germany. It has all the earmarks of a dictatorship, and suppresses free speech, and does it all in the name of war and patriotism." [4] "I am charged with radicalism for opposing government repression," said Senator William E. Borah of Idaho, "but it is radicalism which consists in the attack principally upon those who use the Constitution of the United States when it protects them, and trample upon it when it comes in their way." [5]

Yet the war period saw a triumph of just such Americans. And their victims were numerous. Pacifists, conscientious objectors, aliens, and recent immigrants, especially those with German names, were harassed and intimidated both by those charged with enforcing the war-time legislation and by self-appointed super-patriots who on occasion took the law into their own hands. More ominously, radicals, particularly members of the Industrial Workers of the World (IWW), the Socialist Party, and the Non-Partisan League, long the subject of conservative hostility and animosity, now afforded their enemies the justification for striking devastating blows at both their leaders and members. For while their overt anti-war stances were logical projections of their general philosophies, cast as unpatriotic interference with the war effort these stands quickly became grounds for patriotic repression of the entire group.

The American Union Against Militarism had emerged in 1915 as a body hopeful of preventing United States involvement in the European war. By 1917, such hopes had been

[3] Peterson and Fite, pp. 16–17.
[4] Claudius O. Johnson, *Borah of Idaho* (Seattle, 1967), p. 214.
[5] *Ibid.*

shattered, yet the AUAM still served as a rallying point for those opposing governmental war-time excesses.[6] Early in 1917, Roger N. Baldwin, a Harvard-trained social worker and former secretary of the National Probation Association, joined the staff of the organization. He was instrumental in establishing a Civil Liberties Bureau within it to handle the numerous Bill of Rights violations brought to the AUAM.[7] In time, the Bureau became independent, operating as the National Civil Liberties Bureau with a board of its own and with the professed purpose of undercutting wartime suppression by fighting to preserve freedom of speech, press, association, and conscience, particularly in conscientious objector cases.

The NCLB, for example, urged President Wilson, albeit unsuccessfully, to prevent congressional attempts to destroy the German-language press in America; fought Postmaster General Albert S. Burleson's frivolous control and vigorous censorship of the mails; and, despite its limited resources, attempted to utilize legal action to undercut mob violence, particularly against Americans who openly denounced the war. The government, apparently sensitive to such criticism, raided the NCLB's offices in September, 1918, and seized all of its files. Subsequently Roger Baldwin was called for military service, which, as a conscientious objector, he refused. There being no alternative service at the time, he was prosecuted and sentenced to a year in prison.[8] The Bureau's direction was then assumed by Albert DeSilver, a New York lawyer, who han-

[6] Donald Johnson, *The Challenge to American Freedoms* (Lexington, Ky., 1963), pp. 8–9; Charles Chatfield, *For Peace and Justice* (Knoxville, Tenn., 1971), pp. 21–30.

[7] The literature on Baldwin, while often more adulatory than objective, is voluminous. See R. L. Duffus, "The Legend of Roger Baldwin," *American Mercury* (August, 1925), pp. 408–14; "Galahad of Freedom," *World Tomorrow*, XIII (January, 1930), 33–36; Travis Hoke, "Red Rainbow," *North American Review*, 234 (November, 1932), 431–39; Oliver Jensen, "The Persuasive Roger Baldwin," *Harper's*, 203 (September, 1951), 47–55; Dwight MacDonald, "The Defense of Everybody," *New Yorker*, 29 (July 11 and 18, 1953), 31–55, 29–59; and Willie Morris, "Barely Winded at Eighty: Roger Baldwin," *New Republic*, 150 (January 25, 1964), 8–10.

[8] For his statement at the time of his sentencing see Lillian Schlissel, ed., *Conscience in America* (New York, 1968), pp. 142–49.

dled the work of the body admirably in the period toward the end of the war and immediately afterward.[9]

This proved to be a crucial time, not only in the history of the NCLB, but in the history of civil liberties generally in the United States. The federal government, which had ruthlessly prosecuted the leaders of pro-labor, social-action radical groups during the war, made clear in the early post-war period its intention to continue supporting the suppression of strikes, their leaders, and the working people who joined in them. While such activity was conducted largely by the Justice Department, with Attorney General A. Mitchell Palmer playing the key role, Congress also set out in 1919 and early 1920 to enact peace-time sedition legislation to authorize continued surveillance of critics of the American system.[10]

Thirty-five states, fearing that such actions were not enough, passed their own repressive laws in the form of either criminal syndicalism statutes, sedition acts, or "red flag" measures (barring the display of revolutionary flags). All seemed aimed particularly at labor and champions of labor who advocated advanced programs of industrial democracy and social justice.[11] The success of powerful economic interests in breaking all the major strikes of this period, largely through the wholesale denial of civil liberties combined with federal and local governmental eagerness to jail or deport or in lesser ways harass those advocating labor militancy, made clear to civil libertarians both their post-war need and challenge.

Roger Baldwin, who after his emergence from prison had participated briefly in organizational work in the great steel strike of 1919, had clear ideas regarding the most pressing demands in the civil liberties area. A philosophical idealist, Baldwin was a tactical realist with a primary interest in social ends. He was convinced that any group which was to attain full civil liberties within American society had to do so by

[9] On DeSilver see Walter Nelles, *A Liberal in Wartime* (New York, 1940).

[10] On the movement for such legislation see Paul L. Murphy, *The Meaning of Freedom of Speech* (Westport, Conn., 1972), Chaps. 4, 5, *passim*.

[11] Eldridge F. Dowell, *A History of Criminal Syndicalism Legislation in the United States* (Baltimore, 1939).

gaining sufficient power to resist suppression. "Those who
have economic power," he was fond of proclaiming, "have
civil liberties and civil rights." But the road to such power was
a rough one, with success clearly tied to the ability to articulate common purposes and to mount successful group action
for their attainment. Here Baldwin saw a role for the newly
founded American Civil Liberties Union, which was formally
organized in January, 1920. "We are not concerned to promote
any radical program, or the causes of any class," Baldwin
stated at the time. "But the circumstances of industrial conflict
today force us chiefly to champion the rights of labor, to meet,
organize, strike, and picket because labor is the class whose
rights are most attacked." [12]

Such work, Baldwin hoped, would be carried out by three
groups: those directly engaged in the labor struggle, who
knew the facts first hand and who represented large constit-
uencies; those who by their writing and speaking were
close to labor problems; and those who stood, on general principles, for freedom of expression. As to techniques, the ACLU
played down political pressure and legal activities ("The
courts do not help much as protectors of rights, for judges
write economics as well as law, and usually on the side of
established property relationships") [13] and emphasized the
technique of direct intervention and manipulated test-cases.
This included particularly the molding of "free speech fights"
in the areas of industrial conflict where employers were clearly
restricting civil liberties. This politics of confrontation—forcing civil liberties where suppression existed or could be
expected to be produced—would, it was hoped, both dramatize the extent of the denial of basic Bill of Rights freedom
and arouse the conscience of concerned middle-class Americans to support remedial action.

Such a program was approved by the governing board of
the new body, which was, in many ways, a microcosm of those
Americans concerned with civil liberties in the United States

[12] American Civil Liberties Union, *The Fight for Free Speech* (*Annual Report*, No. 1, 1920–21), pp. 4–5.
[13] Roger N. Baldwin, "The Myth of Law and Order," in Samuel D.
Schmalhausen, *Behold America!* (New York, 1931), p. 664.

in the 1920s. The old pacifist-oriented Board of the National Civil Liberties Bureau was transferred in its entirety to the new ACLU, and maintained an ongoing interest, particularly in freeing political prisoners still in jail for anti-war expression. But the forty-five other individuals who joined the group gave it a distinctly different flavor. Such people included many pro-war liberals, and ranged from social workers and reform-minded churchmen to businessmen, college professors, lawyers, authors, and publishers. Despite Baldwin's hope, only twelve of the ultimate sixty-four members were labor people, with only fifteen decidedly pro-labor in their general views.[14]

Thus, while the new body's proposed "dramatic campaign of service" to labor was not disputed, there was strong sentiment that such a campaign should not be conducted at the expense of meaningful action against other clear threats to civil liberties. These included especially the excesses of federal repression arising out of fears of the successful Russian Revolution; the deportation of aliens for their radical beliefs; the challenge of the Ku Klux Klan; and the continued pattern of local suppression of personal freedom in everything from censurious assaults on political and social unorthodoxy to direct action against individuals whose behavior offended the local militant majority. Such forms of civil liberties violation were clearly evident in the case of Negroes, Indians and other ethnic minorities; but also in the harassment of authors, publishers, educators, and a broad range of political and social nonconformists.

The national civil liberties situation in January, 1920, made clear the need for such an organization. At few times in American history were the forces of reaction so completely in the saddle. As the ACLU pointed out in its first annual report,

> The revolutionary changes brought about by the war and industrial conflict are nowhere more apparent than in the new machinery for the suppression of opinion and of tra-

[14] For a general analysis of early membership patterns, especially of the Board, see Barton Bean, "Pressure for Freedom: The American Civil Liberties Union" (doctoral dissertation, Cornell University, 1955), pp. 158 ff.

ditional minority and individual rights. That machinery consists chiefly of the reactionary decisions of federal and state supreme courts, the growing use of injunctions in labor disputes, the sweeping provisions of state sedition and criminal syndicalism laws, an array of city ordinances and police regulations restricting free speech and assemblage; the arbitrary power of the Post Office Department over the press and the mails, state constabularies and private gunmen, and the lawlessness of such organizations as the American Legion and the Ku Klux Klan.[15]

Behind that machinery stood the property interests of the country, so completely in control of the political system as to establish in effect a class government and verify Calvin Coolidge's remark of the time, "the business of America is business."

Yet within a few months certain signs of encouragement reached civil libertarians. The overkill tactics of the Palmer raids (arrest and deportation of aliens because of their political beliefs) produced a national backlash, particularly among citizens fearful of the reestablishment of powerful central government in a period which they hoped would bring a return of laissez-faire practices. Businessmen joined lawyers and noted journalists in viewing with alarm the flouting by government officials of accepted legal guarantees, practices, and procedures. The election of Warren G. Harding in November, even though campaign leaders had successfully obscured contemporary civil liberties issues, nonetheless evoked a landslide vote for policies of governmental noninterference. This led Albert DeSilver, a few months after the new president's inauguration, to comment favorably on the March, 1921, repeal of the war-time sedition act, and to observe with some relief that "the new attorney general [Harry M. Daugherty] is a nice fat man with a big cigar in his face, and instead of getting excited as Palmer used to do, he grins when somebody talks about revolution and says, well he thinks it probably best 'not to agitate the agitator' too much." [16]

[15] ACLU, *The Fight for Free Speech*, p. 4.
[16] Quoted in Nelles, *Liberal in Wartime*, p. 204.

Yet such policies in no way lessened the need for vigorous civil liberties action. Indeed, the ACLU had already begun to take part in 1921 in a series of conspicuous free speech fights in such places as the textile town of Passaic, New Jersey; the steel city of Duquesne, Pennsylvania; conservative and wealthy Mount Vernon, New York; and several smaller Connecticut communities, where the ACLU had joined with the Socialist Party to force a favorable decision through the state Supreme Court forbidding discrimination against speakers on public streets.

The more sustained campaigns for free speech of the early years of the decade concerned themselves heavily with overt forms of suppression, both past and current and also threatening future developments. In the first category came the ongoing commitment of many Americans to the struggle for amnesty for war-time civil liberties victims. The issue raised not only immediate problems for devoted civil libertarians, but forced them into considerable soul-searching. The injustice of the situation was pointed out clearly by many leaders of the period.

A bitter editorial in the *Washington Times* possibly summarized it best by arguing that "all of the war-time profiteers, wealthy draft-dodgers, and capitalists who had defrauded the government on war-time contracts had not so much as tasted penalty, while the radicals whose 'crime' had been primarily speech were still in jail." Such an example, the writer contended, "could hardly encourage a public image of a nonpartisan government." [17] The issue also had immediacy. With social unrest prevalent, and national labor problems brewing, government arbitration would very likely be necessary. It was thus essential that the government reestablish itself as an impartial agent. This it could best do by recreating an atmosphere of respect both for government and for basic American traditions. Yet the question of which were the best tactics to induce the government to adopt such a policy remained.

Sensitive civil libertarians in the government had actually

[17] Quoted in General Defense Committee, *Public Opinion: Where Does It Stand on the Question of Amnesty for Political Prisoners?* (Chicago, 1924), pp. 5–6.

begun to take action. In 1919, two members of the Justice Department, John Lord O'Brian and Alfred Bettman, had reviewed numerous cases. They so drastically reduced sentences in two hundred of them that prisoners went free in a short time. Contemporaneously, numerous amnesty committees were formed to work for the release of the remaining prisoners. The Central Labor Bodies Conference for the Release of Political Prisoners was created to rally the labor movement behind the cause. For a time it looked as if the 1920 convention of the AFL would endorse release, and resolutions were introduced calling for a total amnesty. But conservative union leaders, fearing the radicalism of many prisoners, balked at blanket endorsement, leaving the CLBC to appeal to individual locals throughout the country for financial and moral support. During the 1920 presidential campaign both major candidates talked of the desirability of general amnesty for political prisoners, a refreshing switch from Woodrow Wilson's hard-line opposition to such a move ("I contest the accuracy of any statement that the rights of a single citizen have been unjustly invaded").[18] But if Warren G. Harding was indeed approachable on the question, concerned civil libertarians were determined to prod him toward amnesty, and not pardon.

The distinction was a basic one. Amnesty involved formal recognition that the crisis during which it was unsafe to exercise the right to criticize no longer existed. It would constitute a restoration of liberty for all those who had been restrained during the alleged emergency. Pardon carried with it no such implications. It simply implied that the "wrongs" of expressing unpopular views were to be forgiven. Amnesty, therefore, revitalized free speech; pardon rejected it.[19] Political prisoners, it was hoped, would be released in spite of their unpopular utterances, which would show that the nation had returned to the essential position that dissent was still alive and protected. But such a posture, while high-sounding, and meaningful in the abstract, ran afoul of certain human aspects

[18] See Johnson, *Challenge to American Freedoms*, p. 177.

[19] For a contemporary delineation of this difference see Oswald Garrison Villard, "Why Amnesty Matters," *The Nation*, 114 (January 25, 1922), 87.

of the situation. It presumed that imprisoned men were fully prepared to sacrifice themselves to the abstract cause of free speech and to refuse pardon on the basis of repentance. It further assumed that those officials in a position to release such individuals were fully wrong from the outset and that critics of the war had been unjustly punished.

The case of Eugene V. Debs was a peculiarly poignant example of the problem. Debs had not only gone to jail for his opinions during the war. He also had run for the presidency while in the Atlanta Penitentiary in 1920 and had polled nearly a million votes. He was now an old man, in ill health and a national figure for whom a broad range of public sympathy existed. Harding and his attorney general, Harry M. Daugherty, were alert to the situation. Harding was prepared to pardon Debs but, on Daughterty's advice, was reluctant to grant amnesty. "To make Debs a martyr to free speech and a conspicuous example of illegal war-time prosecution," Daugherty argued, was very risky.[20] Rather, the attorney general saw the opportunity of turning Debs's release into a gracious act of mercy to a sick man, thereby undercutting the amnesty crusade before it had gone too far.

Thus, although twenty-four other men were actually released with the ailing Socialist leader on Christmas Day, 1921, civil liberties champions were greatly disappointed by the action. Such release failed to recognize the principle of free speech they were trying to establish. Public reaction to such a posture, however, was disturbingly hostile. It ultimately became so sharp that leaders of the campaign qualified their insistence on amnesty and agreed to work for individual pardons in individual cases. This, however, displeased numerous IWW members in Leavenworth who were dedicated to maintaining the amnesty position for which they had suffered long and bitterly. They particularly assailed Roger Baldwin and the ACLU for, on the one hand, allegedly pretending to stand for civil liberties, and, on the other, urging them to waive those civil liberties through the pardon process. Even under such fire, however, the Union continued to submit frequent ap-

[20] Preston, *Aliens and Dissenters*, p. 259.

plications to the Justice Department asking for the release of the prisoners.

Happily, other pressures were being felt at the White House. Al Smith, upon taking office for a second term as governor of New York, in his initial message to the legislature in January, 1923, called for repeal of that state's repressive postwar Lusk laws, and a restoration of complete freedom of expression. His statement encouraged defenders of various prisoners arrested during the "red scare" (of the Palmer and local red-raid era) under the old New York criminal anarchy law to seek their immediate release. This Smith very shortly granted, coupling pardon with a strong statement that "political progress results from the clash of conflicting opinions." National opinion was generally favorable. "We are still listening," wrote *Collier's Weekly,* in response, "for President Harding to say about the political prisoners in Leavenworth words as bold and ringing as those of Governor Al Smith." [21] And with further prodding from Senators William E. Borah and George W. Pepper, Harding responded with pardons, which, however, required that any man so pardoned promise to be "law-abiding . . . and not encourage, advocate, or be willfully connected with lawlessness in any form."

After Harding's death, Calvin Coolidge surprisingly extended the process. In December, 1923, he recommended release of the remaining prisoners. This action also drew widescale commendation. Civil libertarians and a variety of national leaders hailed it as a vindication of the right of free speech and free press, and editorial comment widely praised the president for restoring the principles of American democracy. For ACLU leaders this was both a tenuous victory and a bitter disappointment. They hastened to proclaim publicly that the president's action recognized fully the principle of freedom of speech. Yet Coolidge's failure to remove the restrictions imposed by Harding upon earlier releases was a setback, and the fact that a number of state political prisoners still languished in various penitentiaries indicated the further need for vigorous local campaigns.

[21] "Fresh Air Blows Away Hot Air," *Collier's Weekly,* LXXI (February 10, 1923), 16.

The sum total of this crusade, then, was somewhat ambiguous, yet also didactic. If victims of repression were to become merely agents for the attainment of abstract principles, civil libertarians ran the risk of seeming callous toward human needs. If, on the other hand, human needs were placed first, the ability to claim that abstract principles had been obtained somewhat compromised the alleged *raison d'être* of such bodies as the ACLU. Thus, as in so many of the campaigns in the 1920s, the Union, and civil libertarians generally, found themselves accused by the right of using free-speech symbolism as a camouflage for putting over the radical movement, and by the left for being so involved with abstract principles as to be unable to work effectively to achieve progressive social ends.

Such a dilemma arose far less clearly in two major contemporary labor clashes with strong civil liberties overtones, one in the coal mining region of West Virginia, the other in the iron fields of Pennsylvania. In each, employers used the law to exploit working people and undermine their protests by denying them basic civil liberties guarantees. The West Virginia mining areas were an especially dangerous powder keg and afforded civil libertarians a good, nationally observed arena in which to try out the politics of confrontation.

As was typical of the period, the labor movement in that area had been encouraged as a result of war-time gains, and the United Mine Workers hoped to expand organizational work among the miners. Mine operators were just as adamantly opposed to any further unionization and, in fact, hoped to undo that which had already taken place. The operators also had a tremendous advantage. Eighty percent of the workers in the coal mining counties of Logan and Mingo lived in company-owned, company-financed, and company-dominated towns, carefully monitored by local authorities subservient to the mine owners. Operators could thus easily enforce rules prohibiting miners from inviting union organizers into their homes, which, given carefully enforced restrictions against public meetings, meant the inability to publicize the union's cause in any fashion.

In early 1920, UMW officials decided to confront the local

establishment. The ACLU and Roger Baldwin promptly offered full cooperation, seeing clearly the right of free speech
and freedom of assembly involved. Baldwin hired a free-lance
journalist, John L. Spivak, to represent the ACLU and to assist
in organizing a free-speech campaign in Logan County.
Spivak was shocked at what he saw of mine-owner tyranny.
Realizing that the unionization campaign would have to fight
not only the mine owners and their hired gunmen but the
state's Democratic governor, John J. Cromwell, who fully
sympathized with them, Spivak wrote New York for strongly
worded posters and pamphlets designed to arouse the workers by putting the issue in civil liberties terms. The New York
office, then manned by Albert DeSilver in the temporary
absence of Baldwin, was disturbed. Posters reading "The
Thugs and Gunmen of Logan County Must Go!", DeSilver
felt, were too violent and provocative and he urged the circulation of materials of a far more "quasi-judicial nature."
Spivak was both annoyed and amused. Writing to Roger
Baldwin on his return, he suggested that those in the New
York office were apparently

> willing to do anything which would not hurt their tender
> feelings about civil liberties. They are still under the im-
> pression that there is some semblance of legal procedure
> here. There is not. You can't hold a meeting here, get
> pinched and then fight it out in the courts. If you try to
> hold a meeting in the southern counties, you'll never live
> to see the courts. . . . The State is on the verge of civil
> war, due to the suppression of the Constitutional rights of
> free speech and free assemblage. That's where you come
> in—or rather are supposed to come in, for the Union, be-
> sides sending me down, has *not* come in.[22]

Local events underlined the validity of his position. As the
UMW organizational campaign began to make some head-
way, miners who joined were systematically fired and evicted

[22] Donald Johnson, "The American Civil Liberties Union: Origins,
1914–1917" (doctorial dissertation, Columbia University, 1960), pp.
307–8. See also John L. Spivak, *A Man in His Times*, (New York,
1967), pp. 56 ff.

from company-owned property by company-employed detectives. Eventually a violent confrontation occurred, with the mayor of the town of Matawan, a detective official, and six deputies, as well as three union men, shot to death. The Matawan Massacre promptly made national headlines and produced demands for federal intervention.

Prompt protests were filed on behalf of the UMW with Governor Cromwell, President Wilson, the secretary of labor and the attorney general. All quickly hedged, with the federal officials insisting it was a local matter and local officials insisting that the union troublemakers were to blame. Two dozen such troublemakers were promptly arrested and charged with perpetrating the episode. The UMW assumed responsibility for their defense, and the ACLU agreed to manage the publicity for the trial, hopeful of thereby showing its sincerity in its willingness to support the miners and the UMW as well as the abstract principles of freedom of speech and assembly.

The risk paid off. The trial was eventually held before a jury of local miners who were secretly delighted to strike a blow at their perennial exploiters. The union men were freed. Emboldened, the UMW decided to respond to the growing evictions by calling a strike. The operators promptly imported black and foreign-born strikebreakers, and civil war again developed, this time in Mingo County. Woodrow Wilson, responding to pleas from Governor Cromwell, sent federal troops to the area to put down local violence. Again protests were heard from across the country, but to no avail. In the meantime, a local court issued a temporary injunction against further union recruiting. Such biased governmental action, however, drew further national criticism, and before the fall election Wilson withdrew the troops, hoping to recreate an image of impartiality.

Harding's sympathies in this situation parallelled those of his predecessor. The new president had no comment when a new Republican governor declared martial law and used the milita to break up union meetings and suppress the local UMW newspaper. Civil libertarians were insistent upon federal action, however, and their demands brought response in

the form of a Senate investigating committee which set out
to hold hearings in the mining area. Such action did not come
soon enough. Goaded to the point of violence by company
tyranny, a force of four or five thousand evicted and discharged miners, many of them army veterans, began a carefully planned assault upon Logan County with the intent of
taking the law into their own hands and ending company control. Although their march was eventually dispersed, the
Senate hearings were reconvened, and a desultory report was
issued blaming both sides (the miners for unjustified violence,
the operators for using paid sheriffs and deputies, which the
committee branded "a vicious un-American policy").[23]

The most important result of the struggle was under the
surface. Operators, realizing that coal could not be dug by
strikebreakers in an atmosphere of constant violence, softened
their own policies. Although the ultimate result was largely
stalemate, operator respect for union resources was enhanced,
enabling the ACLU to claim that exploitation through the
denial of civil liberties could no longer go on. The ACLU thus
emerged from the conflict having won considerable respect
from the workers for its willingness to fight in their behalf in
a situation which took courage and pertinacity. The ultimate
payoff came in 1924, when a new Republican governor, Howard M. Gore, took office. With a liberal attorney general joining him, a suit was brought in the Circuit Court of Charleston
attacking the Logan County system of armed guards paid
by the companies and deputized as sheriffs. The result undercut the atmosphere of intimidation and onesidedness which
had prevailed earlier, when state authority had been so clearly
lined up behind the operators.

The Pennsylvania situation, while similar in many ways,
had important civil liberties variations. In this, one of the
most employer-oriented states in the country, the coal and
steel concerns had emerged from the great strikes in those
industries in 1919 with virtually unqualified victories and
tacit assurances of further strikebreaking support, not only
from their own local government lackeys, but from state and

[23] U.S., Congress, Senate, Committee on Education and Labor, *Personal Views of Senator Kenyon et al.* (Washington, 1922), pp. 6–7.

federal authorities as well. The one aspect of the situation which it was felt might be exploited was public revulsion with the excesses of owner autocracy. Here basic denial of civil liberties guarantees was the most flagrant symptom. Further, if this issue could be successfully exploited, the potential pay-off was great. The state contained probably the largest number of economically depressed citizens in the country who were not only being denied their basic civil liberties, but were so intimidated that they were reluctant to protest such denial for fear of reprisals. To assist them in gaining the protection of their basic civil liberties was not only important, but could have valuable side benefits as well.

The activities of the Pennsylvania Coal and Iron Police were particularly outrageous. Recruited and paid by the companies, but commissioned and given official sanction by the state, the organization was largely composed, as a later report authenticated, of men "of a character which permits them to viciously club and shoot men who are entire strangers— peaceful pickets." [24] And their brutal record of violence over a fifty-year period led local workingmen to refer to them as "Cossacks." In 1905, partially on the pretext of replacing this unpopular force, the legislature set up the Pennsylvania State Constabulary, the first state police force in the country. The real motivation, however, had come from employer complaints that the National Guard had not behaved satisfactorily during the great anthracite coal strike of 1902–3. The meaning of the move quickly became clear. No serious attempt was made to disband the Coal and Iron Police, but rather an early working arrangement grew between that body and the new constabulary so that workers were now terrorized by two organizations instead of one. To make the repressive situation virtually complete, the press of the state was almost entirely employer-oriented. Civil liberties advocates had great difficulty obtaining accurate reports of local conflicts, and even more in getting their own activities correctly reported, a situation which was more the rule than the exception throughout the country during the decade.

[24] John P. Guyer, *Pennsylvania's Cossacks and the State's Police* (Reading, Pa., 1924), p. 21.

The tactics followed in challenging this monolith paralleled those used in West Virginia. Civil liberties leaders made clear early their willingness to assist in any way possible challenges to local repression, and volunteered to enter closed towns to foment free speech fights and challenge the legitimacy of civil liberties violations. They also raised national demands for a federal investigation of the denial of civil liberties throughout the state. When President Harding appointed a United States Coal Commission in September, 1922, to study the problems of the coal industry, the ACLU, noting that its membership was almost totally pro-management, joined with the League for Industrial Democracy in sponsoring a joint Committee of Inquiry on Coal and Civil Liberties to supply facts concerning violations of civil liberties to the federal commission. This unofficial Committee of Inquiry included such figures as Zechariah Chafee, Jr., of the Harvard Law School; national liberal Catholic leader Father John A. Ryan; the Reverend Arthur Holt, social service secretary of the Congregational Church; and Kate H. Claghorn of the New York School of Social Work. It later published its findings in a widely distributed pamphlet by Winthrop D. Lane entitled, "The Denial of Civil Liberties in the Coal Fields." [25] The action undoubtedly prodded the federal commission to include the civil liberties question as part of its concern and to concede that "free travel, free speech and public assemblage have been practically abridged" in parts of the coal fields, before hastening to add: "Men have, of course, the inalienable American right to go into strange communities and diagnose the evils under which the community suffers and offer remedies for a cure. But many times it is not expedient to exercise this right. Men not connected with the industry have no right to make inflammatory speeches leading to the use of violence." [26] The Commission further made clear that it felt no responsibility to take any action which might affect the civil liberties situation.

[25] Winthrop D. Lane, *The Denial of Civil Liberties in the Coal Fields* (New York, 1924).

[26] U.S., Congress, Senate, *Report of the United States Coal Commission,* 68th Cong., 2nd sess., Sen. Doc. 195, Part I (Washington, 1925), pp. 176, 179.

But operators were not merely content to sit back and have others shield them. In April, 1923, a squad of federal Department of Justice agents, working closely with city police and county detectives (a number in the pay of the companies), staged a "red raid" on Worker's Party headquarters in Pittsburgh, ransacking the files, seizing party leaders, and holding them without bail for ten days. The Pittsburgh newspapers quickly fell into line, announcing that a "May Day plot" had been nipped in the bud. But the ACLU wired a strongly worded protest to the newly elected governor, Gifford Pinchot, calling the action a flagrant violation of the right of freedom of speech. The newspapers cleverly ran the story of the ACLU wire with another report indicating that the arrested workers had planned to dynamite public buildings, wording the story in such a way as to seem that the ACLU was protesting against the arrest of persons intent upon violence. As a further gratuitous display of local power, city police raided the home of the chairman of the Pittsburgh branch of the Labor Defense Council, arresting the chairman and two New York attorneys who were residing with him while preparing briefs for the arrested workers.

Governor Pinchot, however, had a long career as a champion of social justice and was anxious to restore reasonable public control. Although concentrating initially upon arbitrating a bitter labor dispute over wages, he indicated his intent to appoint a commission to explore critically the relationship between the Coal and Iron Police and the State Constabulary; this indicated to civil libertarians that Bill of Rights guarantees might, for the first time in years, have some chance of being respected in the state. Emboldened, civil liberties leaders Reverend Harry F. Ward and Arthur Garfield Hays went to Pennsylvania, intent upon pushing the issue of public meetings to further dramatize civil liberties needs.[27]

The report of Pinchot's commission provided the needed fillip. A devastating exposé of company tyranny, it listed in detail over a hundred cases of lawless violence by public officials in the single strike year of 1922. These revelations put

[27] Hays tells the story colorfully in his book *Let Freedom Ring* (New York, 1928), pp. 102 ff.

such officials on the defensive. They were anxious to erase
the image of tyranny surrounding them, so many then moved
quickly to allow dissent, protest, picketing, and, for the first
time in memory, even expressions of anti-company sentiment.
Thus, even though much company control was reasserted
when Pinchot, unable to succeed himself as governor, was
forced to step down, the fact that there had been a period of
respect for personal rights encouraged local laboring people
and local civil libertarians to resist a total return to pre-war
industrial feudalism.

Heartening as the recognition of dissent and protest was in
the Pennsylvania episode, new stormclouds gathered over
First Amendment rights. The Bridgman, Michigan, Communist
case of 1922–23 raised questions regarding future potential
suppression of dissident expression. Again, the situation had a
variety of intricate and intriguing civil liberties overtones.
Millions of Americans had found Attorney General A. Mitchell
Palmer's "red raids" of early 1920 offensive and threatening
both to the Bill of Rights and, indirectly, to themselves. If
the federal government was to flout such basic guarantees
as the right to counsel and protection against unreasonable
search and seizure, to deny bail and habeas corpus, and to
deport aliens merely for their political beliefs, it was time to
blow the whistle on that government. And, despite Palmer's
loud protestations to a congressional committee that "loyal
Americans could easily see that the sole purpose of the Department of Justice had been to enforce the law fairly and
impartially," [28] many local citizens agreed with attorney Swin-
burne Hale when he concluded that Palmer's position was
"compounded of false testimony and equivocal boasting." [29]
Such a view was further validated when Federal Judge
George W. Anderson, in the 1920 decision of *Colyer* v. *Skeffington,* reversed many convictions, stating categorically that
the Palmer raids had been a "sordid and disgraceful spectacle." [30]

But although Palmer left office discredited in the eyes of

[28] Johnson, *The Challenge to American Freedoms,* pp. 162.
[29] *Ibid.*
[30] *Colyer* v. *Skeffington,* 265 Fed. 17 (1920). See Johnson, *The Challenge to American Freedoms,* p. 163.

millions of Americans, his successor, Harry M. Daugherty, had no intention of withdrawing from politically advantageous harassment of radicals and militant labor leaders. Under his rule, the "radical division" within the FBI remained intact, and its director, William J. Burns (head of the profitable Burns Private Detective Agency), continued to use undercover agents to keep track of the political acitivity of radicals. One of the organizations of which Burns was most suspicious was the American Civil Liberties Union. Burns was convinced, despite Daugherty's doubts to the contrary, that the ACLU was one of the most dangerous radical organizations in the country, and his agents continually monitored its mailing list, its literature, copies of its minutes, and the speeches of Roger Baldwin. Such action was also carried out regarding a wide range of radical organizations from Communist bodies to militant labor unions.

By mid-1922, Burns was inspired to more aggressive action. In mid-year Daugherty, in an effort to break a national strike, had thrown the support of the Justice Department against the railroad shopmen, urging the massive use of injunctions to prevent both strike action and sympathetic expression of support for the strikers. Despite bitter criticism and a move by one congressman to impeach Daugherty for interfering with fundamental rights of free speech and press,[31] the strike was broken. Burns was pleased at his own success in intimidating and curtailing strikers, and in late August he moved on his own. At the time, he was badly in need of a situation which would demonstrate the necessity for further large congressional grants for the "radical division." Since disruptionist radical activities in the country had virtually disappeared, Burns had been reduced to hysterical statements regarding "red infiltration of all aspects of American life—education, religion, the news media, even the movies and vaudeville." [32] But he desperately needed some evidence other than rhetoric.

Communism in the United States at the time constituted an

[31] Johnson, *The Challenge to American Freedoms*, p. 165.

[32] U.S., Congress, House, Committee on the Judiciary, Hearings, *Charges of Hon. Oscar E. Keller Against the Attorney General of the United States* (Washington, 1922), p. 2.

ineffective, faction-ridden dialogue among a few thousand alien radicals and native American malcontents. Its leadership had rejected the tack of infiltrating existing labor unions and workers' groups to gain power through direct economic pressure. A bitter internal dispute was raging over whether a combined body should seek open legal status as a formal organized political party or small factions should operate as splinter groups underground. In the hope of arriving at some common policy, a secret convention was scheduled at Bridgman, Michigan, in August, 1922. The group that met was sharply divided.[33] William Z. Foster, organizer of the 1919 steel strike, was only reluctantly allowed to attend since his desire to work through economic coercion was a path which had previously been rejected.

Into the midst of this debilitating and acrimonious confrontation Burns sent secret agents, who managed to arrest a few fleeing delegates and gather up a number of documents representing proposals for divergent and often contradictory tactics. Aroused civil libertarians, sensing an opportunity to expose Burns for what he was, promptly offered defense to the arrested Communists and decried the seizing of delegates and Party records and materials as a serious threat to the rights of free speech and assembly. ("The essence of the charge against the men is that, holding Communist views, they dared meet together for discussion. While we thoroughly disagree with the Communist attitude toward free speech, with their melodramatic secret tactics and with their talk about revolutionary violence, we shall defend their right to meet and speak as they chose.") [34]

Frank P. Walsh, a co-signer of the National Popular Government League's devastating indictment of the Palmer raids, agreed to serve as counsel. Skillfully casting the whole issue as a free speech question and charging federal agents with the

[33] On the background of Bridgman see Theodore Draper, *The Roots of American Communism* (New York, 1957), pp. 345 ff.; and Irving Howe and Lewis Coser, *The American Communist Party* (Boston, 1957), pp. 98 ff.

[34] *New York Call*, December 16, 1922, quoted in Johnson, *The Challenge to American Freedoms*, p. 167.

intention of suppressing basic guarantees, Walsh succeeded in more than convincing the courts to free Foster and other seized leaders. He used the occasion to introduce a witness who testified at length regarding Palmer's and Burns's role in the "red scare" and who contended that the whole episode had been used to shake down business firms for protection money through the creation of false hysteria and unwarranted apprehension. The same witness charged that the Justice Department, in the Bridgman situation as in the Palmer raids earlier, had actually written many of the seized documents upon which the Communists were now being tried.[35]

Undaunted, in a subsequent appearance before the House Appropriations Committee Burns insisted that the Bridgman raids had proved that "radicalism is becoming stronger every day in this country." He further linked its growth with the increasing influence of the "parlor Bolsheviks," whom he maintained had "sprung up everywhere, as evidenced by this American Civil Liberties Union of New York. Wherever we seek to suppress these radicals," Burns complained, "a civil liberties union promptly gets busy." [36] But the shrillness of Burns' charges, the lack of hard evidence of destructive activities, and the embarrassment his actions were causing both the Department and the government, meant that his days were numbered. "He is the only man in the United States," editorialized Pulitzer's *New York World,* "who can still see that famous Red revolution coming."

> He has called attention to it repeatedly; he has shown that liberals are capturing some of the colleges; that radicals are occasionally allowed to speak on street corners, that the Civil Liberties Union has defended free speech for communists as well as for other people. But he has

[35] "Charges Inciting of Red Outrages," *New York Times,* February 13, 1923, p. 1; "Death Threats Here Laid to Burns Man in Spy Testimony," *New York Times,* February 14, 1923, p. 1; See also "Memorandum of Albert Balanow" and "Deposition of Albert Ballin Alias Albert Balanow," February 12–17, 1923, *Frank Walsh Papers* (New York Public Library).

[36] U.S., Congress, House, Subcommittee on Appropriations, *Department of Justice Appropriations, 1925* (Washington, 1924), p. 93.

failed miserably to arouse the citizens to a sense of their own danger. They are not aware of the cateclysm impending. It is the tragic fate of Mr. Burns that nobody is aware of it but himself.[37]

The revelation of the scandals of the Harding administration, with particular emphasis upon malfeasance in the Justice Department, created a level of public indignation which brought major changes. Among Calvin Coolidge's first appointees was a new attorney general, Harlan Fiske Stone, former dean of the Columbia University Law School and future chief justice of the United States. Among the first to fly before Stone's new broom was William J. Burns. In naming his successor, Stone made clear that the Bureau of Investigation was to be taken out of politics. Far more significantly, from the standpoint of civil liberties, Stone ordered an end to the Bureau's radical-chasing activities. In a public statement on May 14, 1942, Stone said:

> There is always the possibility that a secret police may become a menace to free government and free institutions because it carries with it the possibility of abuses of power which are not always quickly understood. . . . It is important that [the Bureau of Investigation's] activities be strictly limited to those functions for which it was created and that its agents themselves be not above the law or beyond its reach. The Bureau is not concerned with political or other opinions of individuals. It is concerned only with their conduct and then only with such conduct as is forbidden by the laws of the United States.[38]

The action, warmly welcomed by a majority of Americans, removed the executive branch of the government from the task of monitoring opinion and public expression and made it possible for civil liberties proponents to channel their major en-

---

[37] *New York World,* February 9, 1923, p. 8.

[38] American Civil Liberties Union, *The Nation-Wide Spy System Centering in the Department of Justice* (New York, 1924), pp. 2–3. See also Max Lowenthal, *The Federal Bureau of Investigation* (New York, 1950), p. 298.

ergies into confronting more local and subtle forms of repressive action.

These kinds of repression the decade did not lack, however. The Ku Klux Klan, revived at the end of the war, flourished both in the South and in a number of Northern areas as well. In its second annual report, the ACLU indicated that Klansmen were responsible for a variety of incidents involving intimidation of individuals and denial of their rights (one official inquiry in the state of Oklahoma alone showed over two thousand cases of mob violence by the Klan in two years, with not a single Klansman prosecuted or even apprehended).[39] The report noted, further, that most of the victims were white. Attempts to suppress Non-Partisan League and IWW speakers were also noted. Margaret Sanger was consistently harassed when she attempted to stage rallies and meetings for the American Birth Control League. William Z. Foster was run out of Denver by vigilantes. The Italian editor Carlo Tresca was jailed and his anti-Mussolini newspaper, *Il Martello,* assailed when the pro-Fascist Italian Embassy in Washington singled it out for suppression. Anthony Bimba, a Lithuanian newspaper editor, who had denounced prayers and Bible reading in the public schools (a practice required by law in seventeen states) as being just as indefensible as the priest-ridden government of Lithuania, which, he said, ought to be overthrown, was indicted for blasphemy under a 229-year-old Massachusetts law written by Cotton Mather; when that charge did not stick he was convicted of sedition. From a broader policy standpoint, the local police in numerous communities seemed to be the officials with major discretion to determine who could speak and what subjects could legitimately be discussed. This fact was made clear by an ACLU study in 1921 entitled: "The Police and the Radicals: What Eighty-eight Police Chiefs Think and Do about Radical Meetings."

The problem of supplying constructive support to counter widely divergent examples of local repression was a pressing one for civil libertarians generally, and especially for the Union, given its small budget, its overworked staff, and the difficulty of finding attorneys outside of the New York area to

[39] Schmalhausen, *Behold America!,* p. 663.

take its cases. A major episode in Los Angeles in May, 1923, however, suggested new approaches.

Los Angeles, like many major cities in that decade, was tightly controlled by conservative businessmen particularly hostile toward unions and the threat of union power. The newspapers, along with the American Legion and the Commercial Federation of California, a right-wing, anti-radical body shortly to change its name to the Better America Federation, fully endorsed the employer's use of the police against union activity, particularly when such measures were considered "preventive." Thus, when in 1922 and 1923 IWW activity picked up and a campaign was launched to release state political prisoners, undermine "fink halls" (anti-union employment offices in various areas), demand repeal of the state's criminal syndicalism law, and gain higher wages on the San Pedro waterfront, the local police were ready to move.

IWW troublemakers began to be picked up and held, generally without bail, from late 1922 on. Employer-hired mobs assisted the police with vigilante actions. When in late April, 1923, a longshoremen's strike was called, police turned back IWW members attempting to join the demonstration. They arrested and ordered out of town as many strikers as could easily be separated from their colleagues, raided IWW halls, seizing leaders and confiscating literature, and eventually announced that in the interests of public security no more street meetings would be permitted in the waterfront area. Street meetings continued, however, now taking on the character of free speech meetings. The police broke these up with regularity, packing Los Angeles jails with those workers who attended the meetings, and soon bullpens had to be built to accommodate the growing number of prisoners.

Writer Upton Sinclair had been a member of the ACLU since its organization in 1920. He and several prominent citizens obtained permission from the mayor of Los Angeles to hold a free speech meeting in San Pedro. Sinclair informed the chief of police of his intent to read the Bill of Rights and the Constitution at "Liberty Hill," a vacant lot that had been made available to the strikers by its owner. A warning by the chief of police, Louis D. Oaks, that "this Constitution stuff does not go at the harbor," further convinced Sinclair that "to challenge such lawbreakers in office . . . was the highest duty that a citizen of this community can perform." [40] Hauled from the platform after they had tried to speak, Sinclair and three others were hurried off and held incommunicado for eighteen hours. Their lawyer, John Beardsley, later a judge of the Superior Court of Los Angeles, tried frantically to discover where they were being held. He finally succeeded in serving a writ of habeas corpus, and the next day all were released. Sinclair promptly launched a public attack upon the legal authorities, and the ACLU filed suits against the police for damages for unlawful arrest. These were dropped with the release of all but twenty-eight of the six hundred IWW's then being held and private assurances of no further persecution of prisoners.

Not content merely to have won his legal point, Sinclair and his supporters immediately rented a large auditorium in Los Angeles and scheduled a series of open meetings to express public grievances. Crowds were so large many were turned away. The meetings underlined the need for a permanent watchdog over California civil liberties, and from those in attendance came promises of support for a Southern California branch of the ACLU. The Reverend Clinton J. Taft, a Congregational minister, resigned from his pulpit to serve as regional director, a post he held for over twenty years.

Sinclair also was able to extract from Los Angeles authorities promises to remove the chief of police and several of his more heavy-handed deputies. Civic leaders agreed that they had given the city of angels a black eye and wanted to "wipe the slate clean." Oakes' immediate successor moved quickly to soft-peddle the Department's anti-radical activities and to create a new image of tolerance and effectiveness.

Unfortunately, the image was temporary. Although the immediate strike was settled, police continued to harass IWW's through the remainder of the decade. Spurred on by the Bet-

[40] *The Autobiography of Upton Sinclair* (New York, 1962), pp. 229–30. See also Martin Zanger, "Politics of Confrontation: Upton Sinclair and the Launching of the ACLU in Southern California," *Pacific Historical Review*, 28 (November, 1969), 389–90.

ter American Federation, the city established a special "red squad" charged with keeping the city free of "subversives" of all sorts. Ernest J. Hopkins, in summarizing the report of the Wickersham Commission, which investigated the abuse of law enforcement machinery late in the decade, found Los Angeles police, stirred by "hysterical propaganda," unable to "distinguish between the economic dissenter and the criminal." [41] Yet the membership of the new ACLU chapter grew as police repression continued. With efficient organization and considerable support, and through the pages of its paper, the *Open Forum,* the chapter often served as the conscience of the community, remedying overt examples of overzealous repression. Further, the example of a local affiliate handling local civil liberties problems was a model gradually emulated in other parts of the country as the decade progressed.

The two most dramatic challenges to repressive local economic power before the Depression both occurred in New Jersey, a state where exploitation of labor, particularly immigrant workers, approached the level of Pennsylvania. Each campaign was carried on in the spirit of confrontation politics designed to achieve broad worker emancipation. Paterson had been the scene of labor disputes and concomitant police repression since well before World War I. In strikes in 1913 and 1919, men had been sentenced to jail for freedom of expression, leading the ACLU executive committee to state: "Paterson is almost unique among industrial communities in this form of police dictatorship backed up by local officials and the courts. We regard ourselves as commissioned to stop it if we can." [42]

Thus, when in August, 1924, six thousand members of an independent local, the Associated Silk Workers, went out on strike, and the police chief suddenly closed their organizational headquarters, preventing strike planning and strike meetings, the civil liberties group moved in. The result was a violent

[41] Ernest J. Hopkins, *Our Lawless Police: A Study of the Unlawful Enforcement of the Law* (New York, 1931), p. 154. See also United States National Commission on Law Observance and Enforcement, *Report on Lawlessness in Law Enforcement* (Washington, 1931), XI, pp. 143 ff.

[42] ACLU, *Unlawful Assembly in Paterson* (New York, 1925), p. 11.

confrontation between the police and several hundred strikers. Roger Baldwin and five of the strike leaders were arrested for unlawful assembly under a 1796 New Jersey unlawful assembly law, never tested in a court, but available as a potential club over any form of public meeting unsavory to local officials. Baldwin was indicted by a grand jury under the blanket charge of instigating hundreds to disturb the public peace and thus violate the unlawful assembly statute.

The Ku Klux Klan of Passaic County passed a resolution endorsing a proposal to the mayor for deporting troublesome strikers. But the local and national press headlined the episode as an unwarranted example of local tyranny, and so castigated the local police chief that he was forced to open the strikers' hall and guarantee them the right of peaceable assembly through the remainder of the strike. Baldwin's conviction was eventually reversed by the New Jersey Supreme Court. The decision also voided the statute, sharply narrowing the basis for an arrest on the grounds of unlawful assembly in the state. The ACLU hailed the action as "the only liberal state supreme court decision in a civil liberties case in recent years." [43] And even the conservative *New York Times* grudgingly admitted that Baldwin had established an important point of law in undercutting the arbitrariness of local police rule.

In neighboring Passaic, two years later, in probably the most significant strike situation of the decade, ACLU members found themselves working in a united front with Communists, Socialists, and local textile workers in a year-long effort to bring some relief to the beleaguered and disgracefully exploited woolen textile operators. The most pressing civil liberties aspect of the situation involved constant police assault upon picket lines, mass meetings, and union halls, with the local sheriff eventually using what he termed "riot law" to forbid peaceable assembly. Since the authorizing law provided for the reading of the Riot Act only when trouble was clearly brewing, his action, although totally unwarranted, did provide a green light to move on strikers at any provocation. From here on police began dispersing crowds even before meetings could start.

[43] ACLU, *The Victory in New Jersey* (New York, 1928), p. 3.

Socialist leader Norman Thomas, prominent in the civil liberties-conscious League for Industrial Democracy, now set out to force the riot law issue by speaking in defiance of it. Hauled from a tree stump and held for ten thousand dollars bail, Thomas was released when a grand jury refused to indict him; he then brought suit against the officers responsible for his arrest. After a U.S. Senate investigation of the situation was urged, an injunction was obtained preventing the sheriff and his deputies from interfering with either the holding of meetings or peaceful picketing. From then on the strikers were unmolested. But although the strike dragged on and —despite national support, particularly from concerned religious leaders—was eventually terminated with only minor gains for the workers, the effectiveness of the free speech argument was again demonstrated as an immediate challenge to tyrannical and unjustified physical oppression and intimidation.[44]

With Passaic, and with their successful participation in a Colorado coal strike the following year,[45] civil libertarians had gone far to establish their legitimacy with working people as a concerned and useful ally in their causes. Writing in 1929 in a national publication, *The Social Work Year Book*, Roger Baldwin saw the role as an ongoing one. "Of the infringements of civil liberties against which organizations in this field protest," he pointed out, "nine out of ten involve rights which labor asserts in its contest with employers or with civil authorities." [46] The formation at this time by civil liberties advocates and labor leaders of a National Committee on Labor Injunctions, designed particularly to put pressure on Congress to undercut the widespread use by judges of injunctions to

[44] On Passaic see Morton Siegal, "The Passaic Textile Strike of 1926" (doctoral dissertation, Columbia University, 1952); "The Passaic Strike: A Study in Contemporary America," *Christian Century*, 153 (August 5, 1926), 964–90; and Paul L. Murphy, *The Passaic Textile Strike* (Belmont, Calif., 1974).

[45] On the Colorado situation see Donald J. McClurg, "The Colorado Coal Strike of 1927," *Labor History*, 4 (Winter, 1963), 68 ff.; and American Civil Liberties Union, *The War on Colorado Miners* (New York, 1928).

[46] Roger N. Baldwin, "Civil Liberties," in Fred S. Hall, ed., *Social Work Year Book, 1929* (New York, 1930), p. 85.

inhibit strike activities, indicated growing support for assailing unwarranted interference with successful organized worker action. And other avenues of legal redress were also being explored during the twenties in the hope of finding effective weapons against other forms of local repression.

One source of encouragement came from the United States Supreme Court. Although that body had not, in its previous history, demonstrated serious interest in enforcing Bill of Rights guarantees against the states, both Justices Oliver Wendell Holmes, Jr., and Louis D. Brandeis, the great dissenters of the decade, began suggesting immediately after World War I the serious desirability of moving in this direction.[47] Liberty, they argued, and particularly the liberty of the due process clause of the Fourteenth Amendment, had to mean more than the liberty to acquire and enjoy property. And in a case in 1923, voiding a Nebraska statute prohibiting teaching in any language other than English, a majority of the Court took steps in this direction.[48]

[47] The immediate post-war cases testing the convictions of outspoken opponents of the war and war-time policies for sedition brought a significant reinterpretation of the free speech and free press guarantees of the First Amendment, while affording little joy to civil libertarians. Holmes, in rendering the first case (*Schenck* v. *U.S.*, 249 U.S. 47 [1919]) set forth his "clear and present danger" test, which he hoped would draw sensitive lines between permissible critical speech and fomenting direct action dangerous to society, which he acknowledged to be punishable under emergency (e.g., war-time) conditions. He and Brandeis quickly deplored the early "translation" of the test into a device for suppressing any expression which had a "tendency" to elicit an unfortunate response. (*Frohwerk* v. *U.S.*, 249 U.S. 204 (1919); *U.S.* v. *Debs*, 249 U.S. 211 (1919); *Abrams* v. *U.S.*, 250 U.S. 616 (1919); *Schaefer* v. *U.S.*, 251 U.S. 468 (1920); *Pierce* v. *U.S.* 252 U.S. 239 (1920). Their dissenting protests against continued utilization of such a restrictive interpretation were in vain throughout the 1920s, however, with the situation tempered only by the fact that the federal government sought no suppression of speech and press during the decade, leaving such matters to state and local governments. It was not until the late 1930s that a new Court restored the "clear and present danger test" to a Holmesian meaning and began using it as a liberal device for the protection of critical expression. For a discussion of these cases see Paul L. Murphy, *The Constitution in Crisis Times, 1918–1969* (New York, 1972), pp. 23–25.

[48] *Meyer* v. *Nebraska*, 262 U.S. 390 (1923).

Sensing a sympathetic ear, civil libertarians in 1920 threw their resources behind a challenge to the 1902 New York Criminal Anarchy Act, a measure under which a prominent radical, Benjamin Gitlow, had been indicted in 1920, during the "red scare" era, for circulating material urging mass revolutionary action by workers. The Supreme Court was clearly impressed, particularly by an eloquent brief and argument by civil liberties attorney Walter Pollak. Although it ruled that the 1902 act, as it applied to Gitlow, did not unduly restrict freedom of speech or press, it accepted the view that the due process clause of the Fourteenth Amendment could include the freedoms guaranteed in the First Amendment. Two years later, the high court invalidated a similar state criminal syndicalism act as applied because it violated free speech as protected through the due process clause, although the Court shied away from a firm enunciation of a general rule of law on that point.[49]

By 1931, however, the Court, now under new leadership, did complete the first stage of "nationalizing" the Bill of Rights. It clearly brought freedom of speech under its protection in the Stromberg case, voiding key sections of California's "red flag" law [50] and extended its protection to freedom of the press in another landmark ruling, *Near* v. *Minnesota*,[51] striking hard at the principle of prior restraint on publication. Both cases, along with the anti-injunction provisions of the Norris-LaGuardia Act of early 1932, were logical culminations of the civil liberties activities of the 1920s, and the Supreme Court's rulings afforded civil liberties advocates important new legal weapons in the war against undue local repression.

Non-economic or non-labor aspects of the civil liberties scene, however, did not go unattended. The 1920s was a period of rapidly changing social values, as manifested in

[49] *Fiske* v. *Kansas*, 274 U.S. 380 (1927). The case involved an organizer for the IWW, by that time virtually devoid of influence, particularly in the Midwest.

[50] *Stromberg* v. *California*, 283 U.S. 359 (1931).

[51] *Near* v. *Minnesota*, 283 U.S. 697 (1931). The case was cited heavily in various of the opinions in the famed *New York Times* Pentagon Papers case of the early 1970s, *New York Times Co.* v. *U.S.*, 403 U.S. 713 (1971).

everything from the flapper, the hip flask, the open roadster, the movies and radio, to commercialized sport, organized crime, and a general rebellion of youth. It was not surprising then that conservative members of the old order and Babbits alike fought against such tendencies by attempting to utilize traditional forms of social control to contain if not repress them.

Thus, the decade was marked by an almost frantic campaign of censorship which took overt form in banning books, closing movies and plays, attacking textbooks in the school, and blacklisting controversial speakers. But more covert forms of pressure were applied to publishers, book dealers, school administrators, organizations prepared to sponsor meetings on controversial topics, jurors, and, needless to say, members of minority groups or aliens who were attempting to claim rights which some members of the WASP majority felt they did not deserve or were not ready to utilize responsibly. The problem of black Americans was typically bad. Laws prevented them from voting in ten states and from marrying whites in thirty. In seventeen they were segregated in schools or in public conveyances and public assemblies. In the South they were frequently bound to a job by legal penalties against anyone attempting to "entice" them from their labor—legislation designed to prevent their migration North.

The task of monitoring such denials of basic rights and liberties, particularly in their more subtle forms, was monumental. The ACLU's interests were so clearly political-economic, and so geared to the rights of anti-militarists, labor, and radicals, that it was only as the decade progressed that the body began concerning itself with other kinds of challenges. Thus, much of the active civil liberties leadership came from organizations more specifically concerned with special forms of repression. In some important instances,— the Sacco-Vanzetti case being a significant one—it came from ad hoc or one-issue bodies. The National Association for the Advancement of Colored People handled many of the problems of black Americans, particularly in voting and housing discrimination. The American Jewish Congress and the Anti-Defamation League fought overt manifestations of anti-

Semitism. The American Association of University Professors concerned itself with questions of academic freedom. Various anti-censorship groups and literary bodies rallied to confront crises of censorship, actual or threatened. Significant co-operative activity did occur, however, and new and more general support developed for the activities of all such groups.

Many liberal groups joined with Al Smith and other New York leaders in fighting the repressive Lusk laws, which contained a variety of restrictions on teachers, including loyalty oaths and demands for promises to teach only what was conservative and patriotic. Similarly, there was broad support for court action against state laws banning the teaching of German in the schools, and KKK-sponsored legislation seeking to eliminate parochial education by making public school attendance obligatory.

The most well-known civil liberties venture of the 1920s was the Scopes "monkey trial" in Dayton, Tennessee. It was planned by the ACLU as a challenge not only to Tennessee's anti-evolution law, but to governmental threats to freedom of speech and thought, academic freedom, and religious liberty generally. The situation was, in many ways, a microcosm of the type of repression indiginous in the average American community. The Tennessee legislature had enacted a statute forbidding the teaching of evolution or any other theory denying the Biblical legend of the Creation. The ACLU's advertisement for a teacher prepared to defy the law not only brought a prompt response, but eventually a dramatic, headline-making confrontation between Clarence Darrow and William Jennings Bryan.

It also brought to focus the talents of a galaxy of legal leaders, scholars, and scientists. But ultimately, a jury of ten fundamentalist farmers, a teacher, and a shipping clerk brought in a verdict of guilty. Teacher Scopes was fined one hundred dollars. He appealed to the state supreme court, which upheld the law but reversed his conviction. This prevented the case from going to the United States Supreme Court.[52] Nonetheless, the case alerted many citizens to the serious threat

[52] The literature on the episode is vast. See especially Ray Ginger, *Six Days or Forever?* (Boston, 1958); Jerry R. Tomkins, *D-Days at Dayton* (Baton Rouge, La., 1965); and John T. Scopes, *Center of the*

of a state legislature exerting its right to control public instruction in the interests of a particular religious group or dogma.

Challenges were also brought against the common local practice of making school buildings and facilities available to patriotic and right-wing groups, but denying them to those of a liberal or left-wing persuasion. And in probably one of the most scandalous cases of the decade, the ACLU succeeded in getting a Seattle judge to reverse an earlier action in which a nine-year-old boy had been evicted from school for refusing to salute the flag, but not before the boy had been taken from his Jehovah's Witness parents and kept for a year and a half in a state children's home, with his parents denied the right to visit him.

Mary Ware Dennett, a Brooklyn mother who had long been an active worker for social reform, had made a short compilation of elementary sex information for her two adolescent sons. The material was subsequently published in the *Medical Review of Reviews* in 1918 and was so well received that the editor persuaded Mrs. Dennett to reprint it in pamphlet form for general use. The pamphlet, called *The Sex Side of Life: An Explanation for Young People,* and contained straightforward descriptions of the human sex organs and their functions. Widely and continuously circulated for years, it won the approval of many educational, religious, and welfare organizations, including the YMCA. As early as 1922 it was banned from the mails by the Post Office Department under the antiobscenity Section 211 of the postal code. But Mrs. Dennett had continued to mail it under first-class seal, making its distribution virtually non-profit for her.

In 1928 the Post Office Department, as the result of an alleged complaint by a member of the Daughters of the American Revolution, brought a court action against Mrs. Dennett. The case, heard in 1929 before a clearly hostile judge, was prosecuted by a remarkably vindictive and obtuse government attorney. But despite the able efforts of Morris Ernst, an outspoken and eloquent opponent of censorship, a jury of

Storm (New York, 1967). For a general overview of the problem see Norman F. Furniss, *The Fundamentalist Controversy* (New Haven, Conn., 1954).

stolid Brooklyn elders (whose ideas of sex, one commentator remarked, "must have been gleaned solely from studying the growth of rubber plants") [53] found Mrs. Dennett guilty. She was fined three hundred dollars or three hundred days in jail. The decision brought varied reactions. Local Comstocks were delighted, but national sympathy for Mrs. Dennett and her plight was overwhelming. *The Sex Side of Life* was clearly so rational and praiseworthy in intent that its suppression aroused the ire of many people whose interest in earlier censorship conflicts had been minimal. The Dennett conviction, editorialized the *New Republic*, "demonstrates why, in other cases, where our sympathies may not be so thoroughly involved, it is necessary to fight for civil liberties." [54] Apparently, an important lesson had belatedly been learned.

The lesson was not lost on the ACLU. Uninvolved in the literary censorship skirmishes of the decade, the ACLU's concerned itself largely with assaults on unpopular political and economic opinions. For example, it had consistently supported the defense of Sacco and Vanzetti, convinced that they were being prosecuted chiefly because of their anarchist views, and had intervened in visa cases such as those of Karolyi and Saklatvala.[55] In 1929, however, the ACLU set up a National

[53] Morris Ernst, *The Censor Marches On* (New York, 1940), p. 41.

[54] Quoted in Paul S. Boyer, *Purity in Print: Book Censorship in America* (New York, 1968), p. 241.

[55] Count Karolyi, who had been the first president of the Hungarian Republic, wanted a visa to visit the United States and see his wife, who was ill. The State Department granted the visa (and Karolyi arrived, January 8, 1925) on condition that Karolyi takes a pledge that "he would not engage in political activity of any kind" while in the United States. The historian Charles A. Beard, protesting this in *The Nation* (April 1, 1925), commented that the State Department first refused Karolyi permission to speak or write, but later modified its dictum to the the extent of permitting him to speak, but not on politics. The ACLU gave a luncheon in his honor at the Hotel Astor on March 7, 1925, attended by 600 persons, at which Beard was the speaker. Later the ACLU sought unsuccessfully to get the "political speech" ban lifted.

Saklatvala, a Communist M.P. from the London borough of Battersea, was to accompany a delegation of M.P.'s to the Inter-Parliamentary Union Conference in the United States in August, 1925. At the last minute his visa was cancelled.

Mary Ware Dennett Defense Committee to publicize the case and raise funds. It hoped to challenge the right of the New York and Boston police departments, the Post Office Department, the Customs Service, and local-appointed and self-appointed censorship groups, operating under standards of their own making, to determine the legitimate reading fare of the American public. The Union's efforts bore fruit in March, 1930, when a United States district court, in a decision written by Judge Augustus N. Hand, overturned the lower court conviction and exonerated Mrs. Dennett and her pamphlet. The decision, followed by the famous ruling three years later by Judge John M. Woolsey in the *Ulysses* case, marked the first substantial steps toward the undermining of frivolous local censorship standards and the substitution of national standards based upon rational considerations and the broader public interest.[56]

As the nation was plummeted into the Depression of 1929, the civil liberties climate in the country changed sharply. The ACLU had begun its 1928–29 Annual Report talking of the quietness of the year, but observed also that "wherever a strong fight is put up, the chances of gaining rights sought are better than in recent years."[57] One year later it noted "the largest crop of court cases involving civil liberties in any entire year since the war."[58] This was blamed generally upon a wave of official suppression of the militant activities of the Communist Party and left-wing strikes. ACLU leaders, however, were also quick to point out that while business in previous halcyon years had been content to utilize the services of far-right-wing publicists and super-patriotic groups to discredit its critics, by the Depression it had turned more and more to direct action. Industrialists now preferred to spend their money for company guards, labor spies, strikebreakers, and arms.

[56] For Woolsey's ruling see *U.S.* v. *One Book Called "Ulysses,"* 5 Fed. Supp. 182 (1933), and Boyer, *Purity in Print,* pp. 256 ff.

[57] ACLU, *The Fight for Civil Liberty* (Annual Report, No. 8, 1928–1929), pp. 3–4.

[58] ACLU *The Story of Civil Liberty* (Annual Report, No. 9, 1929–1930), p. 3.

Once again the development raised new questions of practical tactics for civil libertarians. With business now determined to muzzle its critics, and even a congressional committee, under New York congressman and legionnaire Hamilton Fish, called to investigate far-left activities in the hope of blaming the Depression on radicals, the wisdom of continued resort to confrontation politics was clearly thrown into doubt. Further, the actions of Communists during a series of strikes in the Southern textile areas raised serious questions as to whether continued united front actions, at least on Communist terms, was any longer fruitful as a path for achieving civil liberties.

Particularly instructive was the strike of textile workers at Gastonia, North Carolina, in early 1929. Fred Beal, a worker and organizer fresh from a labor struggle in New Bedford, Massachusetts, had been designated by the Communists to fight a potential wage cut at Gastonia's huge Loray Mill as a step toward organizing the plant. When the company discharged those who joined his cause, a strike resulted. The National Guard was sent in by the governor, himself a mill owner, ostensibly to maintain law and order, but actually to assault striking workers and their headquarters. Over the summer months, seven strikers were killed, twenty-four wounded, seven kidnapped and beaten, and scores arrested.

But local grand juries were unable to find evidence to indict anyone, until worker retaliation led to the killing of the local chief of police, whereupon seventy-one strikers were arrested and sixteen indicted for murder. These included Beal and other organizers of the Communist-led National Textile Workers Union. Promptly the Communist legal organ, the International Labor Defense, took over the case. Although approached, the ACLU was reluctant to intervene openly in a legal test, since the issue was principally a factual one, self-defense, with issues of freedom of conscience and denial of civil liberties clouded. It thus agreed to finance the ILD with ACLU funds, through an urgent appeal for public support and a substantial grant from the American Fund for Public Service, a large bequest from the son of a wealthy New England family that was turned over to Roger Baldwin and a board of liberal leaders early in the 1920s to be administered for radical purposes.[59]

But as time went on, ACLU leaders quickly realized they were being used by the Communists, who were happy to take their money but had little interest in the workers and less in their civil liberties. Rather, they hoped to use the episode as propaganda for Communist organizational activities, locally and throughout the country. This fact became more clear when the ACLU, after providing bail for convicted strike leaders and retaining former United States Senator Thomas W. Hardwick of Georgia as counsel for the appeal to the North Carolina Supreme Court, saw Beal and other Communist leaders jump bail and flee to Russia, where the Soviets paraded them around as proletarian martyrs of capitalist injustice. The ACLU condemned their action as violating the principle of due process, a step which led William Z. Foster, who had become a Communist, to resign from the ACLU National Committee.[60]

But the episode had broader implications. Such duplicity ultimately weakened the Communist Party and strengthened the bona fide civil liberties movement. The ruthlessness of Communist tactics, plus the complete lack of concern for the individuals they claimed they were out to assist, plus the refusal to stand by workers generally, while callously exploiting their misfortunes, brought growing disillusion with Communism to many American laboring people. Rather, worker sympathy gravitated toward sincere civil libertarians. There were broad expressions of outrage that the work of civil liberties activists had been crippled by Communist tactics. Specifically deplored was the effect such tactics had in encouraging the courts, already inclined to set excessively high bail for militants, to further increase bail, thereby decreasing the funds available for future emergencies.

[59] On the Garland Fund see Merle Curti, "Subsidizing Radicalism: The American Fund for Public Service, 1921–1941," *Social Service Review*, 33 (September, 1959), 277 ff.

[60] On Gastonia see Paul L. Murphy, *The Meaning of Freedom of Speech* (Westport, Conn., 1972), Chap. 11; and Irving Bernstein, *The Lean Years: A History of the American Worker, 1920–1933* (Boston, 1960), Chap. 1.

Partly as a result of the sobering Gastonia experience and partly as a result of the times, the stratagem of civil liberties activists shifted. With the country in the throes of major social upheaval and threatened with economic catastrophe, wisdom dictated soft-peddling the free speech issue as a basis for major social reorganization. There was a need now for heavier concentration on direct defense work, protecting individuals whose civil rights had clearly been violated by overzealous local police or local courts, or by strong-arm methods utilized by nervous employers. All this had a positive effect on the budding ACLU, which ceased to project the image of a disruptionist, trouble-seeking, Communist-oriented body and became an agency for human relief. Membership grew sharply, income rose, further local affiliates began to be planned, and the work-load was multiplied. The press became increasingly well-disposed to ACLU activities. Not only liberal magazines but moderate newspapers took a long second look and decided that the organization served a real function, especially in a period of public tension and growing feelings of personal injustice. With its legitimization came the general validation of the civil liberties crusade as a valid reform movement geared to the wider achievement of fundamental American values.

The 1920s ended upon a note of civil liberties upswing. The decade had produced many grim moments. At the outset repression had been so great and had come from such powerful forces that civil libertarians sometimes despaired of their ability to take meaningful action. By mid-decade the orthodoxy of normalcy had so engulfed American life that the ACLU, for example, reported with discouragement that in 1927 only fourteen left-wing meetings had been broken up. This fact was interpreted as a clear indication of unwillingness on the part of dissenters to take controversial positions publicly, knowing the kind of retaliation which could be expected to follow.[61] But by 1929, the old order, which had previously looked so unassailable, itself began to be disrupted. Hope was now clearly seen in a new climate in which people were pre-

[61] ACLU, *The Fight for Civil Liberty* (*Annual Report,* No. 7, 1927–1928), pp. 3–5.

pared to tolerate critics of the system, no matter how offbeat, who offered options and alternatives to the discredited status quo.

Other causes for optimism sprang from the types of commitments the decade had elicited from a growing number of Americans. Prior to World War I most Americans assumed that minority rights would be automatically protected by the self-restraint of the majority. The war period and the post-war "red scare" had illustrated that simple majority respect for minority rights was not enough. It was also clear that minority groups, particularly in a period of national tension, were incapable of protecting their own rights, because of their lack of political and economic power and leverage. In the words of Roger Baldwin, "the pretense of our constitutional protection of 'guaranteed rights' is plainly exposed."

The 1920s found many Americans prepared to shoulder the public responsibility of the majority to make democracy work by protecting those who could not protect themselves. For the first time in American history, Catholics and Jews were no longer left alone to confront Klansmen or other religious bigots. Outside their own group they found allies who saw their cause as directly relevant to civil liberties generally. The cause of black and Indian Americans was embraced by some whites with a similar sense that what inhibits the freedoms of some groups threatens those of all. Concerned non-teachers joined in actions to protect those in the classroom from chauvinistic harassment, realizing that society suffered fully as much from such intimidation as the immediate victims. When Socialist assemblymen were denied their seats in the New York legislature, national figures such as Charles Evans Hughes and Al Smith, plus myriads of concerned Republicans and Democrats, not only rallied to their cause but worked to make clear to conservative citizens the threatening implications of this action for the civil liberties of all.

Thus, although the decade had been one in which a policy of laissez-faire had been business's professed desire (even though conservative leaders were perfectly prepared to utilize the state and its agents as vigorous instruments of repression), a growing number of Americans came to embrace the position that the Bill of Rights did not operate automatically. In a period of governmental unconcern, especially, concerned citizens had a special responsibility to take positive action in its behalf. Ironically, even the Depression gave rise to a favorable attitude. Positive government responsibility for the protection of the economic needs and the social demands of citizens could not be clearly divorced from comparable governmental responsibilities for the same citizens' civil liberties and civil rights. Such a lesson was especially suggestive to the judiciary, highly suspect by the depressed classes, but anxious to project an image of concern for human needs. And the new chief justice, Charles Evans Hughes, appointed in 1930, had a special sensitivity in this area.

And although the twenties ended with the country in economic distress, civil libertarians had new hopes that once conditions improved American life would be resumed with a new sense of national obligation to rights which early Americans, in the Bill of Rights and in their statements of national purpose, had assured all Americans were their national heritage.

THE DEPRESSION DECADE

JEROLD S. AUERBACH

The struggle for civil liberties is always waged within shifting boundaries set by the prevailing social and political context. During the 1930s, the vulnerability of industrial capitalism in a depression decade, the efforts of workers to unionize, and the domestic implications of the European clash between Communism and Fascism shaped the paramount civil liberties issues. Traditional categories remained—academic freedom, censorship, police practices, vigilantism, freedom of speech and assembly—but their content changed. Whether the protagonists were union organizers and employers, soapbox orators and police, teachers and administrators, or criminal defendants and prosecutors, the prototypical Depression victim of civil liberties infractions was an industrial worker, a union organizer, or a radical critic of capitalism. The institutional setting shifted, as it always has, from factory to school to street to jail to courthouse. But the fight for substantive rights and for procedural due process, wherever it was waged, drew its sustenance from the public issues that agitated Americans during that troubled era.[1]

Diverse perspectives are necessary for accurate perception of this struggle. The first part of this essay provides an overview of civil liberties problems during the Depression. From this most expansive vantage point, broad patterns are discernible, and the ebb and flow within a single decade is apparent. In the following section the focus narrows to the most conspicuous, and for libertarians the most compelling, problem of the first half of the decade: civil liberties in industrial relations. Not only was the battle for workers' rights intrinsically important; it also generated a momentous revision in libertarian thought regarding the role of the federal government in protecting freedom.

In the next two portions of the essay the setting is narrowest: the board of directors of the American Civil Liberties Union; and the chronological span most compressed: the final year of the decade. Yet, paradoxically, the problem was more critical than any other that confronted libertarians: the problem of means and ends. It has always been, is now, and will inevitably remain at the crux of every tactical decision in the endless quest for freedom. Are civil liberties ends in themselves, or are they instruments for social change? From the 1790s to the 1970s no other question has so consistently engaged libertarian passion and energy. As the sole national civil liberties organization, led by men and women maximally committed to the Bill of Rights, the American Civil Liberties Union provides the most appropriate setting for analysis of

[1] The primary focus of this essay, reflecting the primary issues of the Depression decade, is on First Amendment freedoms of belief and expression. Occasional reference is made to other provisions of the Bill of Rights affecting due process of law, especially for criminal defendants. Because civil rights issues, involving equality of treatment for minority group members, present quite different analytical problems, they are omitted from the essay. This analytical distinction is consistent with the emphasis of civil libertarians during the thirties, when the ACLU left the fight for the rights of black Americans largely to the NAACP. For a concise statement of this distinction between substantive and procedural civil liberties, and civil rights, see Alan Reitman, "Civil Rights and Civil Liberties in the 1960s," in *Encyclopedia of Social Work* (New York, 1965), p. 160.

this critical issue. The conclusion to this essay will offer an evaluation of the success of Depression libertarians in resolving their destructive, yet ultimately inescapable, dilemma about means and ends.

The most immediate impact of hard times on the Bill of Rights was a rapid acceleration of civil liberties infractions. Fear of unrest and disorder amid economic catastrophe produced more civil liberties cases in the early months of 1930 than in any single year since World War I. The number of free speech prosecutions jumped from 228 in 1929 to 1,630 in 1930; the number of meetings prohibited or disbanded increased from 52 to 121; incidents of mob violence more than quintupled; and lynchings nearly tripled. Indeed, for the first half of the Depression decade, there was a dismaying uniformity to the pattern of civil liberties violations. Radicals, especially Communists, were the primary victims of suppression for their unionizing efforts, hunger marches, public demonstrations, picket lines, and advocacy of social change.

Wherever it looked between 1930 and 1932 the American Civil Liberties Union discerned "the prevalent notion that radicals have no rights." In the House of Representatives, Hamilton Fish chaired the first of many widely publicized congressional investigations of Communist activities. In one local community after another, police used disorderly-conduct and disturbing-the-peace statutes to disrupt radical meetings and disband picket lines. In California five young women were convicted for displaying a red flag at a summer camp for children; in Atlanta six Communists who conducted an integrated meeting were indicted for inciting Negroes to rebellion. Mob violence toward radicals accompanied official lawlessness; their deadly combination was most evident in Harlan and Bell counties, Kentucky, where eleven union sympathizers were killed and more than a hundred were indicted on criminal syndicalism and related charges for attempting to organize local miners.

A less violent but otherwise similar pattern of repression emerged in academic freedom issues. The most conspicuous violations arose when teachers and students expressed pacifist, liberal, or radical opinions. During 1932–33 a California law school teacher was dismissed for serving as counsel to the American Civil Liberties Union and the International Labor Defense; the University of Pittsburgh demanded loyalty oaths of its students; a Denver high school banned a chapter of the League for Industrial Democracy; and students at Brown University were threatened with prosecution for publishing an anti-war pledge in their newspaper. Radical aliens also were especially vulnerable. With jobs declining and political acrimony rising, the Hoover administration, encouraged by the American Federation of Labor, initiated an increasing number of deportations—primarily of alien members of left-wing unions.[2]

The coming of the New Deal brightened certain corners of this dismal picture. The Department of Labor quickly liberalized its alien regulation and admissions policies and, for the first time in a decade, permitted radical aliens to visit the United States. President Roosevelt declared a Christmas amnesty that restored rights to those convicted under the World War I Espionage Act. Early New Deal encouragement of labor organization raised expectations in this vital area of libertarian concern. Yet its very encouragement inadvertently abetted attacks on the rights of radicals and workers. "The determination of employers to keep the labor movement in check, and passionate opposition to Communism," declared the American Civil Liberties Union, "conspire to provoke attack upon all symptoms of working-class militancy, and all heresy to capitalism."

As political controversy engendered by the Roosevelt administration stirred the embers of conservative discontent, patriotic organizations roused themselves to a level of repressive activity that rekindled memories of the postwar "red scare" in the 1920s. Under pressure, state legislatures enacted teacher loyalty oath bills and sedition statutes, and four states passed laws which barred from the ballot political parties advocating force, violence, sedition, or treason. Academic freedom still pivoted on political radicalism: investigations were conducted of left-wing political activism at the University of

[2] American Civil Liberties Union, *Annual Reports*, Nos. 9–11 (1929–30, 1930–31, 1931–32).

Wisconsin and the University of Chicago; students who engaged in a nationwide anti-war strike or who demonstrated against the ROTC were dismissed, their meetings were prohibited, they were arrested for distributing handbills and, on several occasions, attacked and beaten; radical teachers, most notoriously Granville Hicks, the Marxist literary critic, were dismissed from universities for their political views. The Roosevelt administration itself elicited libertarian concern with its National Recovery Administration codes for the newspaper and motion-picture industries, which raised disturbing questions regarding government control of the communications media.[3]

Not until 1936–37, for the first time since the stock market crash, did libertarians perceive brighter horizons. The stunning organizing successes of the CIO, Roosevelt's reelection, and the mood of liberal euphoria during the Popular Front era contributed to their optimism. The National Labor Relations Act, and the Supreme Court's validation of it, promised settlement of the most compelling civil liberties issues of the New Deal era—the right of workers to enjoy First Amendment freedoms in their unionizing activities. As ACLU executive director Roger Baldwin declared:

> However important or significant may be the struggle for the political rights of fifteen million Negroes; however important or significant the defense of religious liberties; of academic freedom; of freedom from censorship of the press, radio, or motion pictures, these are on the whole trifling in national effect compared with the fight for the right of labor to organize.[4]

Within a year more issues arose affecting the rights of Nazis than the rights of Communists. The enabling resolution for a congressional investigation of un-American activities reflected this changed emphasis—although shifting political winds would blow chairman Martin Dies far to the right in 1939. With the exception of Jersey City, New Jersey, under the

[3] ACLU, *Annual Report* (1932–33, 1933–34, 1934–35).
[4] Roger N. Baldwin and Clarence B. Randall, *Civil Liberties and Industrial Conflict* (Cambridge, Mass., 1938), p. 17.

reign of Mayor Frank ("I Am the Law") Hague, local prosecutions of political and economic radicals had virtually halted
by mid-1938. Nor, at the peak of liberal-left cooperation under
the Popular Front, were there many instances of prosecution
of Communists for their political activities. By 1939, the 150th
anniversary of the adoption of the Bill of Rights, the American Civil Liberties Union joyously reported "unprecedented
suport" for constitutional freedoms.[5]

No institution of government had provided more exemplary
support for civil liberties than the Supreme Court, which began to earn praise as "a Bill of Rights court." [6] Even before
the seating of Roosevelt's appointees, it expanded both the
meaning and scope of constitutional safeguards for individual
rights. Most significantly, the Court read provisions of the Bill
of Rights into the Fourteenth Amendment, thereby protecting
them against state as well as federal invasion. In *Near* v.
Minnesota (1931) it brought freedom of press within the
liberty safeguarded by the due process clause of the Fourteenth Amendment; having done so it proceeded, in 1936, to
invalidate a discriminatory tax imposed by Huey Long on
New Orleans newspapers opposed to his administration. The
following year the Court, reversing the conviction of Communist Party member Dirk De Jonge under Oregon's criminal
syndicalism law, extended similar protection to the equally
fundamental right of peaceable assembly.

In *Hague* v. *CIO* (1939) the prevailing opinion of the Court
upheld broad use of streets and parks for the purpose of dis-
cussing public questions. California's red flag law was held
partially invalid in the *Stromberg* case (1931); here the Court
began to move toward a more expansive definition of "speech"
that went beyond mere talk. It advanced significantly further in *Thornhill* v. *Alabama* (1940), when it brought picketing within the free speech provision of the First Amendment.
Finally, in *Herndon* v. *Lowry* (1937), the Court reversed
Georgia's conviction of Communist organizer Angelo Herndon
under an insurrection statute enacted in 1832 after Nat Turn-

---

[5] ACLU, *Annual Reports* (1935–36, 1936–37, 1937–38, 1938–39).
[6] C. Herman Pritchett, *The Roosevelt Court: A Study in Judicial
Politics and Values, 1937–1947* (New York, 1948), p. 137.

er's slave revolt but not used until a century later, holding the state to a standard of guilt more precise than the alleged dangerous tendency of meetings and literature sponsored by a black radical. Taken together, the *Stromberg, De Jonge,* and *Herndon* decisions blanketed with constitutional protection radical protests that fell short of overt acts constituting a clear and present danger to the government; the *Hague* and *Thornhill* decisions demonstrated the relationship between workers' rights and civil liberties.

The Supreme Court was also impressively libertarian in its treatment of procedural rights. In two decisions involving Scottsboro defendants, innocent victims of the legal travesty known locally as the "nigger rape case," the Court voided convictions on the ground that failure to provide adequate counsel denied due process of law (*Powell* v. *Alabama* [1932]) and, subsequently, because the systematic exclusion of Negroes from Alabama juries was held to deny equal protection of the laws (*Norris* v. *Alabama* [1935]). In *Brown* v. *Mississippi* (1936) the Court brought immunity from self-incrimination under Fourteenth Amendment due process when it reversed a conviction based solely upon a confession extracted by torture. And, in *Nardone* v. *United States* (1937), it held that evidence secured by unauthorized wiretapping was inadmissable.[7]

Ironically, however, just when libertarians believed that they were witnessing the new dawn of freedom, international developments plunged them into despair and disarray. As the decade ended, Nazi victories in Europe, which greatly increased the likelihood of American involvement in war, stimulated waves of intolerance against aliens and German-American Bundists and mob violence against Jehovah's Witnesses, the most conspicuous violators of compulsory-flag-salute laws. The Nazi-Soviet alliance made liberty equally precarious for Communists. Members of the Communist Party were excluded from private employment in interstate commerce and from public jobs. Aliens were placed under tight control by the Smith Act, which not only provided for their registration, fingerprinting, and deportation, but contained (in

[7] *Ibid.,* Chap. 5.

the words of constitutional scholar Zechariah Chafee, Jr.) "the most drastic restrictions on freedom of speech ever enacted in the United States during peace." [8]

The Dies Committee conducted, without procedural safeguards, sweeping investigations of liberal reform groups whose activities were redefined as un-American amid mounting hysteria over the war and heightened opposition to the New Deal. Suddenly the impressive post-1935 libertarian gains evaporated. Just when the issue of workers' rights was finally settled, eliminating the civil liberties violations and blunting the radical critique that emanated from it, Soviet cooperation with Nazi Germany revived anti-radicalism as the paramount civil liberties issue. With Communists perceived as red Nazis as the decade of the forties began, a dangerous undertow of repression began to erode libertarian gains won during the floodtide of the Depression years.

Long before the Depression—indeed as early as the triumph of industrialization and corporate capitalism at the end of the nineteenth century—aliens, radicals, and workers were indiscriminately mixed but collectively identified as the primary targets of repression for their hostility, real or suspected, toward the new industrial order. After 1914 the left condemned a war fought by the masses but allegedly waged by the ruling classes to maximize profits and preserve a reactionary international power balance. Conscientious objection and pacifism gave birth to our first national civil liberties defense organization, the progenitor of the American Civil Liberties Union, which uttered its initial cries of protest against federal espionage and sedition laws.

It was hardly coincidental that every major First Amendment case to arise out of the war or its aftermath—*Schenck, Abrams, Debs, Gitlow*—involved left-wing protest. During the inter-war decades opposition to capitalism in left and libertarian circles manifested itself in the explicit identification of workers' rights with civil liberties. As the American Civil Liberties Union conceded in 1923, "the circumstances

[8] Zechariah Chafee, Jr., *Free Speech in the United States* (Cambridge, Mass., 1941), p. 441.

of industrial conflict today force us chiefly to champion the rights of labor to organize, strike, meet, and picket, because labor is the class whose rights are most attacked." During the Depression decade, the ACLU declared ten years later, the battle between capital and labor was "the central struggle involving civil liberties. . . ." [9]

Economic collapse undercut the myths and promises of the post-war decade of prosperity and left the American business system highly vulnerable to criticism. Radical critics, virtually moribund during the twenties, seized their opportunity. They were galvanized first by the demonstrable failures of the existing system, then by the sense of possibilities elicited with the coming of the New Deal and always by the depths of suffering experienced by millions of ill-fed, ill-clothed, ill-housed, and unemployed Americans. Understandably, the industrial worker inspired their fondest hopes. In radical hagiology he was the primary agent of national redemption. Overworked and underpaid even in the best of times, he was pushed beyond the pale of the Bill of Rights whenever he tried to alleviate his plight through collective organization.

For decades, the experiences of industrial workers had underscored the relation between economic power and individual liberty. Union organization depended on the constitutional freedoms of speech, press, and assembly, but employers consistently abridged these rights. Their reliance on espionage, blacklisting, strikebreakers, private police, and, ultimately, armed violence nullified the Bill of Rights for those workers who had the temerity to resist their employers' unilateral exercise of power. With labor-management discord often resolved by violence rather than through the legal process, the struggle for civil liberties in industrial relations became the paramount radical and libertarian concern.

Ever since World War I, civil libertarians, occasionally impelled by feelings of class consciousness, had shared the radi-

[9] William Preston, Jr., *Aliens and Dissenters: Federal Suppression of Radicals, 1903–1933* (Cambridge, Mass., 1963); Donald Johnson, *The Challenge to American Freedom: World War I and the Rise of the American Civil Liberties Union* (Lexington, Ky., 1963); ACLU, *Annual Report* (1923), Foreword; *Annual Report* (1934), p. 9.

cals' conviction that strong unions could remake American
society. The fight to project the Bill of Rights into industrial
relations was a tactic sanctified by the historical evolution of
civil liberties in the United States. Disadvantaged groups advocating social change that would re-allocate power in their
interest invariably had discovered that the Bill of Rights offered an advantageous sanctuary for their forays against hostile majorities or unfriendly governments. In the eighteenth
century anti-federalists and Jeffersonians used civil liberties to
establish the legitimacy of their political opposition. Similarly,
nineteenth-century abolitionists gathered recruits in their crusade against slavery with their vigorous defense of the right
to dissent. So, too, twentieth-century advocates of unionization perceived that an appeal to libertarian values would expand their constituency and strengthen their cause. Such
libertarian instrumentalism was not disingenuous; it was an
essential stretching process if the Bill of Rights were to fit
changing circumstances.

In one vital respect, however, civil libertarians found it
quite difficult to cope with the changes wrought by the Depression and the coming of the New Deal. Since colonial times
libertarians had been conditioned to measure liberty by the
absence of central government power. They revered Thomas
Jefferson, the patron saint of negative libertarianism, whose
jeremiads against central governments (whether British or
American) became key articles of libertarian faith. The First
Amendment, written in this spirit, restrained Congress—albeit
insufficiently for World War I dissenters, whose memories of
the restrictions imposed by selective service, espionage, and
sedition legislation remained vivid more than a decade later.

ACLU executive director Roger Baldwin and other Union
leaders retained a deep distrust of the federal government.
Baldwin, a conscientious objector, went to prison for violating
the Selective Service Act; far into the 1930s, neither he nor
his libertarian colleagues could relinquish their hostility to
federal power. The war experience, argued ACLU general
counsel Arthur Garfield Hays, demonstrated that "a new
theory of government based on . . . [the] need of legal restraint, is displacing liberty." The Constitution, he reiterated,

restrained only the government. "This was thought necessary to preserve liberty," wrote Hays, who, quite clearly, still thought so.[10] The history of liberty, Woodrow Wilson had said before the war, was the history of the limitation of government power. For libertarians, Wilson's own presidency provided the ironic confirmation of that credo.

Post-war federal intervention in labor-management disputes, invariably on the side of management, reinforced libertarian anti-statism. At the beginning of the Depression decade, therefore, "civil liberties" were defined as "a right of the individual as against the authoritarian state" by political scientist Robert E. Cushman, who warned that "the increasing governmental control necessitated by the complexities of modern social and industrial life results in continuous encroachments upon rights fundamental to the older philosophy of individualism." [11] Although the Depression undercut the intellectual underpinnings of this philosophy, neither it nor the coming of the New Deal undermined the civil libertarian creed. President Roosevelt's request for emergency powers, and the myriad of laws that Congress enacted during the First Hundred Days, portended federal intrusion in civil liberties more severe than those the war years had brought. Midway through Roosevelt's first term the American Civil Liberties Union cautioned: "The enormous increase of the power of the federal government under New Deal policies carried with it inevitable fears of inroads on the right of agitation." As yet, the ACLU conceded, there was no significant suppression, but this provided slight consolation "because there is as yet no significant opposition to suppress." [12] Libertarians were still frozen in their Jeffersonian mold; it was inconceivable to them that the government might exercise power to protect, rather than subvert, liberty.

Labor-management relations provided the critical test of this proposition. The enduring commitment of the Roosevelt

[10] Arthur Garfield Hays, *Let Freedom Ring* (New York, 1928), pp. xvi, xix.

[11] Robert E. Cushman, "Civil Liberties," in *Encyclopedia of the Social Sciences* (New York, 1930), III, 509–11.

[12] ACLU, *Annual Report* (1934), pp. 3, 9.

administration was to revitalizing the economy, not to encouraging union organization. The president, described by one of his close advisors as labor's patron, was unenthusiastic about labor legislation that focused on unions as instruments of social progress. His plan for industrial recovery rested upon a partnership between business and government. Under the National Industrial Recovery Act, the anti-trust laws were suspended and businessmen were authorized to draft codes for entire industries covering production quotas, prices, labor relations, and wages and hours. At the insistence of Senator Robert F. Wagner of New York, workers were guaranteed the right to organize and bargain collectively through unions of their own choosing. Once they sought to exercise this right, however, they encountered determined employer intransigence. Bitter, often violent, confrontations erupted between labor and management. The instruments of industrial warfare —spies, strikebreakers, police, and munitions—were utilized to prevent organization and to deny the civil liberties upon which organization depended.

Civil libertarians were profoundly and predictably distressed. As infractions of the Bill of Rights multiplied, civil liberties issues were cast in the plausible guise of class conflict. The ACLU perceived a "great increase in repression . . . due to the fear of unrest and disorder during the economic depression." [13] This pattern persisted: In 1934 the ACLU identified "the struggle between capital and labor" as "the most vital application of the principle of civil liberty. . . ." [14] For the civil liberties organization, workers' rights were paramount. By 1935 the "attack on anti-capitalist forces under the cloak of protecting the government from advocacies of its overthrow assumed really formidable proportions." [15] The ACLU depicted "an era of constant repression by defenders of the status quo, directed against all movements of change, particularly by organized workers." [16]

Unremitting intrusions upon the workers' right to organ-

[13] ACLU, *Annual Report* (1931), p. 3.
[14] ACLU, *Annual Report* (1934), p. 5.
[15] ACLU, *Annual Report* (1935), p. 4.
[16] ACLU, *Annual Report* (1936), p. 8.

ize—and by extension upon the freedom of expression, assembly, and association—posed a discomfiting dilemma to civil libertarians after 1933. The only institution with sufficient power to redress the imbalance in labor-management relations and to protect workers' rights was the federal government, traditionally the *bête noire* of libertarians. Their commitment to workers' rights could no longer coexist with their antipathy to federal power, especially when it became apparent (as it did by 1935) that the Roosevelt administration was prepared to implement legal sanctions to protect the unimpeded right of workers to organize. During the first two years of the New Deal libertarians vacillated in their approach to the exercise of federal power in labor-management relations. They wanted the protection that only the federal government could provide, yet their posture reflected their exprience that no federal agency could fairly determine workers' rights.[17]

This nagging libertarian ambivalence was underscored during the months immediately preceding enactment of the National Labor Relations Act—the keystone of New Deal labor policy. Roger Baldwin's opposition to the statute provoked discomfort within the ACLU. Arthur Garfield Hays conceded that libertarians had "heretofore taken the position that governmental interference or power ordinarily results in a denial of rights to the workers; that labor can advance only through its own power, not through legislation." But the Wagner Act, far from denying workers' liberties, protected them. Therefore it deserved—indeed required—libertarian support.[18] Under pressure, Baldwin rescinded his earlier statement of opposition and notified Senator Wagner that the ACLU would maintain neutrality toward his bill. This *volte-face* terminated negative libertarianism. Once the federal government held out the promise of safeguarding workers' rights, libertarian

[17] Roger Baldwin to Robert F. Wagner, April 1, 1935, ACLU Papers, Vol. 780. (The reference here and in succeeding footnotes to the ACLU Papers is to the ACLU Archives at the Princeton University Library in Princeton, New Jersey. A microfilm copy is also available at the New York Public Library.)

[18] Hays to ACLU, May 7, 1935, ACLU Papers, Vol. 780.

antipathy toward federal power receded and the American Civil Liberties Union relaxed its hostility toward the state.[19]

Released from obeisance to the past, libertarians could accept federal power. Convinced that "effective control over the exercise of civil liberties in the United States rests where it has always been—with the masters of property," they were slow to perceive that the federal government might, at least temporarily, loosen the effectiveness of those controls.[20] The Wagner Act wrenched them from their eighteenth-century commitments, reinforced by World War I memories. Both the federal government and the civil libertarians traveled along the paths of expediency and inadvertance toward their joint destination. The Roosevelt administration, uncommitted to unions, accepted labor organization as a necessary means to economic recovery. The American Civil Liberties Union, antagonistic toward the federal government, accepted federal power as the necessary means for securing workers' rights.

The labor movement was the magnet that pulled civil libertarians toward the federal government. "It was when labor sought to exercise its 'right' to organize or strike," wrote an NLRB attorney, "that the most fruitful soil was prepared for the wholesale violation of our civil liberties." [21] The Wagner Act, by prohibiting interference with the right to organize, extended First Amendment guarantees of speech, press, and assembly to workers who had enjoyed civil liberties, if they did at all, solely on their employers' sufferance. For the first time advocacy of unionism, traditionally consigned to the mercy of employer and community intolerance, enjoyed legal protection. By prohibiting employers from abridging their workers' freedom of expression, the act extended First Amendment prohibitions to private persons. That statute, Roger Baldwin believed, was the New Deal's "major achievement"

[19] For a full account of these and related developments, see Jerold S. Auerbach, *Labor and Liberty: The La Follette Committee and the New Deal* (Indianapolis, Ind., 1966).

[20] ACLU, *Annual Report* (1934), p. 10.

[21] Joseph Rosenfarb, "Protection of Basic Rights," in Louis G. Silverberg, ed., *The Wagner Act: After Ten Years* (Washington, D.C., 1945), p. 93.

in the protection of civil liberties. And the Supreme Court decision that upheld it, more than any other judicial decision in Baldwin's memory, "affected civil liberties in the one major area where they had been most grossly violated." [22]

During the Depression decade a momentous transfer of power to the federal government, intended to hasten economic recovery, undercut the antipathy of civil libertarians to the state. Philosopher John Dewey argued that the only hope for liberalism was the realization that social control "is necessary in order to render secure the liberties of the individual, including civil liberties." [23] Libertarians were urged to heed anti-libertarian forces more dangerous than the federal government. "Perhaps it is time," wrote a social scientist, "to think of civil liberty as protection *by* the state rather than protection *against* the state." [24] Americans traditionally had been content to provide sanctions against governmental incursions upon civil liberties. But, a contributor to the *Yale Law Journal* noted, "we have given little thought . . . to the importance of providing sanctions against the use of private power of the employer to the same end." [25] In the nineteenth century governmental non-intervention meant liberty; within the economic configurations of the twentieth century, it had come to mean unlimited opportunity for private power to destroy liberty. Although federal intervention to safeguard liberty was a series of improvised responses to specific needs, not an articulated policy, the results were equally pleasant for libertarians to contemplate.

Federal defense of civil liberties overflowed the boundaries of labor-management relations. During the New Deal years each branch of the government contributed significantly. The congressional response—a four-year investigation of employers' infringements of workers' civil liberties—was most di-

[22] Roger Baldwin, Columbia University Oral History Collection, 176, 201.

[23] John Dewey, "Liberalism and Civil Liberties," *Social Frontier*, 2 (February, 1936), 138.

[24] Frederic Heimberger, "Our Outworn Civil Liberties," *Christian Century*, 53 (April 22, 1936), 599–600.

[25] T. Richard Witmer, "Civil Liberties and the Trade Union," *Yale Law Journal*, 50 (February 1941), 622.

rectly attributable to labor-management turmoil. Between 1936 and 1940 a Senate subcommittee chaired by Senator Robert M. La Follette, Jr., of Wisconsin publicized violations of free speech and rights of labor in industries where major organizing drives occurred. The La Follette Committee stripped the veneer of respectability from unethical (and, after the Wagner Act, illegal) anti-union activities, exposed the menace to civil liberties from the concentration of power in private hands, and advocated the application of strong governmental power to protect the Bill of Rights.[26]

During Frank Murphy's brief tenure as attorney general toward the end of the decade, the Department of Justice, for the first time in its history, acted decisively to protect civil liberties. Here, too, the labor movement served as the inadvertent vehicle of change. Murphy repudiated the conviction of his predecessors that the federal government was powerless to intervene to protect civil liberties. As governor of Michigan during the hectic days of the General Motors sitdown strike, he had learned that "in times of social unrest, there is an increased necessity for vigilance in those charged with the protection of constitutional privileges and immunities." Shortly after his appointment to Roosevelt's cabinet, he publicly stated that "the Department of Justice ought to be active, alert, and defensive of civil liberties in this country."

Early in 1939 Murphy established a civil liberties unit to prosecute violations of the Bill of Rights. As he explained to Roger Baldwin, "I am anxious that the weight and influence of the Department of Justice should be a force for the preservation of the people's liberties." Various Reconstruction statutes, which made civil rights violations federal crimes, were reexamined for their contemporary applicability. "For the first time in our history," he reported to President Roosevelt, "the full weight of the Department will be thrown behind the effort to preserve in this country the blessings of liberty, the spirit of tolerance, and the fundamental principles of democracy." Although Murphy's achievements lagged significantly behind his rhetoric, he could justifiably take pride in his claim that

[26] See Auerbach, *Labor and Liberty*, pp. 205–18.

this was "one of the most significant happenings in American legal history." [27]

These developments, in conjunction with favorable Supreme Court decisions, pleased libertarians immensely. Roger Baldwin acknowledged that he appreciated only belatedly "how much further the New Dealers were prepared to go than we in federalizing the protecting of civil rights." Roosevelt's reelection in 1936, he recalled, marked the beginning of "a new chapter," and obviously an auspicious one, in the history of civil liberties in this country.[28] Chroniclers of that history have echoed their euphoria. During the thirties, according to one political scientist, "the United States left the paths of tribalism for the high road of due process of law and substantive justice and equality. . . . [By 1940] civil liberties and minority rights had become part of American public policy." [29] A historian, evaluating the New Deal civil liberties record, concurred: "By the eve of World War II the federal government's commitment to the principle of protecting civil liberties seemed irrevocable." [30]

Such judgments required substantial reconsideration and modification.[31] The ad hoc responses of particular members of a liberal administration at a certain time for specific reasons constituted something less than an enduring federal commitment. Not only did libertarian "public policy" fail to survive

[27] *New York Times,* April 16, 1939; *Progressive,* February 4, 1939; Murphy to Baldwin, February 3, 1939, copy in ACLU Papers, Vol. 2070; Murphy to Franklin D. Roosevelt, July 7, 1939, Franklin D. Roosevelt Library OF 2111.

[28] Baldwin, Columbia Oral History Collection, 182, 197; Lucille Milner, *The Education of an American Liberal* (New York, 1954), p. 242.

[29] John P. Roche, *The Quest for the Dream* (New York, 1963), pp. 134, 183.

[30] Auerbach, *Labor and Liberty,* pp. 216–17.

[31] In reconsidering my own earlier thoughts on this subject I have been prodded by three reviewers of *Labor and Liberty:* Otis L. Graham, Jr., *New England Quarterly* (June, 1967); Stanley Coben, *Journal of Economic History* (June, 1968); and Douglas Chaffey, *American Political Science Review* (September, 1968); and especially by William Preston's extremely persuasive "The Limits of Dissent: Contraction or Enlargement" (unpublished manuscript).

the hostile environment of a subsequent era; competing public policies, especially the policy of anti-Communism, crippled it in its own time. Consequently, the positive civil liberties record of the 1930s, resting heavily upon a re-allocation of power in labor-management relations, should not be taken to imply consistent governmental support for civil liberties generally. The protection of workers' rights, an achievement of considerable magnitude, was nonetheless a circumscribed achievement. There was an ominous side to the libertarian picture.

Especially toward the end of the decade, when opposition to the New Deal and hostility toward the Soviet Union increased, the specter of Communism was introduced to justify serious infringements upon civil liberties. The Roosevelt administration, under siege from its conservative critics, practiced "irresolute libertarianism." [32] The president was ambivalent toward the Dies Committee investigation of un-American activities, indulging in what one critic has labeled "the rhetoric of condemnation and the policies of appeasement." [33] He signed the Smith Act, the first peace-time federal sedition law since 1798 and the first federal criminal statute to introduce the principle of guilt by association. He authorized the use of wiretaps against suspected subversives, tolerated loyalty oaths, and supported limitations upon the freedom of expression of expression of government employees.

Thus the federal government "used the machinery of repression inherited from previous administrations and . . . added more effective devices of its own." [34] The federal bureaucracy persisted in its intrusions upon the personal liberties of aliens, radicals, and alleged subversives. States enacted compulsory-flag-salute laws, strengthened their sedition statutes, and prescribed loyalty oaths for teachers. In local communities private vigilante groups—often with the tacit support of public

[32] Preston, "The Limits of Dissent," p. 20.

[33] *Ibid.*, p. 25.

[34] *Ibid.*, p. 23, Richard Polenberg, "Franklin Roosevelt and Civil Liberties: The Case of the Dies Committee," *Historian,* 30 (February, 1968), 177–78.

officials—harassed dissenters under the guise of protecting society against subversion by outside agitators. At every level of government anti-radicalism, more explicitly anti-Communism, wove these various strands into a rope of repression.

With the rights of radicals at stake, libertarians became acutely discomfited over the problem of means and ends. In their struggle for workers' civil liberties they had managed to bypass this issue. But it erupted spasmodically, and with gathering force, toward the end of the decade: first over restrictions upon employers' freedom of expression, then over the Dies Committee investigation, finally—and disasterously —after the Nazi-Soviet pact drove a wedge deep into the united front of liberals and radicals.

Ever since the American Civil Liberties Union had first committed its energies to the protection of workers' rights ("because labor is the class whose rights are most attacked"), libertarians had encountered the charge of double standards and divided loyalties. Although they drew no political lines, and indeed accepted the responsibility of defending deviants of all political persuasions, the objective situation required them to channel their energies toward radicals on the left, who, as critics and therefore as targets, raised the most frequent and compelling civil liberties issues. This circumstance, in turn, molded the sympathies of many libertarians. For a time it was possible to blur the distinction between a principled defense of civil liberties, in which workers' rights were paramount because workers were the primary victims of repression, and a partisan defense, in which workers' rights were paramount because transcendent political commitments made them so.

Both positions, however, pointed toward the preponderant defense of workers' rights. Some libertarians used First Amendment provisions primarily as instruments for social change, as means rather than as ends. These instrumentalists defended civil liberties because the new social and political order that they sought depended upon wider boundaries for radical agitation. Thus Roger Baldwin wrote in 1933: "Civil liberties, like democracy, are useful only as tools for social change." [35] And ACLU chairman Harry F. Ward, speaking in 1936, declared that "the struggle for civil rights is entering a new phase. . . . The fight is to use these rights for peaceful political evolution." [36] Other libertarians viewed the Bill of Rights as an impartial shield, not as a partisan weapon. These idealists felt uneasy when civil liberties were subsumed in the labor crusade, stripped of their neutrality, and manipulated for partisan purposes. Arthur Garfield Hays distinguished between libertarians who "regarded free speech as merely a means toward a better social or economic end as against others of us who felt that the right of self-expression is an end in itself. . . ." [37]

Given the compatibility between labor's interests and civil liberties, instrumentalists and idealists found it easy to agree upon immediate objectives without wrangling about ultimate goals. In reply to the allegation of critics that libertarians adopted the political commitments of radicals whose rights they defended, the American Civil Liberties Union disclaimed political bias and reiterated that its purpose was "solely to protect the agitation of public issues and the guarantees of personal liberty set forth in the Bill of Rights." But, it added, the organization did not exist to protect property rights; such protection, it insisted, "has nothing to do with the maintenance of democratic processes." [38] If, as the ACLU properly argued, the circumstances of industrial conflict compelled it to champion the civil liberties of workers, it is also apparent that the sympathy of many libertarians for unionism shaped their approach to civil liberties issues. The objective situation and personal predilections were mutually reinforcing.

Early in 1938 libertarians first confronted the issue of employers' rights to freedom of expression. The National Labor Relations Board found the Ford Motor Company guilty of

[35] Baldwin to the Editor, *New York Times*, April 8, 1933, published in the *New York Times*, April 11, 1933.

[36] Copy of Ward speech, ACLU Papers, Vol. 863.

[37] Arthur Garfield Hays, *City Lawyer* (New York, 1942), pp. 229–30.

[38] ACLU, *Annual Report* (1937), pp. 14–15.

violating Wagner Act prohibitions against unfair labor practices. Not only did it order Ford to cease its intimidation and
coercion of employees who exercised their legal rights; it also
ordered the company not to circulate or distribute among its
workers statements that criticized unions or advised employees
not to join them. Such statements had comprised an integral
part of Ford's anti-union campaign, which included discriminatory discharges, intimidation, and physical assault. The
question for libertarians was whether the NLRB prohibition
against anti-union statements to workers violated the constitutionally protected freedom of expression of employers.
Based upon the labor board's finding that Ford's anti-union
literature constituted "a direct address to fear of physical
violence," and that such violence had consistently accompanied its dissemination of literature, an ACLU committee on
labor rights concluded that "when speech *is thus implemented
by force* or by threats of discharge or violence it is not the
free speech about which the ACLU is concerned." [39]

When the committee circulated its report the Civil Liberties
Union erupted in protest. Critics insisted that the right to
join a union had been elevated above the right to freedom
of speech. The nationally known clergyman John Haynes
Holmes, a member of the board of directors since the found-
ing of the organization, warned that "the very life, not to say
the integrity" of the ACLU was at stake.[40] In a lengthy exchange of letters with ACLU chairman Harry F. Ward,
Holmes defined the libertarian idealist position. "Under the
impact of our real sympathy for labor's cause," he warned,

> we are allowing ourselves to become mere advocates of
> the rights of labor to the denial of those rights as exer-
> cised by those who are against labor. . . . More reluc-
> tantly than I dare to confess, I find myself believing that
> our enemies have good reason for charging us with being
> partisan in the labor struggle, and using the civil liberties

[39] ACLU Committee on Labor Rights, Memorandum on Ford Case,
February 28, 1938, ACLU Papers, Vol. 1078. Among the six members
of this committee were lawyers Nathan Greene, Abraham Isserman, and
Osmond K. Fraenkel, and ACLU executive director Roger Baldwin.

[40] Holmes to Baldwin, February 2, 1938, ACLU Papers, Vol. 1081.

principle as a means of fighting labor's battles and the cause of radicalism generally.[41]

Ward agreed that support for labor was not a proper ACLU objective. He insisted, however, that in any conflict between the right of labor to organize and the right of employers to oppose organization, "both rights stop where persuasion ends and coercion begins." [42] Holmes was unconvinced. Certain that some members of the ACLU Board believed in civil liberties not on a principled basis but "as a means toward certain ends—namely, the advancement of labor, and the revolution" he rejected Ward's "coercion" test and insisted upon "violence" as the sole justification for restricting expression.[43]

Torn by these serious internal disagreements, the directors of the Civil Liberties Union finally declared that the NLRB order did not properly distinguish between expressions of opinion and "directly coercive" language. The Union declared its opposition to "any interference with the expression of opinion on the part of employers as well as on the part of anyone else. We oppose prior restraints upon the use of language which expresses the opinions of anybody." [44] A substantial toll of organizational friction and personal mistrust was exacted before the ACLU reached this libertarian position. With the shift from workers' rights to employers' rights, the misalliance between idealists and instrumentalists began to fracture.

The Dies Committee investigation of "un-American activities," initiated during the summer of 1938, wrenched these uneasy associates further apart. Playing variations on the theme of Communist infiltration and subversion, the Committee heard and repeated verbal broadsides against the Roosevelt administration, the CIO, the Boy Scouts, the American Civil Liberties Union, several hundred other private associations, public officials of liberal political persuasion, and child

[41] Holmes to Ward, February 8, 1938, ACLU Papers, Vol. 1080.

[42] Ward to Holmes, February 10, 1938, ACLU Papers, Vol. 1079.

[43] Holmes to Ward, February 8, 1938, ACLU Papers, Vol. 1079.

[44] "Policies Concerning Civil Rights in Labor Relations" (adopted August, 1938), ACLU Papers, Vol. 1078.

star Shirley Temple. It offered a national forum to those who were convinced that liberalism and Communism were indistinguishable and that the New Deal was a radical conspiracy. The Civil Liberties Union was an attractive target, not only to witnesses but to the Committee chairman. During its earliest hearings the Union and its executive director, Roger Baldwin, were alleged to be linked to the Communist Party. Dies, in a radio address, charged that the ACLU was a Communist-controlled organization that served the Party under the guise of preserving democracy.[45] Although the Union offered affidavits to rebut the charges, and Arthur Garfield Hays requested an opportunity to testify, the Dies Committee disdained evidence that ran counter to the political convictions of its members.

Harassed by sniping from Dies, buffeted by domestic issues, and alarmed by the spread of totalitarianism in Europe, civil libertarians wrestled with the implications of these ominous developments for the Bill of Rights. In April, 1939, the board of directors of the American Civil Liberties Union issued a statement entitled "Why We Defend Free Speech for Nazis, Fascists, and Communists." Offered in rebuttal to "critics who would deny liberty to those they characterize as enemies of democracy," it was a ringing affirmation of the loftiest promises of the libertarian creed.[46]

First, the ACLU enunciated principles of organizational self-restraint: "The Union does not engage in political controversy. It takes no position on any political or economic issue or system. . . . It is wholly unconcerned with movements abroad or with foreign governments." Then it moved to the offensive. It supported only "the suppression of *acts* in violation of civil liberty, or actual preparation for the use of force." It proclaimed its willingness, consistent with that principle, to defend "even the rights of those who might, if they came to power, suppress civil liberties." Its idealist and instrumen-

[45] Memo on Charges before the Dies Committee Involving the ACLU, December 12, 1938, ACLU Papers, Vol. 2075.

[46] The statement appears in full in Corliss Lamont, ed., *The Trial of Elizabeth Gurley Flynn by the American Civil Liberties Union* (New York, 1968), pp. 181–84.

talist members agreed that "free speech as a practical tactic as well as an abstract principle, demands defense of the rights of *all* who are attacked in order to maintain the rights of *any*." Finally, it declined "to indulge in characterizing movements as democratic or anti-democratic." No other policy, the Union concluded, "will preserve democratic institutions."

Four months later, in August, 1939, Germany and the Soviet Union signed a pact of mutual non-aggression. Soon thereafter both nations invaded and divided Poland, thereby indelibly establishing their popular identity as totalitarian regimes.[47] The implications of the Nazi-Soviet pact for civil liberties in the United States can hardly be exaggerated. Within six months, after incessant internal discord, the American Civil Liberties Union repudiated every basic libertarian principle enunciated in its April policy statement. It yielded its overt-acts test. It adopted a test of opinion for membership on its board of directors. It characterized political movements as anti-democratic and became obsessed with foreign policy issues. It expelled one of its own directors solely for belonging to a political organization. Judged by its own enunciated standards, it adopted a policy directly contrary to what it had insisted in April was necessary to preserve democratic institutions. If the question of employers' rights to freedom of expression had exposed the vulnerability of the radical libertarian faction to divided loyalties, the question of Communists' rights to freedom of expression exposed the vulnerability of the rival, anti-Communist, faction.

The Nazi-Soviet pact prompted some libertarians (those whose associations made them vulnerable after the demise of the Popular Front or whose anti-Communist politics had suddenly become respectable) to reconsider their antipathy to

[47] According to two recent students of "red Fascism," Americans "casually and deliberately articulated distorted similarities between Nazi and Communist ideologies, German and Soviet foreign policies, authoritarian controls, and trade practices, and Hitler and Stalin." The result of this analogy was "a potent and pervasive notion that significantly shaped American perception of world events in the cold war" (Les K. Adler and Thomas G. Paterson, "Red Fascism: The Merger of Nazi Germany and Soviet Russia in the American Image of Totalitarianism, 1930's–1950's," *American Historical Review*, 75 [April, 1970], 1046).

the Dies Committee. Allegations of Communist sympathies, dismissed before the pact as trivial or politically motivated, seemed especially ominous after Stalin became Hitler's ally. As the political winds shifted late in the summer of 1939, lines of communication were extended between the ACLU and the Dies Committee. By October, according to the ACLU staff counsel, the organization was concerned with "taking advantage of any opportunity we have of clearing ourselves after the job he [Dies] has done on us." [48]

Late that month ACLU General Counsel Morris Ernst and Arthur Garfield Hays met with Dies and Congressman Jerry Voorhis, a liberal member of the Committee. The substance of their conversation has remained a matter of dispute. Ernst and Hays maintained that their sole purpose was to convince the congressmen to hear rebuttals to the charges against the ACLU; no other issues were discussed.[49] But five ACLU members in Washington were deeply troubled by published and private reports that Ernst had held several conferences with Dies "in the interest, we are told, of preventing the American Civil Liberties Union from being 'smeared' further by the Dies Committee. . . ." [50] More recently Corliss Lamont, then an ACLU director, has accused the Union of making "a deal with Dies," citing "abundant circumstantial evidence that the organization itself would take the necessary steps to 'cleanse' itself of Communists." [51]

Whether or not an explicit *quid pro quo* was arranged, a tacit understanding seems to have existed between the Civil Liberties Union and the Committee. After more than a year of harassment Dies suddenly changed direction and announced in public hearings, in late October, that the ACLU

[48] Jerome M. Britchey to Morris Ernst, October 21, 1939, ACLU Papers, Vol. 2076.

[49] Baldwin to Gardner Jackson, December 16, 1939, ACLU Papers, Vol. 2077. For Ernst's conviction that he had saved the ACLU from being smeared by Dies, see Ernst to Lamont, January 12, 1940, Morris Ernst Papers, University of Texas (Austin).

[50] Gardner Jackson, Walter Gellhorn, et al. to ACLU Executive Board, December 14, 1939, ACLU Papers, Vol. 2077. They requested a complete report on Ernst's "discussions and possible agreements" with Dies.

[51] Lamont, *Trial*, p. 21.

was "an organization that the Committee has already said is not a Communist organization." [52] And in December, after more than a year of hostility toward the Committee, a special ACLU committee (which included Morris Ernst) issued a report that referred to the Dies Committee's "culpable conduct" but praised it for performing "a useful and important service. . . . [It] has usefully revealed much propaganda and many activities by those who desire to destroy or suppress American principles and democratic institutions and who would set up in their place some form of dictatorship whether of the right or left." [53]

According to one member of the ACLU committee, the report was designed to serve a political purpose: to guide liberals to "a position of 'pragmatic realism.'" [54] The report was roughly treated by other ACLU directors, who insisted upon more severe criticisms of the Dies Committee's work. As finally issued, it conceded that the inquiry had "performed a service" in compiling a record of activity and propaganda that was a proper subject of investigation, but it warned that the Committee's investigatory methods were subject to "valid and serious disapproval," and it "strongly condemned" the Committee's political partisanship. [55] Without these changes, declared one of the directors, the report, "an unworthy attempt to curry favor with Mr. Dies," would have been "a shocking disgrace" to the American Civil Liberties Union. [56]

The Dies Committee episode revealed the swiftness with which some libertarians were prepared to apply anti-Com-

[52] Transcript of Harry F. Ward Testimony before the Dies Committee, October 23, 1939, ACLU Papers, Vol. 2076. There is evidence that Ernst was in Washington on business relating to the Dies Committee during the week of Ward's testimony and Dies's announcement. See Sol Alpher to Jerome Britchey, October 26, 1939, ACLU Papers, Vol. 2076.

[53] Special ACLU Committee on the Dies Committee, Report, December 1939, ACLU Papers, Vol. 2077.

[54] Gardner Jackson to Board of Directors, December 25, 1939, ACLU Papers, Vol. 2077.

[55] Report on Dies Committee, December 29, 1939, ACLU Papers, Vol. 2077; Minutes, Board of Directors, December 26, 1939, ACLU Papers, Vol. 2063.

[56] Osmond K. Fraenkel to Holmes, September 5, 1940, ACLU Papers, Vol. 2066.

munism as a test of commitment to civil liberties. If there was anything intrinsically meritorious about the application of such a test it had certainly escaped the perception of libertarians until the Nazi-Soviet pact. But social and political forces exerted considerable impact, then as always, upon the cluster of value judgments that surround the application of the Bill of Rights to concrete situations. In this instance, the result was a deepening ambivalence toward the application of constitutional guarantees to those who either acknowledged their Communist sympathies or who refused to deny them.

Throughout 1939, the Civil Liberties Union was wracked by internal discord that accompanied domestic and international political developments. Early in the year Norman Thomas had urged the adoption of an explicit declaration of opposition to totalitarian dictatorships, whether of the left or right. Failure to do so, Thomas warned, would "unnecessarily weaken" the organization.[57] Others expressed similar unease. John Haynes Holmes complained: "So many of us are partisans of other causes, that again and again the cause of civil rights is so bent to the advantage of these other causes as to be warped and strained beyond recognition." [58] Amos Pinchot, the veteran reformer, referred to the reputation of the ACLU for considering "the identity of the violator as more important than the nature of the violation." [59] And John Dos Passos, pushed beyond endurance by the Soviet invasion of Finland, resigned from the ACLU national committee because the board of directors included persons "still able to compromise with Communist-directed organizations." [60]

These criticisms prompted the directors to reexamine their position on civil liberties "in the light of changed conditions." Upon reconsideration, however, the Board issued a statement

[57] Thomas to Executive Committee, March 6, 1939, ACLU Papers, Vol. 2063. For Thomas's concern over the Dies Committee's examination of the ACLU record, see Thomas to Elmer Rice, February 22, 1939, Ernst Papers.

[58] Holmes Statement, October 26, 1939, ACLU Papers, Vol. 2063.

[59] Excerpts of letter from Amos Pinchot, November 1, 1939, ACLU Papers, Vol. 2063.

[60] John Dos Passos to Baldwin, November 20, 1939, ACLU Papers, Vol. 2160.

noting merely that ACLU members differed sharply in their political views and were free to express these differences without implicating the organization.[61] As Roger Baldwin explained, "We can hardly apply in our Board or membership the test of political or other views. . . . I don't see how we could adopt any such policy without doing violence to our fundamental principle." [62] Any test of political views, Baldwin told Dos Passos, would have dire consequences. "Once we begin drawing such a line, there is no end to it." [63]

But the pressure to draw that line increased. The anti-Communists, incensed by Stalin's alliance with Hitler, were certain that their political rivals were guilty of "tolerance of intolerance" in their "temporary, partial, and fragment[ed] defense of civil liberty. . . ." [64] They disregarded warnings that a test of belief would commit the civil liberties organization to the very principle it had consistently opposed in statutes, prosecutions, and administrative proceedings. As discord increased, both factions could agree only that mutual hostility and distrust was crippling the work of the Civil Liberties Union; each placed sole responsibility upon the other.[65] The anti-Communists, however, possessed one vital advantage: given the prevailing hostility toward Nazi Fascism, they could more easily capitalize upon international developments and their domestic implications as long as Stalin and Hitler re-

[61] Board of Directors, Special Meeting, December 4, 1939, ACLU Papers, Vol. 2063.

[62] Baldwin to Robert A. Hoffman, December 4, 1939, ACLU Papers, Vol. 2064.

[63] Baldwin to Dos Passos, December 4, 1939, ACLU Papers, Vol. 2160.

[64] Thomas to Fraenkel, December 19, 1939, ACLU Papers, Vol. 2063. See also Ernst to Margaret DeSilver, December 9, 1939, and Holmes to Richard E. Childs, December 22, 1939, *ibid.*

[65] Ward to Richard S. Childs, December 19, 1939, ACLU Papers, Vol. 2062. Ward, a particular target of the anti-Communists, insisted that the sole test for membership had been, and should be, "attitude toward the violations of the Bill of Rights that come before this Board, and actions in regard to the Bill of Rights outside this Board." See Ward to Childs, January 9, 1940, ACLU Papers, Vol. 2162; Baldwin to Childs, December 30, 1939, ACLU Papers, Vol. 2062. Despite the factional conflict, according to Baldwin, board decisions "have not represented compromises which weaken us. . . ."

mained allies. In the ensuing clash between ideological politics and libertarian values, the Bill of Rights was the major casualty.

In January, 1940, attorney Morris Ernst, who, with identical tactics, had already precipitated a similar struggle in the National Lawyers Guild over the same issue, drafted a resolution that made a test of political opinion a condition of membership on ACLU governing committees.[66] That resolution, adopted by the Civil Liberties Union in February, disclaimed tests of opinion as a condition of membership in the organization itself or in determination of whose right to expression would be defended. But the personnel of governing committees and staff "is properly subject to the test of consistency in the defense of civil liberties in all aspects and all places." Such consistency was "inevitably compromised by persons who champion civil liberties in the United States and yet who justify or tolerate the denial of civil liberties by dictatorships abroad." It was, therefore, "inappropriate" for any person to serve on ACLU governing committees "who is a member of any political organization which supports totalitarian dictatorship in any country, or who by his public declarations indicates his support of such a principle."[67] In an accompanying press release, the Union conceded that the resolution "appears to set up a test of opinion," but it claimed that it was consistent with Union policy not to elect leaders whose support of civil liberties "for everybody without distinction" seemed qualified. In fact, as the ACLU acknowledged, "the occasion for raising this issue at this time is the increasing tension which has resulted everywhere from the direction of the Communist international movement since the Soviet-Nazi pact."[68]

The February resolution triggered an impassioned response from libertarians who believed that their organization, guided by political expediency, had compromised its commitment to

[66] Ernst to Baldwin, January, 1940, ACLU Papers, Vol. 2163. In mid-January, by a one-vote margin, the board of directors had dismissed the need for such a test. Minutes, Board of Directors, January 18, 1940, ACLU Papers, Vol. 2162.

[67] Ernst to Baldwin, January 1940, ACLU Papers, Vol. 2163. The full text of the February resolution is reprinted in Lamont, *Trial*, pp. 42–43.

[68] Statement to Press, ACLU Papers, Vol. 2060.

the Bill of Rights.[69] According to its critics, the ACLU had adopted the principle of guilt by association in making mere membership in an organization sufficient ground for disqualification from ACLU leadership. Furthermore, by disqualifying people for their public declarations, it had repudiated its traditional distinction between expression and action. Finally, the term "totalitarian dictatorship" represented an excessively vague standard by which to measure culpability.

It was apparent to some members, including the venerable libertarian Alexander Meiklejohn, that one faction had "taken advantage of the current intense feeling against Communists and Communist sympathizers to purge a minority with whom they have for a long time conducted a bitter feud." [70] It was especially ironic, perhaps, that if these criticisms were correct, those responsible for the resolution had disqualified *themselves* for leadership by violating the principle of "consistency in the defense of civil liberties in all aspects and all places." If consistency in defense of civil liberties was a valid test, then those who sponsored and supported the February resolution, thereby denying the freedom of association to their political opponents in the ACLU, had hoisted themselves by their own libertarian petard.

Stung by criticism, the Civil Liberties Union attempted to justify its action. It emphasized that the February resolution was merely a "statement of propriety," rather than a basic change in policy. It insisted that the acts-opinions dichotomy was applicable "only to restraints by law, not to selection of the personnel of the Union." And mere membership, it asserted, "may be a sufficient indication of a point of view inconsistent with civil liberties"—a principle it had consistently repudiated prior to August 1939. As the ACLU explicitly

69 ACLU local chapters were "practically unanimous" in their condemnation of the resolution. Baldwin to Holmes, March 15, 1940, ACLU Papers, Vol. 2163.

70 Ward to ACLU, March 4, 1940, ACLU Papers, Vol. 2059; Alexander H. Frey to Baldwin, March 4, 1940, ACLU Papers, Vol. 2163; "Open Letter to the ACLU from Seventeen Liberals," March 18, 1940, ACLU Papers, Vol. 2066; George P. West, Alexander Meiklejohn, and Edward L. Parsons to National Committee, March 21, 1940, ACLU Papers, Vol. 2160.

acknowledged, the ultimate justification rested upon another consideration: "There is no question but that the Union has been greatly strengthened in public opinion by this action." [71] As John Haynes Holmes, the new ACLU chairman, conceded: "An attitude we could tolerate during a period of a democratic co-operation became difficult to tolerate when differences became so sharp. It was the changed behavior of the Communist movement . . . which prompted our action." [72]

Driven by the inexorable logic of its position—to say nothing of its intent in adopting the February resolution—the ACLU Board of Directors requested the resignation of Elizabeth Gurley Flynn, a charter member of the Union, a member of the Communist Party since 1937, and a director who had been unanimously reelected prior to the Nazi-Soviet pact with full knowledge of her Party membership. Miss Flynn refused to resign, claiming that the board had no right to exclude her for political beliefs and associations. Three charges were then brought against her. According to the first, consistent with the February resolution, her membership in the Communist Party disqualified her as a director. According to the second and third, she was further disqualified by her authorship of two articles, published in the *New Masses* and *Sunday Worker* after the request for her resignation. In one of these, Miss Flynn had accused the Board of Directors of an unseemly quest for public respectability: ". . . they play with Mr. Dies for a whitewash. Maybe the price of same was to wash out the red—who knows?" In the other she declared that the charge against her violated "every principle the ACLU has fought for in the past." [73]

[71] "A Statement to Members and Friends," May 1940, ACLU Papers, Vol. 2163.

[72] Holmes to West, Meiklejohn, and Parsons, April 5, 1940, ACLU Papers, Vol. 2060. As early as 1934 Holmes had urged that any Communist Party members be retired from the board of directors. They were, he wrote, "a group of savages, who, like their Nazi competitors, make war upon all members of the human race excepting themselves." Holmes to Baldwin, February 20, 1934, ACLU Papers, Vol. 676.

[73] Elizabeth Gurley Flynn, "I Am Expelled from Civil Liberties," *Sunday Worker*, March 17, 1940; "Why I Won't Resign from the ACLU," *New Masses*, March 19, 1940, ACLU Papers, Vol. 2062.

In an impassioned, acrimonious confrontation that lasted until the early morning hours, Miss Flynn was tried by the Board of Directors in early May, 1940. In her own defense, Miss Flynn challenged the legitimacy of the February resolution as contrary to ACLU purposes, principles, and traditional policies. The additional charges, she contended, would if upheld censor her right to publicly defend herself against public accusations. "The demand for my resignation," she asserted, "is an attempt to force a minority to conform to the political view of the majority or get out. . . . If this trial occurred elsewhere it would be a case for the ACLU to defend!" [74]

At the core of the trial was the issue that had haunted libertarians since their campaign for workers' rights, and then had irreconcilably divided them after the Nazi-Soviet pact: idealism versus instrumentalism—the problem of means and ends. In the new political context created by the pact, this abstraction was entangled in Soviet foreign policy and American Communism. A critical question was posed to Miss Flynn by Arthur Garfield Hays: ". . . do members of the Communist Party believe in civil liberties and democracy as a way of life, or merely that they are useful methods to be used in a democracy towards bringing about a Communistic system and a dictatorship of the proletariat?" [75] Miss Flynn demurred: rejecting the question as hypothetical, she nonetheless suggested that it might cut as deeply against those directors who, as the resolution and trial demonstrated to her, were themselves using civil liberties instrumentally, as means toward anti-Communism. [76]

In the end, attitudes toward Communism controlled the verdict. As Corliss Lamont asserted during the trial:

> We have been in a first-class political fight here for over a year. The battle has waged back and forth, and has become very bitter whenever this issue comes up. . . . Since we passed the resolution . . . saying that the Union

[74] Lamont, *Trial*, pp. 45–47, 99.

[75] *Ibid.*, p. 124. Hays's opposition to the expulsion of Flynn, on grounds of principle and expediency, appears in Hays to Holmes, February 21, 1940, Arthur Garfield Hays Manuscripts, Princeton University.

[76] *Ibid.*, p. 125.

would make no statement in opposition to any form of government, Mr. Morris Ernst and a group associated with him on this Board have constantly brought up this Communist issue—week after week, and month after month. It has embittered our work and made it almost impossible at times.[77]

And Hays, when asked whether that issue had ever been revived by any member of the left-wing group, replied simply: "No."[78] But the anti-Communists had the votes—barely. On the vote to sustain the critical first charge, based upon Miss Flynn's Party membership, the directors divided 9–9. Chairman John Haynes Holmes, who presided over the trial, then cast his decisive affirmative vote. The second and third charges were sustained 12–8, whereupon a final vote, to expel Miss Flynn, carried 11–8.[79] The final word, however, belonged to Lamont, who, earlier in the evening, had said: 'I think that tonight it is not only Miss Flynn who is on trial, but the members of this Board. . . .'"[80]

Editor's Note: Jerald S. Auerbach's description of this highly-controversial internal ACLU dispute has been challenged by Roger Baldwin, the Union's executive director from 1920 to 1950, who was deeply involved in the events surrounding the conflict. As there are differences in interpretation and fact I have asked Mr. Baldwin to supply his own personal account. His own comments follow:

As the executive director of the Union during the 1930s, I owe the record a correction of the account of the

[77] *Ibid.*, pp. 168–69. A corroborating view of Ernst's role is in Fraenkel to Holmes, September 5, 1940, ACLU Papers, Vol. 2066. Fraenkel insisted that political controversy had been injected into board deliberations not by Communists or fellow travelers, but by "an entirely different minority, of which Morris Ernst was perhaps the chief spokesman." Fortified by the Nazi-Soviet pact and the Soviet invasion of Finland, that group became the majority. My own reading of the sparse minutes of board meetings supports the Lamont-Fraenkel claim.

[78] Lamont, *Trial,* p. 170.

[79] *Ibid.*, pp. 174, 176–77.

[80] *Ibid.*, p. 69. The board's decision to expel Flynn was sustained by the national committee, 27–12, with twelve not voting. ACLU Papers, Vol. 2162.

controversy in the Union over formulating for its leadership a test of consistency in defense of civil liberties. The author devotes twenty-two out of fifty-five pages to this single internal dispute in treating the civil liberties history of a whole decade. This disproportionate attention reflects his view that the Union abandoned its principles by excluding from its councils those who support dictatorships and anti-democratic movements.

But no principles were changed. No such persons had ever been elected initially. What had changed was the need for a clear policy on our choice of leadership following the turnabout of the Communists and their supporters after the Nazi-Soviet pact.

The policy then adopted is policy to this day, embedded in a wider constitutional provision and resolution concerning the qualifications for leadership, with the sole omission of the 1940 ban on membership in specific organizations. It was not the result of pressure, as the author states, by some few Board members. It was the result of a situation long debated. I wrote the 1940 resolution at the request of some Board members and it was handled in prescribed fashion at the annual meeting of the Board and advisory committee, and overwhelmingly adopted.

The author's account is incorrect, biased and misleading. The sufficient answer to its assumption, that the resolution was a departure from principles, is that it has remained in substance Union policy ever since.

The author is wrong in interpreting evidence to conclude that the Union's counsel made a deal with the chairman of the House Un-American Activities Committee to get rid of Communist influences in return for his laying off attack on the Union. The record shows that the only purpose of meetings between them was to arrange for the Union to be heard by the Committee, a simple civil liberties requirement of fair hearing. When the chairman publicly exonerated the Union of any need for investigation it was not due to any deal, but presumably to a personal hearing I had as director with the Committee's investigators.

It is perhaps difficult today to appreciate the shock of the Nazi-Soviet alliance after Communists everywhere had been the most vigorous opponents of Fascism and Nazism. There was strong feeling of betrayal of democratic principles by the Communists. The author thinks that they still should have been welcome allies in civil liberties. That led him to the conclusion that to have been anti-Communist then was to be anti-civil liberties. He does not say the same for being anti-Nazi.

The burden of defending the Flynn trial and expulsion fell to Holmes. He was hard pressed to rebut the allegation, made by one member of the ACLU national committee, that the board majority "convict themselves of having been moved by popular fancy and fleeting public opinion, generated by a war hysteria. . . . Their only excuse for such conduct seems to be that Adolf Hitler signed a treaty with Soviet Russia." [81] Holmes justified the action by rejecting the notion that the Civil Liberties Union was, or should be, "a free society, the members of which may agree or disagree on the question of civil liberty." The Union, he insisted, was "a closed corporation; it is not a free church but a church with a dogma; it has a creed to which all of its officers and members must necessarily subscribe." The right of private voluntary associations to establish their own restrictions upon members was, to Holmes, "one of the priceless guarantees of this republic." The Civil Liberties Union could only serve the cause of liberty if it limited association to "those who believed in liberty." Holmes, however, backed himself against the wall of political expediency. The directors, he explained, had confronted the specter of "loyalties to outside political and economic issues and systems." Consequently, "if we were to transact any business at all, we had to exorcise this ghost—get rid of this political controversy." Like other liberals, Holmes explained, "we were lenient toward the Communists. . . . We leaned over backward in this endeavor, and at last we toppled over in confusion and dismay." [82]

[81] A. F. Whitney to Baldwin, August 16, 1940, ACLU Papers, Vol. 2060. Whitney's long, critical letter was given to Holmes for reply.

[82] Holmes to Whitney, August 26, 1940, ACLU Papers, Vol. 2060.

Holmes's position rested upon the premise that anti-Communism and liberty were identical; that a member of the Communist Party 'is not free either to think or act for himself, and therefore for this reason is not qualified to sit as a member of our Board." [83] According to his unfolding syllogism Miss Flynn, as a Party member, could not think or act independently; therefore, she could not remain a director. Given the premise, no proof was necessary that Miss Flynn had *in fact* ever spoken or acted detrimentally to liberty. Indeed, no evidence was ever presented to suggest that she had done so, and she offered unchallenged evidence to demonstrate that she had not. To rest an entire case upon the fact of Communist Party membership seemed sufficient to some board members. They did not, however, confront the question why, if mere membership justified disqualification, Miss Flynn had been unanimously reelected to the Board of Directors when her Party membership was publicly known.

Holmes labeled her reelection a "grievous fault"—a reflection of the undue leniency of liberals toward Communists.[84] But this judgment required a retrospective projection of values from one political climate to an earlier, quite different, one. Reelecting a Communist to the Board of Directors was not a "grievous fault" early in 1939; it was perceived as such only *after* the Nazi-Soviet pact. The problem was not to justify Miss Flynn's reelection, since there was no evidence at the time that she held commitments antithetical to libertarian values. The problem was to justify her expulsion by demonstrating that European power politics were alone sufficient to destroy the credentials of one whose commitment to liberty had hitherto been unchallenged and against whom no new evidence of culpability was, or could be, offered. Holmes, like the other anti-Communist libertarians, asserted this claim but beyond his *ipse dixit* no evidence was presented to sustain it.

Holmes' proposition that the Union was a "church with a dogma" was unimpeachable if the "creed to which all its officers and members must necessarily subscribe" was in fact liberty, not something else. "How otherwise can we serve our

83 *Ibid.*
84 *Ibid.*

cause, be faithful to our ideals, transact our business?" Holmes properly inquired.[85] During the crisis of 1939–40, however, it is not altogether clear that liberty was the sole dogma. Libertarians like Holmes had acutely perceived the instrumentalism of those who had used civil liberties as tools for workers' rights, but not for employers. They failed to perceive that once the issue shifted from labor-management relations to Communism they were themselves guilty of instrumentalism in pursuit of political objectives. After the Nazi-Soviet pact the dogma that Holmes, Ernst, and others defended was anti-Communism, with the freedoms of speech, press, and association within their own organization reserved only for those who repudiated Soviet foreign policy. In practice, Holmes's desire to limit association to those who believed in liberty yielded to a policy that limited association to those who disbelieved in Communism, a test that was less self-evident than the anti-Communists assumed.

When Holmes asserted the right of the Civil Liberties Union not to be free he meant, of course, to impose restraints that preserved rather than destroyed liberty. Although the anti-Communists believed that their restrictions upon liberty served the cause of liberty, their claim did not make it so. Indeed, by the standards of their own test—"limiting association with us to those who believed in liberty"—they were as vulnerable as Miss Flynn to expulsion. The hypothetical question put to her regarding her belief as a Communist in civil liberties as a means or as an end could also be asked of them. Miss Flynn, in fact, did so implicitly during her trial when she claimed: "It would be equally logical for me to object to any upholder of capitalism remaining on the Board on the assumption that real civil liberties are impossible of realization under such a society, a reasonably demonstrable proposition from the 20 years' record of the ACLU!"[86] Unless belief in liberty and anti-Communism were compatible, there was no justification for Miss Flynn's expulsion. To establish their compatability some evidence beyond mere membership in the Communist Party was necessary.

The dilemma that libertarians confronted before World

[85] Holmes to Whitney, August 26, 1940, ACLU Papers, Vol. 2060.
[86] Lamont, *Trial*, pp. 99–100.

War II was not amenable to easy resolution. Committed to the test of overt acts, to the principle of free expression of political views, and to the repudiation of membership in political organizations as a test of libertarian *bona fides,* they found themselves in a quandry after the Nazi-Soviet pact. Retention of these principles exposed their political vulnerability. Repudiation required the sacrifice of libertarian principle to political exigencies. Buffeted by the winds of international and domestic politics, many libertarians chose the second alternative. On each critical issue, libertarian principle was sacrificed. The February resolution repudiated a prior commitment to free expression of political views. Implementation of its mandate in the trial and expulsion of Miss Flynn substituted mere membership in a political organization for overt acts in determining individual culpability. In a tragic twist of irony, an organization whose *raison d'être* was the defense of civil liberties imposed a political test that curtailed freedom of expression and made guilt by association the inevitable consequence. Although the members of John Haynes Holmes's "church with a dogma" pursued the holy grail of liberty, many of them ended their quest by worshipping at the altar of anti-Communism.

With the resurgence of anti-Communism on the eve of World War II, the story of civil liberties in the Depression decade ended as it began: the right to dissent was reserved for those who repudiated Communism. Where economic and civil liberties issues had overlapped, and economic recovery dictated tolerance of workers' rights, libertarians had registered impressive gains. Applying instrumentalist weapons they stretched the First Amendment to cover industrial relations, hitherto the domain of employers' prerogatives, not workers' rights. But whenever anti-radicalism and civil liberties issues coincided, libertarian achievements were circumscribed. With the rejuvenation of anti-Communism the rout of libertarians began. Not only were they helpless in the face of the Smith Act, the Dies Committee investigation, and bureaucratic incursions upon liberty; they contributed to their own demise by debilitating their defense organization in the name of liberty. By 1940, anti-Communists guarded the gates to the First Amendment. The implications for dissent were chilling.

The civil liberties struggles of the Depression decade raised a perennial question in a new setting: were the provisions of the Bill of Rights means to political ends, or ends in themselves? The fact that idealists and instrumentalists crossed like ships in the night over this issue suggests that means and ends were interrelated. During the thirties this issue underwent three discrete phases: first, the fight for workers' rights; then, equal treatment for employers; finally, civil liberties for Communists and fellow travelers. During the first phase libertarians were undifferentiated partners in a common cause. They shared a commitment to the Bill of Rights as a means to a common end, the right to unionize. Once that battle was won, however, their alliance disintegrated. The question of employers' rights exposed quite divergent ends. Idealists properly (by libertarian standards) refused to discriminate; more radical instrumentalists demonstrated that their primary commitment was to anti-capitalist social change rather than to impartial application of the Bill of Rights. Stung by this exposure of divergent ends, wounded by Dies Committee attacks and shocked by the Nazi-Soviet pact, the idealists on labor-management issues picked up the gauntlet of instrumentalism. By 1939 their commitment to anti-Communism took precedence over libertarian values, just as the radicals' commitment to anti-capitalism had been paramount only a few years earlier.

To chart these meanderings is easy; to evaluate them is not. It is always easier to stand in historical judgment than to stand at the libertarian barricades. Yet the necessity for judgment remains. Anti-radicalism, a conditioned reflex deeply imbedded in the American psyche, invariably has failed to distinguish critics from defenders of the right to criticize. Consequently society has exerted considerable pressure upon libertarians to bend their principles to "social necessity." Invariably, however, "social necessity" is defined to justify anti-radicalism. Libertarians who permit themselves to be maneuvered into this definitional trap find escape impossible. In practice, they accept freedom of expression only for those who repudiate the freedom to express radical alternatives. Freedom of expression then becomes nothing more than the freedom to express conformity to prevailing political institutions and doctrines. By accepting such constraints, anti-Communist libertarians set self-imposed limits upon their capacity to resolve critical civil liberties problems of their time. More seriously, by imposing anti-libertarian solutions they accentuated these problems. Anti-Communism and liberty might, in particular circumstances, be compatible. They are not inherently identical. Those who believed in their identity displayed the fatal flaw in libertarian thought during the Depression decade. Their belief did incalculable harm to freedom of expression prior to World War II.

Justice Holmes once conceded: "Persecution for the expression of opinion seems to me perfectly logical. If you have no doubt of your premises or your power and want a certain result with all your heart you naturally express your wishes in law and sweep away all opposition." [87] Although Holmes opted for "free trade in ideas," he was exceptional. Most Americans, certain that capitalism and democracy are identical, have preferred ideological monopoly. The definition of noxious ideas has changed—from anarchism to peace to unionization to Communism to racial integration and back to peace—but hostility toward ideas labeled subversive has persisted. Official and unofficial sanctions have strengthened anti-radicalism, assuring its spread as a virus endemic to modern American life.

[87] *Abrams* v. *United States,* 250 U.S. 630 (1919).

SHADOWS OF WAR
AND FEAR

WILLIAM PRESTON, JR.

During World War II the Armed Forces Radio Service interpreted the mandate to "inform, educate, and entertain" the troops largely in terms of the third category, thereby lining up with the historic priorities of broadcasting itself. At one point, however, a documentary script describing the adjustment of black workers in previously all-white factories arrived for transmission to Uncle Sam's boys. When the AFRS officer-in-charge heard the disc, he called in the producer, with whom he then had the following crisp exchange:

"Are you responsible for this?"

"Yes."

"Now get this straight and you'd better remember it! No nigger-loving shit goes out over this network!" [1]

That brief dialogue captures some essential qualities of the 1940s, both in war and peace: the crude censorship, the blunt, unfeeling racism, and the administrative vindictiveness aroused

[1] Quoted in Eric Barnouw, *The Golden Web: A History of Broadcasting in the United States, 1933–53* (New York, 1968), pp. 196–97.

by challenges to the status quo. The decade did not necessarily welcome the free trade in ideas on which the American democratic experiment must assuredly depend. And radio was not the only sinner.

Hollywood immediately comes to mind; the movie moguls and their banker allies were then at the height of their power. A schizophrenic industry, movie-making combined monopoly arrogance in production and marketing with cowardly subservience to the dictates of moral canons at least a century outdated. The frightened men who ran the industry positively avoided the controversial. A bland screen was a profitable one, and much of the output quarantined the public from any ideas that might prove deleterious to juvenile innocence. As one producer reportedly put it, "If I want to send a message, I'll call Western Union." Social issues were out.[2]

The atrophy of free speech at the mass communications level was only one of the civil liberties problems of the forties. Other fundamental freedoms were also threatened. Wiretapping became a persistent illegal intruder. Even Eleanor Roosevelt had her hotel room bugged during World War II by devices that could hear any conversation therein. And Judge Learned Hand was so disgusted by the trend in searches accompanying arrests that he remarked, "It is a small consolation to know that one's papers are safe only so long as one is not at home." If privacy and procedural due process faced some new challenges, the concept of equality continued to suffer from violations decades old.[3]

Long denied the equal protection of the laws and numbered among the most "constitutionally underprivileged" minorities in history, American blacks remained trapped in the ghetto of tokenism. The white majority still believed that the Negroes were "going too fast" in their call for civil rights. In 1947 the black community's indignant desperation led to an attempt to unmask the arrogance of this position. The NAACP took the

[2] *Ibid.*, pp. 105–6. See also Ira H. Carmen, *Movies, Censorship, and the Law* (Ann Arbor, Mich., 1966).

[3] Harriet F. Pilpel, "The Challenge of Privacy," in Alan Reitman, ed., *The Price of Liberty* (New York, 1968), p. 24; Judge Hand quoted in Jacob W. Landynski, *Search and Seizure and the Supreme Court: A Study in Constitutional Interpretation* (Baltimore, Md., 1966), p. 117.

case of its fourteen million people to the United Nations in "a frank and earnest appeal to all the world for elemental justice against the treatment which the United States has visited upon us for three centuries." [4]

Indians, Mexican-Americans, Puerto Ricans and colonial subjects in Guam and Samoa might also have composed militant appeals to world opinion in the 1940s. Nor would the Japanese-Americans soon forget their war-time imprisonment in concentration camps, a preventive detention of a whole people allegedly justified by military necessity and ratified by the Supreme Court itself. Typically, the nation obscured the reality of this suppression in rhetoric more congenial to the abstract libertarianism it professed to follow. It called the camps "relocation centers" and pretended the internees were there on a sort of holiday from the West Coast. [5]

Equally ominous from the viewpoint of civil liberties was the decade's manic preoccupation with loyalty. Faced with a seemingly endless security emergency during war and cold war, the country panicked, allowing a pathological fear of dangerous internal minorities (a nativist reaction almost as old as the nation) to overcome any realistic assessment of the actual dangers. Nor could those investigating the threat define its characteristics with any precision. By the end of the 1940s the security obsession had made serious inroads into free inquiry and due process—so much so that Zechariah Chafee, Jr., could offer an appropriate epitaph for the decline while testifying on the Mundt-Nixon Bill of 1949: "If we no longer want to be the land of the free," Chaffee suggested, "at least let us be the home of the brave." [6]

These vignettes suggest that the age-old tension between freedom and repression was still alive and well during the decade of the forties and that "eternal vigilance," as the

[4] NAACP Press Release, October 24, 1947, ACLU Papers, Box 8, Vol. 18, 1947. The reference here and in succeeding footnotes to the ACLU Papers refers to the ACLU Archives at the Princeton University Library, Princeton, New Jersey.

[5] Chief, Aliens Division, to ACLU, September 25, 1942, ACLU Papers, Scrapbook 2444, Princeton University.

[6] Quoted in Alan D. Harper, *The Politics of Loyalty: The White House and the Communist Issue* (Westport, Conn., 1969), p. 35.

American Civil Liberties Union has always insisted, would
still be "the price of liberty." The New Deal had not been,
therefore, a fundamental turning point in the history of American civil liberties, however much it may have done to promote
due process and substantive justice and equality. In fact, the
legacy of the 1930s was an ambiguous one, dramatic testimony
to the political pragmatism of a broker state whose partisan
commitments did not always respect human freedom. An uneasy equilibrium of forces thus characterized the civil liberties
atmosphere as the 1940s began.

On the positive side, labor had won its long-contested right
to exist and organize, validated by the Wagner Act. The New
Deal had also created a variety of administrative commissions
to defend and extend individual and minority rights, and it
had staffed those boards with dedicated libertarians. The
Supreme Court, now the Roosevelt Court, seemed intent on
reaffirming the priority of the first ten amendments.[7]

Yet a darker, even repressive, mood had survived the onslaughts of liberal reform, for currents of arch-conservatism
and rock-ribbed super-patriotism ran strongly during the thirties. Infiltrating more than one congressional committee, this
vigilante spirit found its true home with Martin Dies and his
know-nothing investigations of "un-American" opinion and
association. Representing an intense popular feeling against
aliens, radicals, and other dissenters, it was largely an anti-
Communist hysteria. This paranoid atmosphere was further
fouled by the backlash against New Deal reform programs
and by the renewed vigor of the conservative coalition in Congress, whose Republican wing repeatedly expected to seize
power in the forties by exploiting charges of Communism in
government and un-Americanism in the nation. And there were
numerous New Deal bureaucrats who sympathized with this
repressive public temper.[8]

[7] Jerold S. Auerbach, *Labor and Liberty: The La Follette Committee
and the New Deal* (Indianapolis, Ind., 1966), John P. Roche, *The
Quest for the Dream: The Development of Civil Rights and Human Relations in Modern America* (New York, 1963).

[8] Walter Goodman, *The Committee: The Extraordinary Career of the
House Committee on Un-American Activities* (New York, 1968), pp. 3–

In 1940 the nation celebrated the 150th anniversary of the Bill of Rights. Whether it could also honor it in practice was another matter. A decade of continuing crisis would certainly test that commitment. If there were those that would fight for the rights of all, there were others whose priorities threatened basic liberties. The country might once again expose its darker side if there were enough pressures, as someone later argued in the McCarthy era, "to give up our fundamental freedoms in order to preserve our democratic way of life."

"If it walks like a duck and talks like a duck, it must be a duck," was not just a crude though humorous aphorism describing the modus operandi of Joe McCarthy's investigations during the 1950s. It was in fact the guiding principle by which the United States evaluated loyalty during the decade of the forties, a shameful historical admission to have to make. The sins for which McCarthy has been condemned were a common feature of American attitudes, policies, and procedures in the nation's quest for absolute security. To condemn McCarthy is to blame Frankenstein's monster and not Frankenstein, his master. And censuring the senator avoided a more embarrassing confrontation with the country's collective guilt, however hard it may be to think of McCarthy as a scapegoat.[9]

The loyalty-security issue was certainly enemy number one on the ACLU's most wanted list for the decade. It is not hard to see why. Consumed by an evangelical fury, the country practiced ideological pacification with scant regard for a series of substantive and procedural rights long considered fundamental. Sensitized to subversion and deception by the real evils plaguing international politics (fifth columns, aggressive war, poisonous propaganda, espionage, and clandestine "fronts"), the populace and its leaders overreacted. Their victims were members of groups that never totalled over one-half of 1 percent of the total population (often much less). Yet so threatening did these enemies seem that no strategy, however extreme, could provide the reassurance so desperately de-

116; Robert Griffith, *The Politics of Fear: Joseph R. McCarthy and the Senate* (Lexington, Ky., 1970), pp. 32, 34, 328.

[9] Quoted in Alexander Kendrick, *Prime Time: The Life of Edward R. Murrow* (New York, 1970), p. 54.

manded; not even the three hundred federal, state, and local laws against subversion, nor the five hundred edicts against the resident Japanese.[10]

This frame of mind, so reminiscent of the witchcraft delusions, craved simplistic conspiratorial explanations and pursued the chimera of absolute security. Totalitarian unity would be achieved by inspecting and labeling beliefs as if human beings could be certified "pure" like food and drugs. Yet the process was seriously flawed. Loyalty itself remained undefined, and no one ever devised exact standards to discover whether or not it existed in a person. No matter, the security establishment had substitute norms as slippery as any in history. One was the idea of a "party line" (Japanese, Nazi, or Communist). Anyone supporting policies favored by the "enemy" became subject to novel quasi-legal charges of "guilt by coincidence" or "guilt by verbal association," also described as "parallelism." And under the Smith Act, passed during the tense summer of 1940, the government could prosecute a conspiracy to propagandize, that is, could attack speech twice removed from overt acts. During the decade Trotskyites, Fascist "seditionists," and top Communists would all fall victim to this extreme abridgment of free speech.[11]

Stereotypes that imposed distorted and frightening images on the public consciousness guaranteed that the "disloyal" would be treated not as individuals but as members of evil and disciplined conspiracies. Even those suspected of being Communists, according to Lawrence Chamberlain, were assumed to have "all the qualities . . . of the most dedicated party operative." This mental set ignored human variety and the capacity to retain multiple loyalties (even contradictory

10 Walter Gellhorn, ed., *The States and Subversion* (Ithaca, N.Y., 1952), *passim;* Mortin Grodzins, *Americans Betrayed: Politics and the Japanese Evacuation* (Chicago, 1949), *passim.*

11 Lawrence S. Wittner, *Rebels Against War: The American Peace Movement, 1941–1960* (New York, 1969), pp. 34, 97, 101; Jacobus ten Broek, Edward N. Barnhart, and Floyd W. Matson, *Prejudice, War and the Constitution* (Berkeley, Calif., 1954), pp. 222–23. Material on the mass sedition case that introduced many of these concepts may be found in ACLU Papers, Scrapbooks 2355, 2503, 2507, 2508, 2545, 2605, 2679, 2986, and Box 1, 1946, Vol. 39; Box 20–26, 1949, Vol. 25.

ones), and justified the harshest policies the evil stereotypes might evoke.[12]

Even these measures, however, did not provide the illusion of security because the country wanted to be further protected from the "crime" of potential disloyalty. Hence the notion of "preventive law" to uncover the seeds of subversion in ideas and attitudes not yet subversive and to punish suspects, as Walter Gellhorn has described the process, "in anticipation of criminality that has not yet occurred and as a means of forestalling it." Even evidence of loyalty itself did not prove satisfactory, for it could as easily signify a conspiracy to mask other more sinister objectives.[13]

From the late 1930s through the Truman administration a sustained offensive took place to eliminate disloyalty and induce one hundred percent Americanism among the population at large. A variety of strategies, some deliberate, others spontaneous, served this end: exclusion (refugees), mobbing (Jehovah's Witnesses), imprisonment (Nisei), conspiracy trials (pro-Fascists and radicals), exposure through congressional and state investigations (leftists, teachers, New Dealers, and Gerald L. K. Smith), and loyalty-security testing (the new Triple-A program to plow under every fourth federal subversive). Political considerations played a significant role in all of these cases, so that the victims of the decade's repression were also cast as scapegoats for reasons ulterior to their actual behavior.

Two groups first experienced the loyalty tremors cracking the facade of libertarianism—European refugees and the Jehovah's Witnesses. The former succumbed to racist and restrictionist attitudes at the highest levels of government, and the latter fell prey to the compulsive patriotism of the small-town American mob; which proves that suppression is not a pre-

[12] Lawrence H. Chamberlain, *Loyalty and Legislative Action: A Survey of Activity by the New York State Legislature, 1919–1949* (Ithaca, N.Y., 1951), pp. 205, 218; John H. Schaar, *Loyalty in America* (Berkeley, Calif., 1957), *passim;* ACLU Papers, Scrapbooks 2160–66, 2174, 2181, 2186, 2264, 2269.

[13] Schaar, *Loyalty*, pp. 133, 172–73; Gellhorn, *The States and Subversion*, p. 362; Henry Steele Commager, *Freedom and Order: A Commentary on the American Political Scene* (Cleveland, Ohio, 1968), p. 82.

rogative of class, position, or education. For five agonizing years (1939–44) the Roosevelt administration blocked the entrance of the desperate people fleeing Hitler's extermination camps. While professing good intentions, the government failed utterly to go beyond "a politics of gesture," a product not only of anti-Semitic and anti-alien prejudice but of fantasies of foreign subversion. FDR would not risk a political battle where supposed national and partisan survival was an issue, regardless of the libertarian values involved.[14]

Jehovah's Witnesses, those persistent advocates of religious liberty, won a place in the vigilante victims' hall of fame by refusing to salute the flag, a defiance that seemed the essence of subversive disloyalty in those years (1940–44). A 1940 Supreme Court decision upholding the salute coincided with a vigorous missionary campaign by the Witnesses. The result was an extended repression in which communities throughout the country expelled from school some two thousand nonsaluting children and mobbed hundreds of Witnesses distributing literature in some of the worst religious riots in American history. After the Court reversed itself in 1943, some of the worst hysteria subsided and the Witnesses themselves shifted their agitation to the draft and the military. Yet eight years of tenacious litigation by the Witnesses and their stalwart and lonely ally, the American Civil Liberties Union, and an astonishing amount of physical abuse did force the country (in the Barnette decision) to recognize the claims of conscience and religion and see the essential error in attempting to coerce "an expression of belief or state of mind." [15]

If the Witnesses won this grudging tolerance for their eccentric behavior, the Japanese-Americans (Nisei) were much less fortunate, as their war-time imprisonment proved. Two and a half months after Pearl Harbor, the claim of military

[14] Henry L. Feingold, *The Politics of Rescue: The Roosevelt Administration and the Holocaust, 1938–1945* (New Brunswick, N.J., 1970), pp. 121, 128, 130–31, 135–36, 146, 159, 296–97; Arthur D. Morse, *While Six Million Died: A Chronicle of American Apathy* (New York, 1968), *passim.*

[15] David R. Manwaring, *Render Unto Caesar: The Flag Salute Controversy* (Chicago, 1962), pp. 26–28, 30, 163, 176–79, 185–87, 225–53; ACLU, *Annual Report* (1935–1936), p. 41; ACLU Papers, Scrapbook 2215; Box 6–10, 1948, Vol. 6.

necessity and West Coast pressure induced Roosevelt to order the removal of 112,000 Japanese-Americans, two-thirds of whom were citizens. The evacuation itself took over six months, and no such program went into effect for the more exposed Hawaiian Islands. This, in spite of a total absence of sabotage (interpreted as a concerted plot to delay violence). Detained behind barbed wire and by military force, the Nisei had to swear a loyalty oath *as American citizens* to repudiate Japan. The War Relocation Authority (WRA), needled by Congressman Martin Dies for "softness," believed it could separate "the questionable minority from the wholesome majority" and released only those "above suspicion."

Yet even admittedly loyal citizens suffered continued detention because of WRA judgments as to how much of an exodus from the camps was "socially desirable" given the mood of public opinion. The Japanese-American victims were thus expected to make the sacrifices that would reassure the larger community responsible for their prosecution, a policy not theoretically different from the purge trials of the Stalin era. The majority thus accepted "loyally" their evacuation, the WRA's definition of release, tremendous economic losses, enlistment in a racially segregrated army, and massive resettlement (54,000 did not dare return home to the West Coast).[16]

If the American Civil Liberties Union has rightly called the evacuation "the worst single wholesale violation of civil rights of American citizens in our history," the Supreme Court approval of it surely ranks as "one of the great failures in its history. . . ." Blandly approving the program as a legitimate security operation given the apparent "dire emergency" and "public necessity," and without challenging the government claims, the racism, or the military control, the decision left available for future use a war-making power almost without constitutional limitations.[17]

Compared to the Nisei incarceration, the war-time Smith

[16] Ten Broek *et al., Prejudice,* pp. 250–51; Robert K. Carr, *Federal Protection of Civil Rights: Quest for a Sword* (Ithaca, 1947), p. 18; Grodzins, *Americans Betrayed, passim;* ACLU Papers, Scrapbooks 2264, 2363, 2394–2397, 2463–2470, 2584–2590, 2662–2664.

[17] Ten Broek *et al., Prejudice,* pp. 211–333; Grodzins, *Americans Betrayed,* pp. 373–74; ACLU Papers, Scrapbooks 2355 and 2363.

Act indictment and trial (eventually dismissed) of Joseph McWilliams, Lawrence Dennis, and some thirty pro-Fascists, Bundists, and their sympathizers may look like a comic interlude. Yet this mass sedition prosecution invigorated widely held attitudes that threatened traditional liberties and forecast what would come to typify cold war repression. Applauded by almost the entire country, including the left and liberal leadership, the prosecution attacked the free speech then despised by the majority by means of dragnet conspiracy charges, using guilt by association and condemning the defendants for views that paralleled Nazi propaganda *before* the outbreak of war. The case thus made the "party line" and past associations the tests of loyalty and abandoned the standard of overt acts. Few people protested this war-time suppression. Since the trial exploited the nation's hatred for the racial views and pro-Axis sympathies of the defendants, even most liberals had been willing to sacrifice free speech in pursuit of higher goals, including national unity.[18]

The anti-Communist crusade that followed was simply a more persistent, pervasive, and damaging extension of those war-time excesses, and would have come sooner had not the Communist Party line and U.S. policy coincided during some four years of anti-Nazi combat. As it was, by 1940 a campaign was already underway to remove Communists and fellow travelers from positions of influence in associational life. Assuming the worst stereotypes to be true, groups generally acted as if Communist Party membership was in itself an overt act requiring no further proof of subversive behavior. These private purges tended to overkill by including supposed sympathizers, added to the conviction that radicals were lepers, and often satisfied reprehensible objectives related to internal organizational conflict. All of it set a bad example for public officials to follow.[19]

[18] Francis Biddle, *In Brief Authority* (New York, 1962), pp. 234–43; Nathaniel Weyl, *Treason: The Story of Disloyalty and Betrayal in American History* (Washington, D.C., 1950), pp. 320–39; ACLU Papers, Scrapbooks 2335, 2503, 2507, 2508, 2545, 2605, 2679, 2686, Box 1, 1946, Vol. 39.

[19] Chamberlain, *Loyalty*, pp. 125–26; ACLU Papers, Scrapbooks 2160–2164.

Their containment of the Communist menace proceeded on three major interrelated fronts: exposures by investigation, Smith Act prosecutions, and loyalty-security programs. Congressional investigations of "un-Americanism," the analogue to Russia's "counter-revolutionism," defined subversion broadly enough to suggest any effort to impede or distort U.S. policy. Presumed by the courts to have a legislative purpose, HUAC and its allies also exploited the libertarian distaste for stealth, anonymity, totalitarianism, and dual allegiance. The investigators defended freedom while simultaneously betraying it.

The price to civil liberties was high. Attacking "fronts," unions, the media, government agencies, minority groups, and Gerald L. K. Smith (for balance), the probers intimidated their enemies and imposed a form of outlawry, infamy, or ostracism on individuals named as suspect (an index of one million subversives was compiled by HUAC). Loss of jobs and blacklisting often followed. The inquisitions into beliefs and associations also threatened the First and Fifth Amendments and violated due process by the star chamber quality of the proceedings. The main obscenity of the forties was, therefore, not something the censors could do much about. It was the indecent exposure of individuals by verbally stripping them in public, and this political pornography, ideological dirt for dirt's sake, had no socially redeeming feature, though it did represent contemporary community standards.[20]

Smith Act prosecutions would also have a "chilling effect" on dissent by suggesting that speech itself could be punished even without a showing of clear and present danger. In 1941, largely at the behest of the Teamsters' Union leadership, the Roosevelt administration indicted and convicted the Trotskyite Socialist Worker Party members who controlled the truckers' local in Minneapolis. Their crime, a supposed conspiracy to advocate the overthrow of the government, was one of opinion only, without evidence of overt acts. If the United States was

[20] Goodman, *The Committee*, pp. 125–51, 172; Martin Shapiro, *Freedom of Speech: The Supreme Court and Judicial Review* (Englewood Cliffs, N.J., 1966), pp. 165, 167; Robert K. Carr, *The House Committee on Un-American Activities, 1945–50* (Ithaca, N.Y., 1952), *passim;* ACLU Papers, Scrapbooks 2180, 2366.

really in danger of overthrow from "a few fanatics who control a single local of a trade union," as John Dos Passos described it, then the country was in bad shape indeed.[21]

The 1948 indictment of twelve top Communist leaders and their subsequent conviction was part of the toughness the Truman administration felt it should exhibit to rebut Republican charges that it was "soft on Communism." Since the Communist Party had been operating for years without the government bringing charges, a trial for advocacy and belief alone hardly met the clear and present danger test. Unable to indict the Party for sedition or conspiracy to commit sedition because it lacked evidence of overt acts, the Justice Department built its case on a conspiracy to advocate. "Thus, paradoxically," Martin Shapiro has pointed out, "the defendants were convicted in an area where they were protected by the supposedly rigorous demands of the First Amendment precisely because they could not be convicted under the routine protections of criminal law." A guilty verdict was inevitable since proof of criminal intent has always been "an empty protection" in sedition trials.[22]

The appeals courts refused to speak out against a peacetime sedition law or convictions for advocacy under it. The Supreme Court would not review the Minneapolis trial. In the 1951 *Dennis* decision it upheld the Communist prosecution and accepted a formula earlier utilized by Judge Learned Hand, which undermined the First Amendment by focusing on "the ultimate consequences of any speech no matter how remote those results may be. . . ." Advocacy "that seems threatening to the nation" and speech "twice removed from action" was thereby made liable should some judges dislike it. Even though it lost its fight to overturn the Smith Act convictions, the

[21] Thomas J. Pahl, "The G-String Conspiracy: Political Reprisal or Armed Revolt," *Labor History*, 8 (Winter, 1967), 30–51; John Dos Passos, "Letter to a Liberal in Office," August 13, 1941, ACLU Papers, Scrapbook 2265; also Scrapbooks 2306, 2527; personal interview with Roger Baldwin, October, 1968.

[22] Shapiro, *Freedom of Speech*, pp. 63–64; C. Hermon Pritchett, *Civil Liberties and the Vinson Court* (Chicago, 1954), pp. 72–75, 244; Leonard W. Levy, *Freedom of Speech and Press in Early American History: Legacy of Suppression* (New York, 1963), p. 153.

ACLU publicized the frightening and unnecessary erosion of free speech. One of its lawyers rightly called the *Dennis* case "more dangerous to American freedom than the Communists themselves." [23]

While investigations and indictments narrowed the field of permissible belief and associations on the left, the loyalty-security program extended the pressure for conformity to untold thousands of government employees, their friends, and their relations. Initiated in the 1939 Hatch Act and expanded during World War II, loyalty testing became an obsession in the post-war years, a hostage to anti-Communism and political imperatives. After the 1946 Republican congressional victory, Truman set in motion a new employee loyalty policy with awesome implications.

Keyed to the notion of absolute security, the program assumed that even one potentially disloyal person was a serious threat. Without defining loyalty or devising accurate measurements of it, the investigations added the unreliable test of membership in front organizations as significant evidence needing rebuttal. Association with any organization on the attorney general's list of subversive organizations (totaling 197 by 1950) became a presumption of guilt. Employees naturally tried to avoid the controversial and fill their dossiers only with positive proof of adherence to approved values and policies, so that loyalty became confused with conformity. The procedures were inquisitional rather than accusatorial, and sadly lacking in the basic elements of due process. Even worse were the conditions in departments authorized to make security dismissals without charges or hearings.[24]

Had it all been necessary? In retrospect the answer seems clearly not. The country should have trusted its counter-

[23] Irving Dilliard, *The Spirit of Liberty: Papers and Addresses of Learned Hand* (New York, 1959), pp. xiii–xv; Shapiro, *Freedom of Speech*, p. 60; Arthur Garfield Hays, "The Trial of the Communists," February 7, 1949, ACLU Papers, Box 1–5, Vol. 5, 1949.

[24] Schaar, *Loyalty*, pp. 133–39; Goodman, *The Committee*, pp. 186–87; Eleanor Bontecou, *The Federal Loyalty-Security Program* (Ithaca, N.Y., 1953), pp. 144–55; ACLU, *Annual Report* (1946–47), p. 31; *Annual Report* (1947–48), pp. 23–26; *Annual Report* (1948–49), pp. 11–19.

espionage agencies. Naval intelligence, for example, had the Japanese situation well in hand before the war broke out. Counter-espionage and intelligence operations (including informers), fingerprint and name checks, normal civil service personnel practices, and criminal penalties for violations of trust would have provided all the security the nation needed. Besides, the Communist presence in government had been vastly exaggerated, and any chance to influence policy negligible. As to private organizations, they could have done without loyalty resolutions and purges, and expelled only those proven guilty of manifest official malfeasance.[25]

In restrospect, it had been a better war than a decade for civil liberties. The incidence of popular violence and the number of mass indictments and jailings did not compare with the repressive excesses of World War I and its aftermath. Procedural due process and federal restraint characterized the government's response to war-time dissent. But the overwhelming national unity in the fight against Fascism, which represented a liberation gain, was also a result of the decline of dissent, the apathy and disintegration of the peace movement, and the zealous pro-war stance of the Communists. The threat to freedom came from the very totalitarian conformity abroad in the land. When radicalism again became suspect, war-time attitudes and precedents seriously undermined civil liberties. If the forties sent fewer dissenters to jail, it also revived the hated oath *ex officio*, inquisitional procedure, and self-incrimination. The loyalty program also had a tremendously inhibiting effect on free speech and association far beyond the confines of public service. American society had not, therefore, kept its constitutional cool during those years of stress and over issues that really mattered. It had not lived up to Justice Robert Jackson's standard that the true test of freedom was "the right to differ as to things that touch the heart of the existing order." [26]

[25] Chamberlain, *Loyalty*, p. 218; Bontecou, *Federal Loyalty*, pp. 21–23; Earl Latham, *The Communist Controversy in Washington: From the New Deal to McCarthy* (Cambridge, Mass., 1966), pp. 94–154, 290, 314–15; Schaar, *Loyalty*, p. 143.

[26] Justice Jackson quoted in Walter Gellhorn, *Individual Freedom and Government Restraints* (Baton Rouge, La., 1956), p. 99.

"It is by the goodness of God," Mark Twain once said, "that in our country we have those three unspeakably precious things: freedom of speech, freedom of conscience, and the prudence never to practice either of them." Like the reports of Twain's death, his observations are "greatly exaggerated," but at the same time they catch the peculiar flavor of America's free market in ideas, a less than classically competitive arena since the beginning. Or to use military jargon, the First Amendment has not been a no-man's land, but the country has had great difficulty turning this "beachhead for freedom into a liberated province." [27]

An atmosphere favorable to free expression does not spring full-blown from the Bill of Rights, and restrictions on the dissemination of ideas may not involve any violation of the First Amendment. The free and open market for speech may, therefore, be a defective instrument for realizing the "blessings of liberty." This was certainly true in the forties. The media exercised a prior restraint that impeded the free flow of information. Monopoly, technology, and economic self-interest had made the power to inform a scarce resource. A leadership that was "the creature . . . of merchandizing" often communicated the mediocre, irrelevant, and bland out of a desire not to offend or create controversy.[28]

Hollywood was a good case in point. During the 1940s the big five producers almost completely controlled the film industry. Through a written code administered by their chosen czar, the producers exercised a prior restraint censorship with real teeth: the threat of a financial and marketing boycott against violators. Determined to police content and pandering to "the ethical specifications of a single pressure group," the Legion of Decency, the producers excluded realism and controversy, restrained the growth of independents with more creative ideas, refused the documentary film entry into their theaters, and grotesquely stereotyped foreign, ethnic, and

[27] Twain's remarks were recalled by Justice Douglas in his dissent in *Scales* v. *United States.*

[28] Fred W. Friendly, *Due to Circumstances Beyond Our Control* (New York, 1967), p. 116; William Spinrad, *Civil Liberties* (Chicago, 1970), pp. 273–75.

racial images. The 1947 investigation of Hollywood Communism forced a new retreat into blandness that had still not dissipated ten years later. Yet there were forces at work undermining the movie monolith. A 1948 Supreme Court decision (*U.S. v. Paramount Pictures*) ended block-booking and forced the division of production and exhibition, thereby opening up prime territory to the independents. Soon some hundred were in the field; a few had even defied the code. When the courts attacked film censorship in the fifties, quality and innovation would at last have the chance that talent and technology had always made possible.[29]

Subtle yet pervasive restraints also inhibited free speech in broadcasting. During the 1930s commercial control and the power of advertising had mastered the medium. Sales took precedence over information, education, or culture. As in the movies, centralized control by the few insisted on an entertainment emphasis that rated inoffensiveness (demand for the sponsor's product) superior to creative or controversial variety on the air. By 1940 local stations, supposedly autonomous, had ceded effective power to the networks. New York and the sponsors controlled prime time, chain broadcasting further narrowed decisions about content, and educational radio remained crippled.[30]

How did this distort broadcasting's impact during the 1940s? Labor's voice, for one, was badly underrepresented. Soap operas rarely dealt with the realities of working-class life; the union viewpoint had little influence. In the post-war reaction a number of liberal news commentators friendly to labor disappeared from the scene. The interests, values, and life styles of the "other America" seemed intentionally or otherwise unfit for any frequency. Broadcasting remained lily-white in its drama and most of its music, the consumer philos-

[29] Jack Vizzard, *See No Evil: Life Inside a Hollywood Censor* (New York, 1970), pp. 11, 20, 36, 83, 94, 103, 187–88; Arthur Knight, *The Liveliest Art* (New York, 1959), pp. 247–51; Michael Conant, *Antitrust in the Motion Picture Industry: Economic and Legal Analysis* (Berkeley, Calif., 1960), pp. 34–106, 110, 112–16, 152–53; Barnouw, *The Golden Web*, pp. 290–91.

[30] Herbert I. Schiller, *Mass Communications and American Empire* (New York, 1969), pp. 1, 8–9, 21–26; Barnouw, *The Golden Web, passim.*

ophy did not receive an airing, and controversial scripts vigorously defending or attacking subject matter were noticeably absent. A decade later, the critical editorializing of Edward R. Murrow's "See It Now" remained the first and only landmark of its kind, and even it did not last.[31]

Conditions in broadcasting grew worse during the decade, and the industry successfully resisted disruptive changes enhancing freedom of the airwaves. The war years reinforced the habits of self-censorship and the lure of commercial gain. Tax deductions for advertising meant that more sponsored entertainment drove the sustaining public-service programs from the scene. Radio also had to deliver more profits to pay the development costs of television. From 1947 on the policies of popularity and audience accomodation were joined by anti-Communist hysteria. Anyone mentioned as suspect or controversial might contaminate show, network, sponsor, and product. Brand names were sacrosanct; those branded or named were sacrificed. Blacklists and clearances drove many performers from the air, and the personnel had to be as bland as the content.[32]

The broadcasters also turned back the challenges of government regulation and technological change. The FCC's 1949 approval of station editorializing, for example, did not win support from an industry instinctively pro-advertiser. Splitting NBC into two networks in 1943 could not create a new ABC noticeably different in broadcasting policy from its predecessor. And the FCC's 1946 threat not to renew the licenses of stations violating their public service responsibility and succumbing to "advertising excesses" became a casualty of the congressional opposition aroused by the industry. Broadcasting also contained two innovations of a threateningly competitive kind. In 1945 the FCC retarded FM development for years by consigning it to the higher reaches of the spectrum, a

[31] Kendrick, *Prime Time,* pp. 48, 335–36, 338–39, 341, 416; Barnouw, *The Golden Web,* pp. 162, 196–97, 241, 289–90; Biddle, *In Brief Authority,* pp. 124, 126; ACLU Papers, Scrapbooks 2212, 2302, 2303, 2350, 2351, 2352, 2494, 2602, and 2650.

[32] Kendrick, *Prime Time,* pp. 60, 298, 301, 332–36, 353, 363; Barnouw, *The Golden Web,* pp. 165, 214–19, 229–34, 241, 253–272; Friendly, *Due to Circumstances,* p. 23.

move making the pre-war sets obsolete and losing FM the audience already won. Two years later the government approved RCA's VHF television system and dismissed the UHF alternative. This decision drastically curtailed the number of local channels and preserved network control of those scarce outlets. Mass communications thus continued as an establishment operation and the cause of free expression paid the penalty.[33]

Similar economic, technological, and capitalistic imperatives limited the freest, most diverse circulation of opinion in the nation's press. Concentration of control (over 80 percent of cities had only one paper) and cost of entry drastically limited access to and competition in the free market of news. The press, therefore, almost totally represented the established order (of 1,860 daily papers, one, with a circulation of six thousand, was Communist). Newspaper owners, although not always overtly, did not welcome all opinion, and omitted, exaggerated, or misinterpreted a variety of issues such as fair employment, ghetto conditions, pacifism, and the Japanese-American detention. Typical of the bias was the fact that "the vested interests and entrenched hostility of the press" largely suppressed the 1947 critical report of the Commission on Freedom of the Press. A radio series, "CBS Views the Press," received equally hostile attention until it was discontinued.[34]

These trends resisted reversal during the decade. Anti-trust remained an illusion since it could not deal with the economics of publishing and could only replace one wealthy owner with another. Although concentration of ownership was unaffected, two important Supreme Court decisions considerably advanced the press freedom of those able to exercise this right. The Associated Press case broke the monopoly by which pub-

[33] Barnouw, *The Golden Web*, pp. 137, 169, 190, 229–36, 242–43; Schiller, *Mass Communications*, pp. 27–28; ACLU Papers, Scrapbook 2352.

[34] "Neglected Books," *American Scholar*, 39 (Spring, 1970), 318–45; Bryce Rucker, *The First Freedom* (Carbondale, Ill., 1967), pp. 7–8, 46, 217; Zechariah Chafee, Jr., *Government and Mass Communications: A Report from the Commission on Freedom of the Press* (Chicago, 1947), pp. 537, 583, 585, 594, 648; Gellhorn, *Individual Freedom*, p. 68; ACLU Papers, Scrapbooks 2356, 2461.

lishers were able to limit competition through denial of AP service to a rival. The other ruling (*Bridges* v. *California,* 1941) increased the freedom of the press to comment on trials without facing contempt of court charges.[35]

What the mass media were doing on one side of the market street, the cultural and intellectual vigilantes were doing on the other. Censorship was still very much alive in an America that thought Jane Russell's breasts and *Forever Amber's* bedroom would set off, as Father Harold Gardiner observed, "a genital commotion" in the susceptible. Obscenity was, after all, a kind of dangerous thinking as subversive of the established order as treason and heresy. So a society that installed political Puritanism (the Smith Act and the loyalty program) would not normally welcome a dissenting voice in morality. The repressive impulse thus tried hard to maintain the old order in the forties. There would be change, but the great breakthroughs against censorship still lay in the decades to follow.[36]

In spite of Hollywood's prior restraint, the censors seemed determined to leave nothing to chance. Seven state boards and over ninety cities and towns still censored films in the forties. Having been characterized in the 1915 Mutual Film decision as "mere spectacles" subject to the police power of the state, movies lacked First Amendment protection unless the controls were proven "arbitrary or capricious." Under contemporary interpretations that meant the censors could apply incredibly loose language and get away with it. They could and did ban the "sacrilegious," the "immoral," or material that "tended to corrupt morals"; films classified as "prejudicial to the best interests of the people," "harmful," "obscene," "indecent," "unsuitable for children," and "dangerous to friendly relations between the races," could not be shown. *The Outlaw, Forever Amber,* and *Monsieur Verdoux* all fell before one or more censorship board decisions. Yet Hollywood, al-

[35] Rucker, *The First Freedom,* pp. 18, 62–63; Chafee, *Government and Mass Communications,* pp. 21–29, 411–12, 431–32, 545–47, 560; Spinrad, *Civil Liberties,* pp. 266–67; ACLU Papers, Scrapbooks 2356, 2461.

[36] Quoted in Charles Rembar, *The End of Obscenity: The Trials of Lady Chatterley, Tropic of Cancer,* and *Fanny Hill* (New York, 1968), p. 24; Gellhorn, *Individual Freedom,* p. 67.

ways timorous, preferred to cut and sell rather than risk reprisals or stir up trouble. The Supreme Court would obviously have to lead the way.[37]

In the late forties a sizable Court minority began to do just that. Its *obiter dicta* put movies on a par with other communications and argued that "ideas and beliefs are today chiefly disseminated to the masses of people through the press, radio, moving pictures, and public address systems. . . ." Then, in the 1952 *Miracle* decision and for the first time in thirty-seven years, the majority voided as unconstitutionally vague a censorship standard, the term "sacrilegious" in New York's licensing law. If prior restraint had not fallen, film-makers had at least won the right to precise definitions of behavior viewed by a court that gave their ideas a preferred position among constitutional liberties.[38]

Emancipation from censorship had advanced farther by 1950 in publishing than it had in the cinema, but Victorian prudery continued in and out of court. The Hicklin test for obscenity, a nineteenth-century British court's still-popular definition, banned anything that might corrupt the young. As Walter Gellhorn has noted, it let "four letters . . . count for more than four hundred pages." Dragnet raids, surprise crackdowns, entrapment, threats to revoke licenses, behind-the-scenes pressure on booksellers, and arbitrary administrative harassment also aided the censors' cause. During the decade several trends further affected the tug-of-war between freedom and restraint. Material tainted as "red" was more subject to suppression, the classic case being the near-elimination of Harold Rugg's social science textbooks from high school use. McCarthyism increased the pressure on all literature suspected of radicalism.[39]

[37] Ruth A Inglis, *Freedom of the Movies* (Chicago, 1947), pp. 178–88; Carmen, *Movies,* pp. 9–14 and *passim;* ACLU Papers, Scrapbooks 2152, 2157, 2260, 2608, 2637, 2687, 2717, and Box 6–9, Vol. 6, 1949.

[38] Carmen, *Movies,* pp. 41–42, 45–54. Morris L. Ernst and Alan U. Schwartz, *Censorship: The Search for the Obscene* (New York, 1964), p. 148.

[39] Ernst and Schwartz, *Censorship,* pp. 35, 201, 206, 221, 223–24; Gellhorn, *Individual Freedom,* 21, 54, 59, 78, 80–82; Rembar, *The End of Obscenity,* pp. 21–22, 119–20, 123 and 496; Spinrad, *Civil Liberties,* 230; ACLU Papers, Scrapbooks 2148, 2149.

Next to sedition, obscenity evoked the most alarm. Massachusetts (not Mississippi) banned *Strange Fruit*. New York and several Northern cities rejected Edmund Wilson's *Memoirs of Hecate County* because of one not very lascivious account of sex in one chapter. Nor had any authority cleared *Lady Chatterley's Lover, Tropic of Cancer*, or *Fanny Hill*. On the other hand, the American Civil Liberties Union and its allies won a memorable victory over Massachusetts's puritans in the *Forever Amber* trial. Psychological testimony and evidence on "the sex mores of the community" successfully set new precedents. In a timely rebuttal to all censors, the presiding judge found *Amber* "a soporific rather than an aphrodisiac . . . conducive to sleep . . . not . . . to a desire to sleep with a member of the opposite sex." Other courts also became friendlier to artistic freedom and "were willing to hold . . . that sufficient literary quality could drown out a certain amount of lustfulness . . . if there was great enough merit, and little enough sex. . . ." [40]

Periodical and pamphlet literature faced greater hazards than books, seeming to be fairer game and less worthy of constitutional protection. Sweeps against smut were, therefore, part of the normal work-load of a variety of forces from mayors of big cities to police to postal authorities. Fiorello La Guardia believed New York should have only magazines fit for "your children." Philadelphia and Detroit tried to "skim off the filth," a campaign that included comic book violence late in the decade. The Post Office Department had, perhaps, the worst record of all. Assuming that use of the mails was a privilege, not a democratic right, its administrative puritanism imposed archaic taboos almost without judicial restraint, since the courts upheld "an exclusionary postal ruling so long as it lies within the outermost fringes of debatable soundness." In the forties, Washington banned sex instruction, birth control information, the word "sex," and nudity, and even material issued by the government's own health service. [41]

[40] Rembar, *The End of Obscenity*, pp. 3, 24; Chafee, *Government and Mass Communications*, pp. 228–29; Gellhorn, *Individual Freedom*, p. 54; ACLU, *Annual Report* (1946–47), p. 40; *Annual Report* (1948–49), pp. 35–36.

[41] Chafee, *Government and Mass Communications*, pp. 281–84, 292–93, 303; Gellhorn, *Individual Freedom*, pp. 74, 96, 98; ACLU Papers,

During the war years the excesses of mail censorship provoked a moderate improvement. A three-front campaign had attempted to insulate the public against periodicals subversive of established values. Included were foreign propaganda "hostile to American democratic interests," radical publications critical of the war's imperialistic or capitalistic overtones, and over eighty nationally known "allegedly obscene magazines," headed by *Esquire*. With the help of ACLU pressure and litigation, the latter won an appeal that chastized the Post Office for closing the mails to magazines it believed "morally improper and not for the public welfare." Such policies were fundamentally at odds with a free press and unauthorized by any statute. Other decisions opened the mails to birth control and marriage counseling information, but did not basically overturn the system of administrative discretion.[42]

Although censorship and prior restraint restricted the free market in speech, a voluminous babble of voices created still other issues in the 1940s. Most of them involved "the unpopular, the weak, the friendless," minorities whose problems might seem unimportant compared with such great issues as loyalty and security. The First Amendment disagrees since any diminution of freedom symbolizes the rights all may lose. In addition, government repression of speech, however, infrequently it may occur, has a tendency to intimidate all speech. A society should be judged, therefore, on its willingness to tolerate and encourage unpopular speech and on the degree to which the courts preclude interference with it in the name of other social needs. Speech should have a preferred position in the courts since they are its only lobby, and there is no guarantee that the government or the people will pay it much respect.[43]

Scrapbooks 2158, 2349, 2434, 2436, 2669, Box 1–5, Vol. 5, 1948, and Box 6–9, Vol. 8, 1949.

[42] Gellhorn, *Individual Freedom*, pp. 83–88; Chafee, *Government and Mass Communications*, pp. 329–30; ACLU, *Annual Report* (1943–44), pp. 41–42; *Annual Report* (1944–45), pp. 8–9; ACLU Papers, Scrapbooks 2434, 2436, 2438, 2440, 2548, 2637, 2717.

[43] This point of view is most persuasively set forth in Shapiro's *Freedom of Speech;* see also Norman Dorsen, *Frontiers of Civil Liberties* (New York, 1968), pp. xx–xxi, 18–19, 29.

Two major challenges to free speech occurred during the 1940s, one the question of prior restraint by municipalities, the other the issue of abusive speech that led to acts of retaliation. Jehovah's Witnesses' leafleting and door-to-door solicitation had led towns to pass ordinances prohibiting this activity or granting board discretion in its control. Condemning this interference with free speech, the Supreme Court ruled that such laws, if acceptable, be narrowly drawn, reasonable, and non-discriminatory. The decisions also opened up company-owned towns and government projects to the unwelcome attention of Witness propagandists. The justices did not, however, prohibit all licensing or prior restraint. In *Cox* v. *New Hampshire* (1941), the majority approved "non-content control of the orderly procedures of speech," recognizing that, if everyone shouts at the same time, it is like an Agnew rally at the University of California's Berkeley campus. The same held true for parades, in that prior approval related to traffic, not thought, control.[44]

The propaganda of hate deeply disturbed the decade. Those who lived very close to the experience of racial, religious, and national genocide wondered whether they had to tolerate "hateful and hate-stirring attacks on races and faiths." Demands for group libel laws reflected this mood, though legislation condemning incitements to hatred and race hostility or penalizing fraudulent and scurrilous remarks would have clearly threatened free speech. When abusive speech kept coming, community reactions naturally led to the nation's highest court.

Between 1942 and 1952 the Supreme Court reviewed five such cases: *Chaplinsky, Terminiello, Feiner, Kunz,* and *Beauharnais.* On balance the results represented a setback for civil liberties. Disallowing a permit system involving prior restraint (*Kunz* and *Terminiello*) would not mean much in a constitutional atmosphere tolerating police interference with any speech that might tend to arouse audience hostility and its overt expression (*Feiner*). The police function should have been maintaining order among the listeners. Creating the

[44] C. Herman Pritchett, *The Roosevelt Court: A Study in Judicial Politics and Values, 1937–1947* (New York, 1948), p. 100; Pritchett, *The Vinson Court*, pp. 34–42, 44–46, 49–53.

category of "fighting words" and upholding group libel legislation also seemed to remove offensive speech (like obscenity) from constitutional protection. Community well-being and social order took precedence, but the range and subjectivity of the standard could easily fetter all speech. These decisions were part of the Vinson Court's downgrading of speech's preferred position, a reevaluation that balanced First Amendment freedoms on a scale weighted in favor of other interests.[45]

While grappling with the speech of unpopular or hateful minorities, the forties also took on the speech issues that accompanied the continuing struggle between labor and management. Their conflict and violence largely excised by New Deal reform, the two old antagonists found new uses for speech. At the same time each suspected that the other's dialogue was something more than mere talk, that it must be inherently coercive. This disagreement forced the courts to evaluate the element of coercion, invent the concept of "speech plus," and devise ways to preserve the communication function while eliminating the coercive.

Speech on the picket line was one side of the coin. Although past interpretation had always condemned peaceful picketing as inherently contradictory, like "chaste vulgarity," the Court now validated it as a legitimate avenue of communication. *Thornhill* v. *Alabama* (1940), however, never equated speech and picketing. The latter could be enjoined or regulated when it pursued an unlawful objective or was part of a climate of violence. Recognizing the facts of economic warfare, the Supreme Court supported even the loosest and most unrefined language, but not violence or obstruction.[46]

The bosses' freedom of expression might also be something more than mere speech. To labor and some libertarians corporate free speech was necessarily intimidating by reason

[45] Pritchett, *The Vinson Court,* pp. 42–44, 57–65; Chafee, *Government and Mass Communications,* pp. 116–17, 122, 125–27; Shapiro, *Freedom of Speech,* pp. 78–79, 109; ACLU Papers, Scrapbooks 2157, 2186, 2457, 2580.

[46] Sidney Fine, "Frank Murphy, the Thornhill Decision, and Picketing as Free Speech," *Labor History,* 6 (Spring, 1965), pp. 99–120; Pritchett, *The Vinson Court,* pp. 50–56.

of its power, anti-unionism, and past abuses. Did employers have a right to speak out against unions in messages to their own workers? Did the Wagner Act or the First Amendment take precedence? In a 1941 case the Court reported a qualified approval for executive spokesmen. The total atmosphere was again decisive. Unless clearly "part of a pattern of coercion," business opinions had constitutional sanction.[47]

If the growth of labor stimulated greater respect for speech on both sides of the bargaining table, the New Deal and the war-time increase in government employment had the opposite effect. Many more people became subject to the inhibitions on speech that accompanied the anti-Communist hysteria and loyalty program. Apart from silencing the bureaucrat as citizen, the security mania encouraged conformity in internal policy discussions. What loyalty testing did on the one hand, files, dossiers, computers, lie detection, wiretapping, and newer forms of electronic investigation did on the other. Since World War II marked a great divide in the science and practice of surveillance, privacy (hence speech) would never be quite the same again. So much of this was secret that it escaped libertarian detection and social control, yet such odious compulsory (involuntary) testimony gave the recipients "catastrophically dangerous" power and violated free speech as much as any active repression. While amassing vast amounts of information about others, the government resisted release of news about itself with equal vigilance. Classification and over-classification, secrecy, and pre-censorship began to impede understanding of public policies during World War II and grew worse thereafter.[48]

Threats to academic freedom were an equally disturbing aspect of the tumultuous forties. When the decade began, the suppression of liberal and controversial topics and teachers in the schools had already become common. Compulsory patriotic instruction and exercises, compulsory flag saluting,

---

[47] Fine, "Frank Murphy," p. 115; Pritchett, *The Roosevelt Court*, p. 229; ACLU Papers, Scrapbooks 2164, 2233, 2268, 2715.

[48] Schaar, *Loyalty*, p. 89; Alan Westin, *Privacy and Freedom* (New York, 1967), pp. 133, 136, 147, 149, 159, 239, 255, 275, 278, 298, Landynski, *Search and Seizure*, pp. 103, 241–42.

special loyalty oaths for teachers, anti-Communist legislation, required or optional Bible reading, and the censorship of textbooks were overt manifestations of the demand for indoctrination. Other pressures to conform came from within, a process Ernest Van Den Haag has called "prevenient restriction—the semiconscious adoption of standards [that] will not offend public opinion." What made the 1940s worse was the intrusion of the loyalty issue so typical of that decade. School, like government, seemed ripe for the subversive influences that Americans found so threatening.[49]

The search for subversion hit in two waves during the early and late forties, submerged only during the deceptive unanimity of the war years. Led by a variety of pressure groups and an honor roll of legislative investigators, this academic witch hunt dealt a heavy blow to "the free spirit of teachers." Committees such as Rapp-Coudert in New York, Broyles in Illinois, Tenney in California, and Canwell in Washington spread the disease. Twenty-six states barred subversives from teaching. Numerous campuses excluded Communist speakers or those cited by HUAC; some banned the student American Youth for Democracy because of its front reputation. Between 1945 and 1950 the American Association for University Professors investigated 227 cases involving violations of academic freedom and tenure and many others not classified as such. With the exception of the ACLU, almost no one was willing to defend the rights of Communists to teach, in spite of no evidence of classroom indoctrination and much contrary proof of classroom excellence. Teachers invoking the constitutional privilege against self-incrimination faced reprisals. Editorial supervision of student newspapers and censorship of books frequently occurred.[50]

[49] Howard K. Beale, *A History of Freedom of Teaching in American Schools* (New York, 1941), *passim;* Beale, *Are American Teachers Free?* (New York, 1936), *passim.*

[50] Spinrad, *Civil Liberties,* pp. 243–44, 343; Chamberlain, *Loyalty and Legislative Action,* pp. 171–72, 178; Robert M. MacIver, *Academic Freedom in Our Time* (New York, 1955), pp. 35, 38–39, 211–12, 216–17, 266; ACLU, *Annual Report* (1945–46), pp. 50–51; *Annual Report* (1946–47), pp. 49–51; *Annual Report* (1947–48), pp. 47–48; *Annual Report* (1951–53), pp. 59–67.

Teachers mainly conformed. Traditional habits favored this response, but so did the nature of the inquiry. No one ever knew for sure what behavior or attitudes might be found subversive. It was a surveillance "interminable because it . . . [was] non-specific, incalculable in effect because it rarely relate[d] to professional behavior." One historical survey found that 46 percent of the teachers admitted they were "apprehensive about their freedom to teach and speak freely." Even the great foundations succumbed by conceding the government's right to inspect their grants and by eagerly insisting "they had not in fact favored radicals or endowed subversives." It was a time when American education behaved as if its members should not question the society's prevailing orthodoxy.[51]

Was Mark Twain right, or had free speech flourished during the 1940s? How does one balance the imperfect market in mass communications against the persistent forward progress made by unpopular minorities (always excepting the radicals)? Some generalizations may stand up. The unprecedented war-time unity, so beneficial to civil liberties at the time, proved deceptive. It obscured trends and attitudes that linked the beginning and end of the decade in a pattern of repression. The marketplace remained less than free, menaced by new patterns of surveillance and dominated by powerful elites that refused a hearing to ideas and values irrevelant or unfriendly to their own position. The cradle of democracy was an educational establishment of cautious and conformist careerists not known for offending the community. Antiradicalism moved the center of debate rightward and cut off some segments of it entirely. If censorship made some gains, it still could not shake the creative arts loose from age-old notions of morality and obscenity. There was no sign that the people, their legislatures, or the executive power were ready to support free speech for any despised or obnoxious minori-

---

[51] Richard Hofstadter and Walter P. Metzger, *The Development of Academic Freedom in the United States* (New York, 1955), p. 506; MacIver, *Academic Freedom*, pp. 35–38; Chamberlain, *Loyalty*, p. 221; Commager, *Freedom and Order*, pp. 98–99, 126–27; Roger Baldwin to Board of Directors, June 23, 1949, ACLU Papers, Box 1–5, Vol. 5, 1949.

ties. While helping expand freedom in certain areas such as licensing, prior restraint, and picketing, the Supreme Court also abandoned the preferred position test for First Amendment liberties and under Chief Justice Vinson gave free speech "the worst battering . . . [it] has received from our government since the Alien and Sedition Acts." Zechariah Chafee, Jr., came to a similar morose conclusion in 1952. Reviewing thirty-five years with freedom of speech, Chafee was "disturbed by the gradual erosion of many fundamental human rights" since 1949. The "inroads" on free speech he found "disquieting." That judgment on the forties still stands.[52]

In 1943 Eleanor Roosevelt complained that Negroes "ought not to do too much demanding." Her attitude (which she later reversed) opposing black pressure for change in the nation's racial equilibrium during World War II bespoke both an administration and liberal consensus. Still mesmerized by paternalism, white America expected meekness and docility from its black population and resented any breach of the rules that discomfited established authority. By the time Mrs. Roosevelt spoke, Negroes had been waiting eighty years for "the lag in public morals" to catch up with the announced principles of the American creed.

But white racism was still so pervasive that almost no one could recognize the absurdity that the then "extremist" policy of tokenism represented. The decade remained in the grip of racial fantasies that interpreted almost any progress as "going too fast" and "pushing too hard." A tremendous resistance developed against minimal desegregation measures that would in no way have altered the power of the two races or alleviated the basic helplessness of the black minority. And this racism had not suffered much of a setback during the New Deal thirties. Since Roosevelt considered the race issue "political dynamite," his broker leadership always conciliated the Southern votes. New Deal programs, therefore, either ex-

[52] Shapiro, *Freedom of Speech*, p. 109; Zechariah Chafee, Jr., "Thirty-five Years with Freedom of Speech," in Harold Nelson, ed., *Freedom of the Press from Hamilton to the Warren Court* (Indianapolis, Ind., 1967), pp. 326, 328–31, 335.

cluded or segregated the black minority. As Barton Bernstein has argued, it was an "ambiguous legacy, . . . marked more by promise than substance."[53]

War and cold war should have promoted the cause of civil rights. Anti-Nazi and anti-Communist propaganda always contrasted the justice and equality of the free world with the racism and repression of the slave. Allied solicitation of the Third World and United Nations slogans of brotherhood implied greater respect for colonial and colored people. If blacks were asked to die for democracy, could they long remain "objects of radical exclusion, brutality, and humiliation"? The tragedy of the forties lay in its answer to that question. It was a response that shocked the black community into crossing a watershed of recognition about white promises and policies. As James Baldwin once wrote, "a certain hope died; a certain respect for white Americans faded." But it would still take time for the lessons to sink in and for new tactics to emerge.[54]

Military attitudes mirrored the nation's white supremacy convictions. Assuming Negro inferiority, the armed forces assigned black recruits to the most menial and unpleasant jobs, segregated their units, deployed them under white officers, and considered them generally unfit for combat duty. Yet the times demanded an "operation integration." A typical lip-service, public relations maneuver, the program provided only a facade of reform behind which all levels of command sabotaged its intent. Not until threats of civil disobedience had materialized and the Korean War was underway did any real changes occur, and even then slowly and without enthusiasm.

Business as usual was the racial response at the lower and local levels. Many communities objected vigorously to the presence of black troops and subjected them to the insults and degradation normally reserved for Negroes. It was not uncommon for black soldiers to be beaten, and even shot, by white

[53] Wittner, *Rebels Against War,* p. 64; Pritchett, *The Vinson Court,* p. 123; Barton J. Bernstein, "The New Deal: The Conservative Achievements of Liberal Reform," in Bernstein, ed., *Towards A New Past: Dissenting Essays in American History* (New York, 1968), pp. 278–79.

[54] Richard M. Dalfiume, *Desegregation of the U.S. Armed Forces: Fighting on Two Fronts, 1939–1953* (Columbia, Mo., 1969), pp. 105–6 and *passim.*

police in the South. The same pattern repeated itself within the service. White and black soldiers frequently clashed in racial incidents, news of which the white press generally suppressed. White military policemen used their power to harass black GI's who violated the racist code of conduct. Race riots and mutinies also accompanied the troops overseas, American discrimination and black resistance being no respecters of geographic boundaries.[55]

Integration of the armed forces was, therefore, a failure. The top service secretaries had racist sentiments that precluded their holding the military to account. They and the top brass did not believe their task to be one of social reform, nor did they want their fighting machine to be an experimental laboratory of human relations. The main priority was winning the war, yet once that crisis had passed, so did most of the pressure to change. Could the Negro minority have speeded events? Mass resentments and a new militancy existed, but its activist expression remained spasmodic and symtomatic rather than purposeful and political. Only a few blacks sought conscientious objector status or refused to serve in a Jim Crow army. No wave of black sedition swept through the ghettos either. It was still a time when black energies were squandered in meaningless violence or nurtured for later revenge.[56]

Segregated survival in the armed services had its civilian companion: discriminatory employment in the defense industry. When war-time prosperity did not improve black job opportunities and the Roosevelt administration refused to put pressure on business, A. Philip Randolph and others created the March on Washington Movement (MOWM) and threatened to put fifty thousand black protestors in Roosevelt's backyard if things did not improve. The president reluctantly agreed "to place the full force of his office" behind the elimina-

[55] *Ibid.;* see also Department of Justice File 158260-52, National Archives.

[56] Dalfiume, *Desegregation,* 53 and *passim;* Wittner, *Rebels Against War,* pp. 46–47, 65–66; Barton J. Bernstein, "The Ambiguous Legacy: The Truman Administration and Civil Rights," in Bernstein, ed., *Politics and Policies of the Truman Administration* (Chicago, 1970), pp. 270–304; ACLU Papers, Scrapbooks 2482, 2504, 2505, 2605.

tion of discrimination. Fair employment practices legislation was the result; it stood as a symbol over which the battles of that decade were fought. The controversy the Fair Employment Practices Commission excited now seems extravagant, but the forties resisted any front-line testing of established positions as though panzer divisions of change would pour through any breach.[57]

According to Louis Ruchames, "FDR was not going to let FEPC embarrass his administration." The agency discovered it was not there to enforce effectively a mandate for reform; it *was* the reform. Hampered by budget restrictions, subverted even by its own leaders, transferred to another agency, and reorganized to disrupt its policies, FEPC could not even clean house within the federal bureaucracy. In the outside world neither business nor labor was ready to undertake such a socially explosive campaign. Trade union opposition was, however, "the greatest obstacle." At least eighteen unions banned black workers, and many locals did the same in defiance of their national constitutions. The closed shop effectively excluded Negroes from the right to jobs in numerous occupations.[58]

In due course FEPC made the grade as a public enemy gunned down by the politically powerful lobbies of Roosevelt's electoral coalition and two red-hunting investigations. It had also fought the win-the-war philosophy from the start; ending discrimination too often seemed subversive of that national effort. The tremendous energy that advocates poured into fair employment brought very little result. Minority job opportunities did improve slightly (from 2 to 7.5 percent of industrial employment), but these figures obscured the nature of the jobs and the amount of segregation and reflected the war-time needs for manpower. FEPC may have additionally stimulated imitative efforts at the state and local level (by 1949 ten states and twenty-eight cities). In spite of this legis-

[57] Dalfiume, *Desegregation*, pp. 115–17; Louis Ruchames, *Race, Jobs and Politics: The Story of FEPC* (New York, 1953), pp. 18, 20.

[58] Dalfiume, *Desegregation*, pp. 117–18; Ruchames, *Race*, pp. 22, 37, 70–72; Pritchett, *The Vinson Court*, pp. 143–44; ACLU Papers, Scrapbooks 2357, 2581, 2668, 2687.

lation, discrimination remained rooted in American employment, subtler perhaps, but still pervasive. White America would have to find something more forceful than fact-finding and further investigation to overthrow such deeply ingrained patterns.[59]

Housing reform seemed equally illusory. The main issue of the decade was the restrictive convenant, the supposed basis of the ghetto. Ever since 1917, when local segregation ordinances had been declared invalid, the restrictive convenent had allowed property owners to make legally binding agreements not to sell or rent to Negroes or other minorities. For thirty-one years, at a cost of over $100,000, the NAACP had fought to eliminate what the *Chicago Defender* had called "one of the ugliest developments in American history." On May 3, 1948, a 6–0 Supreme Court decision, *Shelley* v. *Kraemer,* outlawed further judicial enforcement of these racially restrictive practices because "state action made available the full coercive power of government to deny equal protection of the laws on grounds of race or color."

Was it a great victory? Atolls of residential racism were no longer protected by the great barrier reef of legal authority. On the other hand, real estate boards and their community supporters mobilized disciplined though informal methods to maintain segregation. Worse yet, the FHA supported these interests in its refusal to insure black loans in white housing areas. Should all else fail, white force and violence came into play. Yet the violence represented historical verification of new residential patterns as well. Blacks did dent hitherto impregnable zones, but not nearly to the degree that optimists had then hoped. In 1961 some forty million units were still off limits to Negroes, proof that landlords and real estate agents could operate an illegal system of housing segregation with the connivance and support of the banking, building, and bureaucratic institutions that dominated the field.[60]

[59] Dalfiume, *Desegregation*, p. 121; Ruchames, *Race*, pp. 24, 134–35, 146, 161, 165, 172–73, 199, 204–12, and *passim*.

[60] Clement E. Vose, *Caucasians Only: The Supreme Court, the NAACP, and the Restrictive Covenent Cases* (Berkeley, Calif., 1959), pp. 205–51; Pritchett, *The Vinson Court*, pp. 139–40; ACLU Papers, Scrapbook 2527; Box 8, Vol. 20, 1947; Box 20–25, Vol. 21, 1948.

The poll tax was to voting as FEPC and the restrictive covenant were to employment, a seemingly crucial issue that aroused strong emotions and promised much more than it could deliver. Other voting barriers—social and economic pressure, education, intimidation, registration procedures, and the white primary—were, of course, more significant. Yet only the latter received public scrutiny and a judicial reversal during the decade (*Smith* v. *Allwright*, 1944). Poll tax repeal, meanwhile, faced successive defeats in a Senate where it represented a civil rights, Northern, New Deal assault on the privileged sanctuary of Southern power. In 1947 seven states still retained the tax. Contrary to the contemporary myths, it disenfranchised poor whites as much as blacks and eliminated those already made voteless by other devices. Repeal would hardly have affected Southern politics, a reality proven by the state repeals (Georgia in 1945; South Carolina and Tennessee in the early fifties) that occurred at the behest of practical politicians (not reformers) who believed the change would improve their own position, not that of the black minority.[61]

Beyond jobs, homes, and voting lay an equally crucial crusade against the entire Jim Crow system in public accomodations. Direct action at the points of discrimination and litigation to overturn the dishonest doctrine of "separate but equal" characterized this largely unsuccessful challenge. One reason was the Supreme Court's cautious tokenism in civil rights cases. Faced with the task of reversing both its own precedents and the social traditions it had sanctioned, the court sought moderation and unanimity. The justices, therefore, sanctioned departures from segregation on the narrowest possible grounds. The trick was to subvert Jim Crow in cases that had the least impact on the white masses, such as segregated Pullman travel or graduate and law school discrimination. If the decisions could not significantly change the daily Jim Crow routine of most black people, they could break with the past and set the stage for further advances in the fifties.

[61] Carr, *Federal Protection*, pp. 94–96; Pritchett, *The Roosevelt Court*, p. 124; Frederic D. Ogden, *The Poll Tax in the South* (University, Ala., 1958), pp. vii, 31, 57, 74, 76, 109–110, 137–38, 173–76, 179–240, 248, 251, 290.

Using the interstate commerce rather than the equal protection clause, the Supreme Court banned discrimination in Pullman and dining car facilities and overruled state-enforced segregation on interstate buses (*Morgan* v. *Virginia,* 1946). No mass movement to the front of buses developed, however, since a score of Negroes had been slain yearly by transportation personnel with the authority to enforce segregation. The Interstate Commerce Commission did not bar all interstate discrimination on trains and buses until 1955, and even then blacks had to risk additional "freedom rides" to put the law into effect.

Jim Crow also dominated the world of education without substantial limitations. In upper academia, however, a few blacks challenged white bigots to erect entire professional schools for their small enrollment and attacked the policy of total segregation within white graduate programs. In 1950 the Supreme Court struck down both alternatives, arguing that neither a separate law school nor a segregated matriculation satisfied the concept of equality.[62]

Not all black people were willing to await benefits that might some day trickle down from above. The same spirit that resisted the Jim Crow army also cropped up in the guerrilla tactics a minority created to disrupt Jim Crow accomodations and recreational facilities. Non-violent, militant members of the Congress of Racial Equality proved that the struggle for social equality might gain as much from direct action as from litigation. Sit-ins helped integrate movie houses in Denver, cafeterias in Detroit, and lunch counters in the District of Columbia. Racial segregation in other cities gave way before the same assertive behavior by demonstrators who were often beaten and arrested. The 1940s had again produced a small but threatening potential that would mature in succeeding decades.[63]

While objects of "radical exclusion," Negroes had to bear other terrible liabilities during the decade. Lynching still sym-

[62] Pritchett, *The Roosevelt Court,* pp. 126–27; Pritchett, *The Vinson Court,* pp. 127–28, 131–36; ACLU Papers, Box 6, Vol. 9, 1947; Box 15–19, Vol. 15, 1948.

[63] Bernstein, "Ambiguous Legacy," pp. 286–90; Wittner, *Rebels Against War,* pp. 67–68, 161.

bolized the racial hostilities then rampant. While public lynching "bees" attracting whole neighborhoods declined, there were still thirty recorded instances between 1940 and 1947. These do not include the common abuses of police power, ranging from beatings and shootings during arrest and custody to the third degree, illegal detention, and denial of medical attention. Other whites rode public transportation and shot to death Negro passengers who offended their sense of racial propriety. Still others assassinated "countless Negroes" in little-known and underground acts of atrocity. Even their country's uniform had not protected black GI's from white violence.[64]

Convinced that New Deal liberalism was for real, the NAACP began early to petition Roosevelt's government for greater protection. Initially it avoided commitment, fearing "undesirable and embarrassing consequences" in Congress and the South. In 1939, however, FDR's Department of Justice formed a Civil Rights Section (CRS), a promise of federal aid to victims of violence. It was not to be so. The CRS never played Lone Ranger. Instead it followed a cautious and limited program. It always preferred negotiation to prosecution and was very solicitous of local sensibilities and the abstraction of states' rights. Yet a start had been made on turning around an entire system of regional injustice. And this meant convincing Southern prosecutors, judges, and juries to indict, try, and convict one or more of their white neighbors for a racial crime. Statistics suggest the difficulty. In 1944, twenty thousand complaints resulted in sixty-four prosecutions and even fewer convictions. Yet federal investigations and indictments did help inhibit illegal behavior; so did unsuccessful prosecutions. Police brutality declined; lynching outbreaks responded to a number of government prosecutions; and the incidence of peonage fell way off. The CRS had made its presence known, but in spite of it, criminal law enforcement on behalf of human rights was an idea whose time had not yet fully come.[65]

[64] ACLU Papers, Scrapbook 2161; Box 6, Vol. 9, 1947; Box 15–19, Vol. 15, 1948.
[65] Carr, *Federal Protection*, pp. 20–21, 36, 48, 68, 83, 105–114, 132, 138–39, 146, 152–54, 159, 162–64, 168–78, 180–81; Department of

Optimism about racial matters and pride in the nation's ability to create an integrated society characterized the decade's reform efforts. President Truman's 1947 Committee on Civil Rights symbolized these hopes and commitments. To face openly the issue of racial injustice after eighty years of inaction was certainly a fundamental break with the past. Yet almost none of the Committee's audacious recommendations entered the arena of serious debate. No bold new initiatives or dynamic programs, therefore, appeared on the agenda to attack the racial crisis as other national emergencies had been met. When tokenism is considered daring, can riot be far behind? The roll call of innovation now seems pathetic; that it engendered passionate controversy absurd. Yet of five mild reforms—military desegregation, FEPC, the restrictive covenant case, the poll tax, and an anti-lynch law—only one had a successful outcome during the decade. The black minority, however, was not ready to repeat the history of World War I and its aftermath. If the white man had not learned anything and still sought inspiration in fact-finding commissions and task-force reports, many blacks had found the value of militant activism and spontaneous resistance. This consciousness redeemed the forties from futility and made it clear that the watershed of accommodation had been crossed.

"The doctrine of fair play," the criminal lawyer Louis Nizer wrote in 1966, "is deeply ingrained in American tradition. . . ." Vincent Hallinan, a West Coast defense attorney, took a contrary view in his 1963 legal memoirs. He condemned the nation's highest law enforcement officials for tolerating outrageous abuses of due process that included perjury, bribery, intimidation of jurors, felonies, and other actions that violated judicial procedure. Perhaps Nizer and Hallinan had different things in mind: one the theory, the other the practices, that govern American due process. Certainly there had always been a wide gap between the rules of fair play and the actual administration of those rights. That gap seemed to have widened in the 1940s. By the end of the decade Walter Gellhorn

Justice, File 158260-10, 58, and 59; ACLU Papers, Scrapbook 2356; Box 1–5, Vol. 3, 1948.

warned his fellow citizens that the country had already made "a steady progression toward the ultimate extinction of our traditional concept of due process." [66]

During the 1940s two tendencies distinctly at odds with procedural safeguards became prominent. One was the administrative revolution that New Deal and war-time programs had produced; it represented a vast expansion in judgments affecting human rights outside the normal judicial process. As Walter Gellhorn has said, there was a startling increase in the power of "inexpert persons whose judgment is altogether beyond external review." The second disturbing trend narrowed the protections afforded all suspects, if not all inhabitants. In constitutionally sanctioned operations, the police won a much freer hand in arrests, searches, seizures, and surveillance. Law enforcement and security were the big winners, due process and privacy the big losers.

Repressive administrative imperialism had a long tradition and an immense survival capacity that even the New Deal had been unable to alter. Deprivations of freedom once limited to alien affairs tended to radiate outward and become all-inclusive. Other agencies found it agreeable and efficient to imitate the high-handed malpractices developed in deportation. The Post Office, State, and Labor Departments, and the Civil Service Commission, for example, operated on the one hand with an "excessive legalism" that carried out the full measure of restrictive authority and on the other hand with a discretion that knew how to circumvent the "inefficiencies of due process." [67]

In the immediate pre-war and war years, Jewish refugees, Japanese-Americans, other alien enemies, conscientious objectors, draftees, and government employees joined the ranks of the "constitutionally underprivileged." They all had a common experience as victims of procedures in which punishment could result without court scrutiny. The State Department and

[66] Louis Nizer, *The Jury Returns* (Garden City, N.Y., 1966), p. 316; Vincent Hallinan, *A Lion in Court* (New York, 1963), p. 230.

[67] William Preston, Jr., "The Limits of Dissent: Contraction or Enlargement" (paper delivered at 1968 American Historical Association convention), *passim.*

its consular officers devised impossible (and secret) qualifications for entry, assumed vaguely derogatory material to be subversive, and instigated long delays to deprive refugees of their right under quotas to asylum.[68]

To be rated "inimical to the welfare of the United States" by minor bureaucrats was the open-ended accusation that would wreak havoc for others besides Jewish refugees. The Japanese-American evacuation and detention followed in the same tradition. Their premises initially searched without a warrant because of the Fifth Column threat (largely imaginary), the Nisei were rounded up and imprisoned without proof that a clear and present danger existed and without a suspension of the writ of habeas corpus. In custody under conditions that Judge William Denman found to be "in important respects worse than in any federal penitentiary," the detainees won release only if the War Relocation Authority believed it to be "socially desirable." Presumed guilty, the Nisei also had to prove their right to live among loyal Americans in hearings that anticipated those that would later plague the federal bureaucracy. Freedom became a function of what was "administratively feasible," a standard unknown to those who wrote the Bill of Rights.[69]

This same tough attitude cropped up in the war-time "disloyalty" cases. Both alien enemy and draft boards had great discretion in interpreting the law without either judicial or national guidelines to follow. Without full procedural rights (counsel, witnesses, public hearings), alien enemies still had to rebut charges unknown to them and produce affirmative evidence of loyalty. Draft board decisions were final, the Supreme Court said, even if they were wrong, and could be challenged only if they had "no basis in fact for the classification."[70]

Protective overreaction and bureaucratic arrogance found

[68] Feingold, *The Politics of Rescue*, pp. 15–16, 121, 126, 128, 130–31, 136–37, 140–43, 146, 154, 159–60, 229–30, 247, 296.

[69] Grodzins, *Americans Betrayed*, pp. 134–35; ten Broek *et al., Prejudice*, pp. 2, 250–51.

[70] ACLU, *Annual Report* (1943–44), pp. 34–35; *Annual Report* (1944–45), pp. 36–37; Wittner, *Rebels Against War*, pp. 70–84, 162; ACLU Papers, Scrapbooks 2662, 2722; Box 1, Vol. 39, 1946; Box 6, Vol. 7, 1947; Box 6–10, Vol. 6, 1948.

their real cause when cold war security pressures became an obsession, for the loyalty program simply created a new set of scapegoats and treated them to the worst that administrative law had by then developed. Since no one knew what behavior was illegal, the hearings began as a guessing game with anonymous, unreliable, and often hearsay information as the rebuttable presumption of guilt. "Derogatory information" might consist of "views on racial relations; . . . sympathy for Russia . . . ; partisanship on the side of labor; [or] criticism of the Un-American Activities Committee. . . ." [71] Conformity to the Communist line on any issue and membership in or association with members of any organization on the attorney general's list usually sufficed to make a prima facie case of disloyalty. Inquisitorial boards combining the functions of prosecutor, judge, and jury, and with their own careers at stake, subjectively interpreted vague guidelines that presumed one disloyal person a serious threat to the national interest. The legal fiction that government employment was a privilege created the figment of legitimacy which characterized dismissals as simple separations from service rather than punishment with loss of reputation, morale, resources, and livelihood.[72]

Business as usual in the immigration, passport-visa, and postal services reflected the prevalence of processes predating the discovery of disloyalty. There, too, bureaucrats thought of themselves as guardians of a privilege which was to be protected against abuses by people with limited rights. Arrogant attitudes naturally developed toward those who were said to abuse the privilege by displaying a demeanor, an ideology, or a morality offensive to those in office.

Deportation was a case in point. The Immigration Service's 1940 transfer from the Labor to the Justice Department symbolized the harder line. Determined to increase the pressure on radicals, the government broadened the Smith Act to make ex-Communists deportable. During the decade the Immigration Bureau used the new provision sporadically at first, then in a wave of arrests in 1948. People who had been Communist Party members as much as twenty-five years earlier faced

[71] Bontecou, *Federal Loyalty-Security*, p. 96.
[72] *Ibid.*, pp. 110, 116, 131, 136–37, 145, 173–79, 206–18, 240–41, 245.

expulsion, regardless of how brief or casual their commitment. Such ex post facto vengeance could only be approved by a Court that had long since conceded Congress the "absolute" and "unqualified" right to deport for any reason. The sixteen-year drive (1934–50) to expel Harry Bridges, the left-wing leader of the longshoremen, revealed the same vindictive spirit. In 1950 Congress further limited due process by exempting aliens from the more favorable terms in the 1946 Administrative Procedure Act and by excluding from entry anyone whose activities "would be prejudicial to the public interest" or "subversive to the national security." Naturalization and denaturalization proceedings also gave government agents an opportunity to stretch administrative flexibility in order to punish individuals (often radicals and pacifists) whom a criminal action could not touch.[73]

Administrative irregularity also hampered both the free flow of domestic and foreign information and the freedom of movement essential to a democratic society. The Post Office continued its arbitrary and irresponsible censorship. Although the *Esquire* decision made hearings mandatory, postal authorities still ignored the courts, pursued obscenity without definite standards, and refused to use expert opinion. Simply assuming it had the power to examine and suppress foreign propaganda inimical to the national interest, the Post Office played 'Big Brother" without notice, guidelines, or court scrutiny. The State Department meanwhile refused admission to radicals it found offensive and played politics with passports. Each consul had 'sole and uncontrolled power to deny visas," an authority inevitably linked with notions of what was in the country's best interests. Neither a review procedure nor a public explanation accompanied passport denials, one of which involved a member of Congress. The ACLU believed the power to be

---

[73] Pritchett, *The Roosevelt Court*, pp. 115–19; Pritchett, *The Vinson Court*, 102–5, 107, 113–17; Biddle, *In Brief Authority*, pp. 107–15, 121, 207–10, 299; Gellhorn, *Individual Freedom*, pp. 12–13, 30, 34; Hallinan, *A Lion in Court*, pp. 231–43, 276; ACLU Papers, Scrapbooks 2176, 2177, 2354, 2362, 2443, 2454, 2455, 2572; Box 5, Vol. 2 and 5; 1947; Box 1–5, Vol. 4, 1948, Box 6–10, Vol. 6, 1948, Box 1–5, Vol. 3, 1949; Box 6–9, Vol. 9, 1949.

"so badly exercised that there is no defense for it" and one that produced "many cases . . . all bad." [74]

"No man's liberties are safe," ACLU General Counsel Arthur Garfield Hays believed, "unless a law is so definite, that is, so clear and explicit that it can be understood and not guessed at." Victims of administrative law had to do too much guessing, and the judgments they challenged often escaped judicial review. The courts would not check executive justice because they accepted the idea that it involved privileges rather than rights. Nor did they wish to subject themselves to charges of judicial legislation and interference. The bureaucratic actions were, nevertheless, a form of vigilante justice that ignored procedural safeguards as effectively as had the lynch mobs of the old West.[75]

Procedural norms that took a beating at the hands of public officials had as little restraining effect on police excesses in criminal law enforcement. Although the right to counsel, self-incrimination, bail, and fair trial aroused some attention, the major 1940 battles dealt with search, seizure, and surveillance. The Fourth Amendment rights, therefore, faced unique challenges during the decade and emerged in 1950 somewhat battered by police lawlessness and judicial interpretation. Technological progress also accentuated the tendency to fight crime by invading privacy rather than by pursuing clues. Electronic intrusion became, in fact, a non-violent third degree that extracted unconscious confessions without physical force and rubber truncheons. The decade ignored the Fourth Amendment at great risk to its liberties, since its protections are "central to enjoyment of the other guarantees. . . ." As Jacob Landynski has also argued, "security in one's home and person is the fundamental without which there can be no liberty." [76]

[74] Chafee, *Government and Mass Communications*, pp. 329–30; Gellhorn, *Individual Freedom*, pp. 25, 83–88; ACLU Papers, Scrapbooks 2158, 2186, 2439, 2440, 2579, 2717; Box 1–5, Vol. 2, 1948; Box 1–5, Vol. 4, 1949; Box 6–9, Vol. 7, 1949.

[75] Pritchett, *The Warren Court*, pp. 47–48.

[76] Landynski, *Search and Seizure*, pp. 2–25, 43–45, 47–56, 164, 262–63.

Judicial precedents and police practices prior to 1940 did not clearly indicate what would happen to Fourth Amendment freedoms during the decade. A broad right to be protected from unreasonable searches and seizures existed, but its enforcement left something to be desired. The exclusion of evidence illegally seized by federal officers in federal criminal proceedings did not prevent the use of similar material taken by state or local police and turned over "on a silver platter" (i.e., with no taint of federal involvement). What is more, the exclusionary rule did not necessarily stop illegal practices. Nor did police officials necessarily honor either the Fourth Amendment or its interpretation by Washington. Court approval of warrantless searches as an incident of an actual arrest suggested another loophole.[77]

The security-minded forties witnessed a further increase in the exceptions rather than a tightening of the rules. In two decisions of 1947 and 1950, the Supreme Court authorized a vast increase in the scope of searches incidental to arrest. The *Harris-Rabinowitz* doctrine, perhaps the worst blow to the protection of privacy in court history, revived the hated general warrant of Colonial ill-fame. Under the new mandate, searches during arrest might now cover an entire house or apartment without need for probable cause, oath, description, or judicial determination. As a result, searches grew more extensive, warrants lapsed into disuse, and, as Landynski wrote, search became "an investigative technique rather than the culmination of an investigation." Other actions also benefited the police enthusiasts. The 1949 decision applying Fourth Amendment guarantees to the states was subverted by the Court's *not* requiring them to adopt the exclusionary rule. And the silver platter doctrine remained in force until 1960.[78]

Law enforcement also outdistanced constitutional restraints in the race between the wiretappers and the Fourth Amend-

---

[77] *Ibid.*, pp. 49, 52–53, 56, 58–67, 70–73, 87–96, 98–101, 123–24, 130, 169–70, 173–74, 177–78, 188, 262–63; David Fellman, *The Defendant's Rights* (New York, 1958), pp. 11–12, 15, 17, 185; Dorsen, *Frontiers*, pp. 29–30.

[78] Landynski, *Search and Seizure*, pp. 72–73, 100–117, 126–34, 158–164; Pritchett, *The Vinson Court*, pp. 147, 150.

ment. Police officials could not resist a technology that promised to produce quickly and easily all the data that had formerly been so painfully assembled by hard detective work, coerced confessions and the third degree. An eavesdropping, dragnet invasion of privacy installed by stealth for an indefinite tenure was much too attractive to be abandoned just because some justice called it a "dirty business." And the fact of the matter was that the Supreme Court had given tappers the green light in a 1927 case, *Olmstead* v. *United States.* Using a technical definition of search, the majority found there had been no entry and no search, only eavesdropping outside the premises or words projected voluntarily by the speakers themselves. Thus, "nothing tangible had been seized," and the evidence was admissible in court. In 1937 the *Nardone* decision reduced this broad grant of authority by interpreting Section 605 of the 1934 Communications Act as a ban on all federal tapping. But *Nardone* had weaknesses. It did not overrule *Olmstead;* covered only wire interceptions, not other electronic intrusions; and left states free to use wiretap evidence. More importantly, *Nardone* could not prevent the government from enforcing the law as it saw fit.

The crisis of World War II revealed how little impact the Court could have. Convinced the nation would be overwhelmed by espionage and subversion without federal wiretapping, Attorney General Robert Jackson reinterpreted Section 605 to prohibit only interception *and* divulgence. Government agents were thereby freed to tap on as long as the evidence stayed inside the executive branch. Jackson had clearly twisted the law. The latter banned divulgence to *any person.* As James Lawrence Fly pointed out, "no tapper acts for sheer amusement; he can't eat the information. He dictates it or its substance to another person. . . ."[79]

Under the influence of the war, the Supreme Court retreated back toward *Olmstead. Goldman* v. *United States* involved the federal use of a detectaphone, a device that picked up telephone conversations when fastened to the outside wall of a

---

[79] Landynski, *Search and Seizure,* pp. 15, 198–208, 225–27, 238; Westin, *Privacy and Freedom,* pp. 174–76; Dorsen, *Frontiers,* p. 29; ACLU Papers, Scrapbooks 2177, 2281, 2458; Box 14–19, Vol. 16, 1949.

room. The majority saw no conflict with the Fourth Amendment because there had been no actual physical entry into the room. Section 605 did not apply unless tapping of the telephone wire had really taken place. Encouraged by *Goldman,* the war, anti-Communism and permissiveness from above, the FBI, the Secret Service, and other federal agencies operated without restraint.

Libertarians could not catch up. Secrecy was one reason. Security was so tight that no hard evidence of federal tapping developed until 1964. Accelerating technology provided ever smaller and more sophisticated devices and helped electronic surveillance stay ahead of the law. The laws that did exist were ineffectual. Those who tapped illegally escaped prosecution, since governments would not punish the very lawlessness they themselves pursued. As Alan F. Westin has demonstrated, when the courts did close loopholes, "the Department of Justice [among many] diligently searched for and discovered new ones." Two decades later the country was still looking for a way to protect privacy and personal liberty from the ravages of this addiction.[80]

If the 1940s made life much more difficult for all suspects facing arrest, search, or surveillance, it did provide somewhat better protection for those who had been arrested. Their need, particularly if they were indigent, was to have a prompt arraignment, avoid self-incrimination, and obtain legal assistance. *Betts* v. *Brady* in 1942 and *McNabb* v. *United States* the following year both improved this situation slightly.

Betts involved the right to counsel of accused indigents. In federal felony cases this assistance was, of course, mandatory. In state trials, however, the majority found it not to be a fundamental right. Using a "special circumstances" rule, the Supreme Court required counsel only in capital cases if the defendant "could show that he would be particularly disadvantaged by the lack of a lawyer." The fact that counsel was not a basic right and the need to interpret the special circumstances provision brought additional cases before the Vinson Court. In twelve appeals between 1946 and 1953, the majority

[80] Landynski, *Search and Seizure,* pp. 208, 210–12; Westin, *Privacy and Freedom,* pp. 119–21, 173–79, 195–97.

found that lack of legal assistance had been unfair in half. It was also apparent that, in spite of the rule, many defendants were unaware of their rights and suffered severe disabilities when trying to conduct their own defense.[81]

If the indigent received a modicum of legal dignity and assistance in the *Betts* precedent, *McNabb* provided a similar small favor in pre-trial proceedings. Arrests, so the *McNabb* decision insisted, were to be followed by prompt arraignment, and confessions extorted while a suspect was illegally detained would be inadmissible in federal court. In spite of the ruling, however, the police often ignored *McNabb* or made arrests for disorderly conduct and vagrancy. The case, therefore, may have left only the slightest fossil trace on the geologic bedrock of customary police routine.[82]

Two alarming trends chartered collision courses with libertarian principles and undermined procedural safeguards during the 1940s. Administrative law sired by welfarism and now the right arm of anti-Communism had vastly enlarged the number of proceedings that imposed punishment without the procedural protections of the judicial process. It was a decade that seemed to welcome "uncontrolled discretion" and liked to create new classes of "quasi-defendants." But if administrative law looked bad in comparison with judicial norms, the latter looked even worse in comparison with the standards usually associated with American jurisprudence. Apart from the decline of the trial tradition in sedition and radical cases, the system offered few guarantees of "fundamental fairness" to millions of Americans, beginning with the blacks and ending with the poor. In addition, due process had lost considerable ground to law enforcement practices that were making a mockery of the Bill of Rights. Electronic surveillance, almost totally free from constitutional restraints, had made great forward strides during the decade and had created a tradition of lawlessness later years would find it almost impossible to reverse. While advocates of national security and law and order raised noisy alarms of subversion

[81] Pritchett, *The Roosevelt Court,* p. 139; Pritchett, *The Vinson Court,* p. 158; Dorsen, *Frontiers,* pp. 194–96, 199–200, 205–9.
[82] Landynski, *Search and Seizure,* pp. 169–70, 178–79.

and criminal coddling, their hue and cry disguised the true nature of events. Far from succumbing to softness, the decade had adopted the tough stand, unleashed its police and security officials and dared civil libertarians to interfere.[83]

In 1940 the Bill of Rights celebrated its 150th anniversary. In the decade that followed, was America a nation "conceived in liberty and dedicated to the proposition that all men are created equal"? The evidence was conflicting and confusing. Certainly the black man beaten to death by a Georgia sheriff who then went free had never had either the freedom or equality so many whites took for granted. The Jehovah's Witnesses who roused the mob fury of small-town U.S.A. and the Japanese-Americans protected from it in concentration camps had met the fearful and short-sighted in unequal contest. There were thousands of other casualties, too, whose histories bore out the dismaying gap between principle and practice. Even the great white majority had been cheated of its rightful share of freedom by a mass media that communicated the banal and blacklisted the programs and personnel that challenged that norm. War and cold war had stimulated the drive for security and conformity. The ever greater proliferation of laws, meanwhile, had complicated constitutional interpretation and widened the area of discretionary enforcement, placing a great strain on procedural regularity and fairness. The dynamic tempo of the country had itself threatened civil liberties by bringing urban groups together in malevolent proximity.

Yet the history of the decade did not entirely read like a civil liberty obituary. Those same Jehovah's Witnesses had wrung a "charter of freedom" from the Supreme Court. The Nisei did find acceptable havens and some financial redress after paying their awful price to American racism. Statistics, whatever they are worth, implied that certain anti-libertarian evils were on the wane. There was less mob violence, less public lynching, less censorship, less interference with leafleting, and less lawless invasion of labor's right to organize. There were also more groups and agencies willing to support civil

[83] Chafee, "Thirty-five Years," pp. 328, 335; ACLU, *Annual Report* (1948–49), p. 9.

liberties. The Justice Department's Civil Rights Section, the NLRB, the FEPC, and the FCC helped the ACLU and its allies defend the heritage of 1791. In 1950 Roger Baldwin retired as executive director of the Union and insisted that "progress. . . . in law, practice, and understanding . . . has been considerable, despite wars, depressions, and police states." [84]

Men on the fighting front, however, do not always see the flow of the battle clearly and fully, especially in the heat of combat. The militant ACLU activists had been in the front lines of the major battles of the decade, and, as often happens in such action, yards of ground gained may seem like momentous victories. Certainly the Union had been the libertarian conscience and watchdog for the nation, but it could not necessarily evaluate the outcome objectively.

Time and historical perspective have had a chance now to survey the scene and estimate the results, just as the strategic bombing surveys corrected the enthusiastic claims of the allied command. It is now apparent that the 1940s were a decisive decade for civil liberties in which tactical gains were impressively offset by strategic losses. Two themes may help fix the character of that era: tokenism and balance.

If the Bill of Rights has any significance, it must assuredly be in the here-and-now guarantees that living Americans count on for protection. Time and again in the forties, those amendments proved unable to halt violations of freedom justified by some higher priority, be it community conformity, law and order, loyalty, or national security. Since the man in the street is always ready to do his own balancing of First Amendment and other freedoms, usually forcefully, the Supreme Court's willingness to pursue the same philosophy was a civil liberty disaster. "Freedom with limits," Howard Beale once wrote, "means bondage to whatever force or person sets the limit."

Balancing in the 1940s left liberty at the mercy of those who judge the circumstances, and the dismal record in loyalty-security cases was only the most prominent comment on how that judgment affected freedom. Apart from the notable instances of deprivation, it is worth remembering that the

[84] ACLU, *Annual Report* (1949–50), p. 3.

Hatch Act turned into the federal loyalty program, the Smith Act was replaced by the McCarran Act, Dies gave way to McCarthy, and the Roosevelt Court was succeeded by the Vinson Court. The result, as Irving Brant has so lucidly summarized it, was that "guarantees planted in a written Constitution as a safeguard against impulsive legislatures, arbitrary executives, and thoughtless popular majorities have been reduced to feeble maxims by those who give them that misnomer." [85]

Tokenism, the popular slogan for measures that seemingly advance liberty while continuing to deny it, took deep root during the war and post-war years. To read the litanies of praise that accompanied much of the meaningless activity of that time is to be reminded of people's unlimited capacity to falsify the record. None of the great Supreme Court decisions, the legislative advances, or the executive pronouncements proved to be Joshua's trumpet, for the institutional walls resisted the inroads of libertarian change. Segregation and discrimination persisted; due process for the victims of administrative processes remained as remote as ever; police officials followed the lines of least resistance, ignoring constitutional statements to the contrary; and technology accelerated already ominous tendencies. The capitalistic and commercial imperatives in the broadcasting, press, and movie industries easily won out over libertarian and regulatory considerations. Those who took heart from an FEPC or a restrictive covenant case, an FCC edict, an anti-trust decision, a Civil Rights Section, a censorship victory, or another presidential commission mistook rhetoric for reality. The forces that threatened civil liberties, popular, economic, and establishment, had vitality and viability that those tokens could hardly touch.

The American Civil Liberties Union had implicitly recognized this inherent intransigence of the status quo when it argued that "eternal vigilance" would be necessary because no fight for civil liberty ever stayed won. Holding the libertarian line was in itself a magnificent effort, to expand the frontiers

[85] Beale, *Are American Teachers Free?* pp. 761–64; Irving Brant, *The Bill of Rights: Its Origin and Meaning* (Indianapolis, Ind., 1965), pp. 493, 507.

of freedom an even more heroic job. If the shadows of war and fear darkened prospects for change in the 1940s, the ACLU helped maintain what light there was. It, too, regretted that the decade treated civil liberties so shabbily, for it had struggled for real progress, not just the illusion of it. The country thought otherwise, and found other priorities consistently more persuasive than the feeble maxims it professed to honor.

McCARTHYISM
RAMPANT

JOHN W. CAUGHEY

Emerging from the Second World War victorious and the richest of nations, the United States neatly carried through the necessary post-war adjustments in its economy. Thoughtful citizens, mindful that the United States not only had made the atomic bomb but had used it, feared that it was a force with which mankind was not to be trusted. Yet the overriding fear as Americans entered the fifties was of Russia and Communism.

At this point in time many Americans retained a gratitude to the Russians for heroic resistance against the Nazis and for turning back the Wehrmacht at Stalingrad. Many also remained firm in their belief that the Russian people had prospects of being better off under the Communist system than they ever had been under the czars. Yet Russia had shown itself blatantly the aggressor in the takeover of Czechoslovakia and intransigent with the Berlin blockade. These actions substantiated the threat of spreading Communism throughout the world. In September, 1949, with the explosion of an atomic device, Russia shaped up as a most formidable rival. In the immediate post-war years the driving force in American foreign policy was restraint of Communism by confronting and containing the Russian fountainhead. That was the purpose of the Truman Doctrine, the Marshall Plan, and NATO. President Eisenhower and his secretary of state, John Foster Dulles, intensified the commitment with brinksmanship threatened and practiced.

Although fear that Communism would sweep the United States was less realistic, this program of making the world unsafe for Communism inevitably nurtured the build-up of anti-Communism on the home front. The display performances had been the attorney general's list of subversive organizations and President Truman's order of a loyalty check of federal employees; the cashiering of the Hollywood Ten (screenwriters, directors, and other creative persons) in 1947 for refusing to answer questions by the House Un-American Activities Committee; the indictment and two trials of Alger Hiss; and the conviction in 1949 of eleven officials of the Communist Party as members of an organization committed to the overthrow of the government of the United States. In 1951, in upholding these convictions, the Supreme Court not only eliminated the element of timeliness in the maxim of "clear and present danger" but shifted to a much looser yardstick of "the gravity of the 'evil,' discounted by its improbability."

Many other experiments in rooting out Communist Party members, associates, and ideas were operative. In 1947 the Los Angeles county supervisors ordered all Communist books removed from the county library. Over faculty recommendations to the contrary, early in 1949 the University of Washington fired two professors who were avowed Communists and another who refused to respond to questions on his political affiliations and beliefs. Following the second of these leads and the government's strategem in the Hiss case, the University of California regents set up a perjury-type oath of denial of Communist Party membership which they called a loyalty oath. As 1949 drew to a close they were in process of requiring its execution by every member of the faculty and every university employee. Domestic anti-Communism as an obsession was slightly in the future, but at the ringing in of the new decade there was widespread acceptance of the tenet that to be a Communist or, for that matter, a fellow traveler overwhelmed any virtues a person might have. Such persons were regarded as pariahs, not covered by civil liberties guarantees. A methodology for dealing with them had come into being. It featured:

Loyalty checks of public employees, federal and local, with the attorney general's list as ready reference on subversive organizations.

Application of the same tests to persons in key positions of influence such as teachers and movie makers.

Exposure by congressional committee or by a state "little Dies Committee," with nonresponsiveness seen as admission of guilt.

Fingering by paid informers.

Dismissal from public employment.

Loyalty oaths of the perjury type as a means of eliminating Communists or fellow travelers from public or sensitive employment.

Prison sentences under the Smith Act on proof of Communist Party membership.

The fifties opened with an assortment of issues and actions such as had been the normal gist for civil libertarians and would be on the agenda throughout the decade. In its annual report covering 1950 the American Civil Liberties Union saw violations of freedom of speech in two convictions for advising non-registration for the draft, which the Supreme Court in a 4-4 division allowed to stand. When the Washington, D.C., transit company began to pipe commercials into its streetcars and buses, it was charged that denying riders the right not to listen was a free speech violation. ACLU protested sporadic censorship of movies such as *Curly*, which showed white and black children playing together; *The Bicycle Thief*, which contained a scene of a young boy urinating in the street; and *Oliver Twist*, allegedly anti-Semitic. Without success, the banning of *The Nation* from New York City school libraries was attacked. A suit was brought to restrain the Los Angeles police from bugging the home of gambler Mickey Cohen. The Union was also preparing a brief on the issue of right to counsel, which had been denied four young Indians in Idaho sentenced for stealing a sheep.

Legal efforts against "released time" from public schools for religious instructions failed. When Cardinal Spellman assailed Eleanor Roosevelt as anti-Catholic for opposing federal aid to parochial schools, the ACLU insisted that the cardinal mistakenly read religious discrimination into the principle of separation of church and state.

Meanwhile the National Association for the Advancement of Colored People was challenging the inferior facilities in "separate but equal" schools; several states enacted fair employment practices acts; a New York statute rejected discrimination in publicly financed housing; and a city ordinance in St. Louis prohibited segregation in public swimming pools. A suit to void the poll tax failed in Virginia, but Idaho by referendum authorized Indians to vote, serve on juries, and hold office.

The press and the public paid much more attention to another set of developments. On January 21, 1950, a federal jury found Alger Hiss guilty on two counts of perjury in denying that he had passed "secret, confidential, and restricted documents" to Whittaker Chambers and in asserting that he had not seen Chambers since January 1, 1937. In the popular mind that registered as tantamount to proof of espionage and served as endorsement, under the banner of anti-Communism, of extraordinary procedures violating civil liberties. Senator Joseph McCarthy began his bluster about Communist infiltration, though at year's end the ACLU report limited itself to refuting his charges against Judge Dorothy Kenyon and urging elimination of congressional immunity and reform of congressional investigations.

In midsummer the Korean War, technically a United Nations action against the Communist invasion of South Korea, heated up the cold war and gave a boost to anti-Communism on the domestic front. Conditioned by the war, Congress enacted a new Internal Security Act, which required Communist front organizations to register, made it a crime to conspire to establish a dictatorship in the United States, authorized depor-

tation of aliens involved in suspect organizations, provided for
war-time internment of subversives, and set up a Subversive
Activities Control Board. President Truman vetoed this measure as "worse than the Sedition Act of 1798," but Congress
promptly passed it over his veto.

The federal government's "loyalty" program ran its ponder-
ous associations-check on federal employees without respect to
sensitivity of assignment. Dismissals occurred with much less
than due process. The University of California regents in February underlined their loyalty oath requirement with a sign-or-
be-fired ultimatum. In April they accepted a compromise formula, but in July and August, irrespective of faculty and administrative clearances, they fired the remaining non-signers. Similar oaths requiring the foreswearing of "false politics," that is
to say, Communism, proliferated widely.

As 1950 came to an end the ACLU noted a spreading and
pevasive atmosphere of fear and intolerance "stifling the good
old American habits of speaking one's mind, joining the organizations one believes in, and observing the principles of fair
hearing and of holding a man innocent until he is proved
guilty." This blighting of civil liberties on such diverse points
as labor, aliens, wiretapping, bail, and discriminatory selection
of grand juries in instance after instance was under the cover
of anti-Communism.

In *The Reporter* (July 21, 1953), in lines entitled "Insomnia,"
SEC outlined the nightmarish scenario.

Count the small liberties as they leap over the stile and
  disappear, one by one!
One, To Differ (those who believe in other ways betray)
Two, To Listen (this lecture is canceled; the thoughts
  might lead astray)
Three, To See (this movie is banned because some call it
  obscene)
Four, To Enter (this man cannot immigrate, he erred at
  eighteen)
Five, To Read (these books are no longer permitted on
  the shelves)
Six, To Be Silent (those who refuse to speak convict
  themselves)

Seven, To Question (this judge who consulted his conscience must be impeached)

Eight, nine, ten, eleven, twelve (the limit is not yet
reached)

Count the small liberties as they leap over the stile and
disappear, one by one.

The man who most unerringly put his finger on the pulse of
the fifties was the hitherto obscure senator from Wisconsin,
Joseph R. McCarthy. Taking a tip from three Republican ad-
visers, he decided that the best way to make a reputation that
would ensure his reelection would be to harp on Communist
infiltration in government. The idea was not new but the tim-
ing was propitious. Within a fortnight came the Hiss conviction, and then, on February 3, 1950, British scientist Klaus
Fuchs confessed that from 1943 through 1947 he had systematically funnelled to the Russians the top British and American atomic secrets. It was easy, though perhaps erroneous, to
assume that such leaks accounted for the speedy Russian
achievement of an A-bomb.

At Wheeling, West Virginia, on February 9, 1950, in the
first of a series of Lincoln's Birthday speeches to Republican
faithful, McCarthy loosed his first salvo, a blast against "trai-
torous action" in the State Department, filled with "bright
young men born with silver spoons in their mouths" and presided over by Secretary Dean Acheson, a "pompous diplo-
mat in striped pants" with a "phony British accent." The
Department, McCarthy fumed, "is thoroughly infested with
Communists." Such diatribes have precedent in American political oratory. McCarthy drove his attack home with something more specific. Brandishing a paper, he rumbled on, "I
hold in my hand a list of 205 names" of persons who he
charged had been made known to the secretary of state as
members of the Communist Party but who were still working
and making policy in the State Department.

The Wheeling speech was not written or recorded, and it
was only perfunctorily reported. Consequently, only para-
phrases of the key sentence exist. At Salt Lake City and Reno,
McCarthy repeated the speech, letting the number change to
fifty-seven or eighty-one and loosening the definition of "Com-

munist." Now the attack made headlines, provoking President Truman and Acheson to tart denials. On the floor of the Senate on February 20 McCarthy was questioned, especially on the numbers. For six hours he parried all questions and held forth with embroidered résumés of what seemed to be dossiers on State Department employees.

A Senate subcommittee headed by Maryland Senator Millard Tydings attempted to pin him down on the number and the concreteness of his evidence. Tydings deflated the notion that there were 205 or 57 or 81 Communists or Communist agents in the State Department. But the rules of the club left a senator much leeway; as one charge was demolished, McCarthy lashed out with another.

Asked for names, after several postponements he named four "pro-Communists" and the next day four more, most of whom it turned out were not State Department employees. On March 20 McCarthy offered to simplify his charge and let it stand or fall on one man, "the top Russian spy," Professor Owen Lattimore. Told that Lattimore had never been a regular employee of the State Department, McCarthy insisted that he still was "the chief architect of our Far Eastern policy." Tydings called Communist and ex-Communist witnesses who said they had never known Lattimore as a Communist. J. Edgar Hoover testified that the FBI files had no such evidence. General Douglas McArthur's chief of counter-intelligence testified that Lattimore had been thoroughly investigated and had top clearance.

McCarthy thereupon shifted the attack to Philip C. Jessup, a member of the United States delegation to the United Nations, as a notorious tool of the Communists. Again the rebuttal evidence was impressive, but in 1951, when Jessup's renomination was up for confirmation, McCarthy browbeat the Senate committee into disapproving, 3–1.

McCarthy went on to attack the most respected member of the Truman administration, General George C. Marshall, as part of a conspiracy to hand China over to Moscow. McCarthy professed not to know "whether we've lost because of stumbling, fumbling idiocy, or because they planned it that way." The American people, he said, should decide "whether these individuals have been dupes or whether they are traitors."

Over the first few months it appeared that "Tail-gunner Joe" was making himself widely known but that none of his charges was sticking. With the outbreak of the Korean War receptivity improved. More Americans began to say, "I don't approve of his methods, but he is doing something that needs to be done." An increasing number enjoyed the spectacle.

If there were disadvantages in operating a one-man crusade, they were more than compensated for by the senatorial immunity McCarthy could claim and the simplicity of being a single-issue promoter. The only thing his supporters had to agree on was anti-Communism. They could come from both parties, all walks of life, and all parts of the country.

McCarthy's southern conservative Democratic colleagues were not disturbed, and the conservative Senate leadership was not disposed to intervene. Moderate and liberal Democrats were less pleased. But they were deterred from an all-out attack because of past identification with the New Deal, fear of political reprisals, and dread of being stamped as pro-Communist. The conservative Republican leadership saw McCarthy as highly useful and urged him on. The gist of Senator Robert Taft's advice was "If one case doesn't work, bring up another." Moderate Republicans were soon appeasing the senator from Wisconsin. In 1952 Eisenhower edited a tribute to General Marshall out of a campaign speech when told it was distasteful to McCarthy. As president he tried not to cross him.

McCarthy and McCarthyism had their strongest appeal to authoritarians irrespective of party or economic status, to the military-minded, to isolationists, and to those eager for strikes against Communist aggression wherever it occurred. The appeal was more to conservatives than to liberals; to Catholics than to Protestants; to Protestants than to Jews; and to the less educated than to the highly educated—which gave rise to the observation that "college-educated Republicans were no more anti-McCarthy than grammar-school Democrats."

With Eisenhower's ascent to the presidency in 1953, McCarthy seemingly lost his main target, the Truman-Acheson operation. But the Eisenhower-Nixon campaigning had stressed the need to clean up "the mess in Washington," and for that

McCarthy as the "Great Accuser" could help. Furthermore, he now would be chairman of the Senate Committee on Government Operations and head its Permanent Subcommittee on Investigations. With larger staff and license to investigate, he could graduate to the methods of Martin Dies and the House Un-American Activities Committee. There would be competition from that committee, now led by Representative Harold Velde, and from Senator William Jenner's Senate Committee on Internal Security, but McCarthy not only monopolized the limelight in his committee but eclipsed the two competing committees as well.

As a Wisconsin judge, McCarthy had built a reputation for volume of cases handled. Now he hurried through a procession of witnesses, content in most instances to pose a question or two that would lead to a damaging admission or refusal to answer based on the Fifth Amendment's privilege against self-incrimination. Thereupon he could brand them as "Fifth Amendment Communists." Voluble with observations on the testimony given or not given and with embellishments on what might have come out, he was master of the art of the daily press release. He made a great commotion about trade by other nations with Red China, permitted and condoned by the United States. He railed about Communists in the Government Printing Office. Because of government contracts he had leverage to probe for Communists employed by General Electric. On the gambit of tax exemption he attacked Harvard University for sheltering an atomic scientist alleged to have Communist ties.

Concurrently the State Department was in retreat from McCarthy on almost all fronts. In spite of prestigious character endorsements McCarthy brought about the dismissal of Theodore Kaghan, an effective employee in Germany. He then dispatched his two callow staffers, Roy Cohn and David Schine, on a sweep through the Information Service libraries in Europe. They brought back a list of "Communist books," 140 of them so defined because the author, editor, or illustrator was an alleged Communist or associated with Communists. The State Department protested but began withdrawing the books and actually burned some of them, to which the American Library Association countered with a ringing endorsement of freedom to read as a First Amendment guarantee and a necessity.

When in impromptu remarks at Dartmouth College Eisenhower spoke out against book-burners, McCarthy denied that the reference was to him. "Who, me? I haven't burned a single book." Eisenhower never took back what he said at Dartmouth, but he did not countermand the State Department retreat.

Interrupting his honeymoon in the early autumn of 1953, McCarthy rushed back to Washington to investigate a reported spy ring in the Army's scientific center at Fort Monmouth. This time he interviewed witnesses in executive session but in his usual fashion issued daily commentaries that forecast uncovering of espionage rising to the level of atomic secrets. Although in the long run the charges appeared to be unfounded, morale in the unit was reduced to a shambles. The Army suspended nineteen scientists and transferred another ten to lesser assignments, a tribute not to the evidence but to the power of a congressional investigator.

In January, 1954, McCarthy shifted his attack to the promotion, along with seven thousand other Army doctors and dentists, and the honorable discharge of an Army dentist on McCarthy's list as a witness. When questioned, Dr. Irving Peress took the Fifth Amendment, whereupon McCarthy brought Brigadier General Ralph Zwicker to the stand and upbraided him for shielding Major Peress and the officers who had promoted him. Secretary of the Army Robert Stevens issued a general order to officers to disregard subpoenas from McCarthy's committee. The then vice president, Richard M. Nixon, thereupon took the initiative of arranging a luncheon meeting between Stevens and the Republican members of the McCarthy committee. At this meeting on February 24 Stevens succumbed to the pleas for party unity and agreed to a "Memorandum for Understanding" featuring a retraction of his order. Cartoonist Herblock realistically showed Stevens surrendering his sword to McCarthy and Eisenhower drawing from his scabbard a white feather.

In its first year in office the Eisenhower administration went beyond tolerating McCarthyism. One indication came in October, 1953, when the White House press secretary released a memorandum stating that under the security program 1,456 federal employees had been separated from government jobs. A little sleuthing revealed that in many departments most of the terminations had nothing to do with security. Yet in his State of the Union message in January, 1954, the fourth anniversary of McCarthy's inspiration, the president took satisfaction in 2,200 dismissals under the security program. A year later his count was 8,008.

Another disclosure in October, 1953, was more partisan. Attorney General Herbert Brownell, speaking for the administration, charged that President Truman had knowingly retained a Soviet spy in the Department of State. When it was pointed out that this amounted to a charge of treason, Brownell substituted "blindness almost to the point of willful blindness." Challenged for particulars, he cited a still classified report containing such an allegation against the late Harry Dexter White. Brownell did not go so far as to say that the file contained proof that White was a spy or that Truman was so informed. In November, former presidential nominee Thomas E. Dewey drew these two threads together, boasting of the 1,456 firings as progress toward a government "not infested with spies and traitors."

At nine Lincoln's Birthday dinners in 1954, four years after his kick-off at Wheeling, McCarthy packaged this message even more forcefully as "Twenty Years of Treason." So that no one would fail to understand, he spelled it out: "The hard fact is that those who wear the label Democrat wear it with the sign of historic betrayal," for it is "a political label stitched with the idiocy of a Truman, rotted by the deceit of an Acheson, and corrupted by the red slime of a White."

In the four years since his curtain-raiser at Wheeling, McCarthy had built up impressive momentum. He also had sold his position and his services very effectively to the American people. The Gallup Poll registered 50 percent favorable to him, as against only 29 percent unfavorable.

The unbridled anti-Communism of the fifties, swept along on the wings of fear, was highly expansive. Its target swelled from Communists to former Communists, anyone accused of being a Communist, socialists, liberals, New Dealers, and Democrats in general. This brand of anti-Communism also offered its handle to many sorts of people in and out of government, and for an astonishing variety of uses.

The sworn enemies of dental health through fluoridation, for example, seized on the bogey of Communism. At the time of the Seattle referendum, fluoridation was branded as the first step in the Communist drive for socialized medicine, and a leader in San Francisco saw fluoridation as a red plot "to weaken the minds of the people" and make them dupes for Communism.

In another example of anti-Communism at the grass roots, in October, 1951, a speaker charged that the children of Los Angeles were being fed "daily doses of Communism, socialism, and New Idealism." The specific she had in mind was a pamphlet, *The E in UNESCO,* which the school district had prepared as a learning aid on the workings of this United Nations agency. The local press gave featured coverage to the attack. The Liberty Belles, the Native Sons of the Golden West, the Women's Breakfast Club, and the Reverend James W. Fifield jumped on this bandwagon. At successive school board meetings the charge was repeated and expanded. Another lady found a much more obscure reference work in the possession of the school district which quoted Communist educators in Czechoslovakia on the function of the school in "correcting the errors of home training" in nationalism.

Representatives of the League of Women Voters, the PTA, the Quakers, Rotary International, labor unions and other groups, and distinguished citizens such as Paul Hoffman, former president of Studebaker, spoke up for the UN and UNESCO. The board and the superintendent temporized. They were worried about a $146 million bond election. They assigned staff to evaluate the pamphlet.

Critics charged that UNESCO intended to abolish parochial schools, that the UN sponsored birth control, and that the UN flag was almost identical to the Red Army battle flag. New critics entered the fray, among them Cardinal McIntyre, Dr. Fifield's Spiritual Mobilization, and State Senator Jack Tenney's America Plus. In August the board cravenly certified that *The E in UNESCO* was not an impartial presentation and therefore would be banned. School Superintendent Alexander J. Stoddard let it be known that his term as director of the American Association for the United Nations was running out.

Although in the early fifties McCarthy rode highest as the great exemplar of anti-Communism, many others in government rushed in to help build and operate a far-reaching apparatus for testing, checking, detecting, exposing, and ejecting the Communist tainted or inclined.

From 1950 through 1952 the House Un-American Activities Committee busied itself primarily in putting former FBI men and other informers on the stand to read into the record name after name and testimony on membership, participation, and support of Communist or Communist-related organizations. In 1948 the committee had claimed to have a million such names in its files. That number rose rapidly.

Occasionally the HUAC achieved a dramatic triumph. Its dragnet pulled in Lucille Ball, star in a feature picture about to be released by Paramount Pictures. The committee granted absolution—itself a rarity—but only after Miss Ball's husband had testified that she was "a political dumbbell" and she had testified that her one-time voter registration as a Communist was merely to please her radical grandfather. Congressman Donald Jackson inadvertently made a revealing confession. "The Committee," he said, "is departing from its usual procedure so that fact may be separated from rumor, and no damage done Miss Ball."

HUAC also was alerted to the specter of Communism in the churches. An informer who was an ex-Communist proclaimed that six hundred Protestant ministers were Communists, and J. B. Matthews, briefly a McCarthy aide, raised the ante to seven thousand. When Congressman Jackson offered the specific that Methodist Bishop G. Bromley Oxnam "served God on Sunday and Communism the rest of the week," Oxnam demanded and was granted an opportunity to rebut the charge, in the format of the committee hearings a very difficult task. He exploded the personal accusations but in cross-examination was trapped into identifying a couple of ministers as Communists or possible Communists. The Committee stipulated that he was not a Communist, but would not retract the charge of "serving Communism."

The U.S. Senate's Jenner Committee less spectacularly concentrated on suspects in the colleges and on the staff of the United Nations, questioning them on suspected past memberships. Refusal to answer on Fifth Amendment grounds was protection against prosecution but in most instances meant that the college or university would dismiss the professor or laboratory technician who was non-responsive. HUAC's Jackson and others called loudly for repeal of the Fifth Amendment. Most committeemen felt that McCarthyism was better served and the complexities of litigation spared by the simpler method of branding such persons as Fifth Amendment Communists. The device was effective, though the syndrome was undermining a cardinal element of the Bill of Rights.

In West Los Angeles a ceramics factory was plagued by pilferage to the extent that almost every employee had taken home a starter set. Management decided on wholesale arrests and prosecution of almost all the employees. Counsel for the defendants outlined a simple way out. So that work in the plant could go on he would ask for agreement that only fifteen witnesses a day be summoned. Then, as each witness was questioned, he would plead the Fifth Amendment. "But," said the union president, "they can't do that. They may be thieves, but they are not Communists!"

As a heritage of the "red scare" of 1917–23, thirty-four states had criminal syndicalism laws and thirty-one had anti-sedition laws. In twenty-four states there were newer and more stringent sedition laws; thirty-two had loyalty oath requirements for teachers; twenty-seven kept subversive parties off the ballot; twenty-eight barred subversives from public employment; eleven forbade use of public buildings by subversive organizations; and six required subversive organizations to register with state agencies. By 1953 Utah was the only one of the forty-eight states without any of these laws.

Many of the state laws and parallel local ordinances could be invoked only at the point when a violation occurred or was imminent, for instance when a meeting was scheduled by a "subversive" organization. The loyalty oath requirements had much wider impact. In California in 1950 the legislature brought every employee of the state or any of its branches under the rubric of civil defense workers and required of each an oath of denial of membership, present or within the past five years, in any organization committed to the violent overthrow of the government.

Not one of the millions in California who executed oaths was sent to jail for perjury. In some instances the threat may have been used to induce resignations. In one case, a couple of years after an oath was signed, it was challenged on the basis of a youth group membership not quite five years prior to the date of signing. The administrator in charge saw a simple remedy: "Execute a new oath dated today and I'll tear up the old oath."

Throughout, it was the non-signer who was penalized. The non-signer became a non-signer Communist in exact parallel to the Fifth Amendment Communist, and lost his job and quite possibly his career. The argument ran that if he was really a subversive, this was a neat and cheap way to get rid of him at the cost merely of the piece of paper and the printing. If, on the contrary, he was a non-Communist, the argument was that he was posing as a conscientious objector where that stand was out of bounds and was giving aid and comfort to the enemy. He too could be treated as a non-signer Communist. For such an individual too, the clear guarantee of the Fifth Amendment was denied, "No person . . . shall be compelled . . . to be a witness against himself, nor be deprived of life, liberty, or property without due process."

In 1867 in *Cummings* v. *Missouri* and *Ex parte Garland* the Supreme Court saw the test oaths of the Reconstruction period as unconstitutional ex post facto laws and bills of attainder. In the 1950s, with only a few exceptions, the courts were much more tolerant of requirements that public employees execute oaths of denial. The underlying attitude was that public employment is a privilege and not a right. So it shines forth in decisions upholding the federal loyalty program and similar statutes affecting Los Angeles employees and employees under Maryland's Ober Act and New York's Feinberg Act. In a few instances oaths were successfully contested in court. Oklahoma State University employees prevailed against that state's oath because it tested for unknowing as well as knowing membership in a subversive organization. The University of California non-signers were rewarded with an eloquent opinion from a district court in 1951 and a technically grounded favorable verdict from the state supreme court in 1952. On that very day, however, this same court upheld a similar oath required of all state employees. Pennsylvania's Pechan oath was upheld in the case of a nurse conceded to be "utterly opposed to Communism."

In the states where the emphasis was on checking organizational connections, a tendency developed to sublet the task. New York's Feinberg Act, for instance, delegated to the State Board of Regents authority to adopt or extend the attorney general's list and to apply it by checking on employee memberships. The New York City schools delegated the questioning to an assistant corporation counsel. Non-responsiveness was basis for dismissal. Maryland's Ober Act had a similar feature.

In the oath states the oaths multiplied. California began with the university oath, the Levering oath for state employees, and by incorporating a revision of that oath in the state constitution. Then came an oath to be executed by veterans and churches seeking to qualify for tax exemptions, a tenants' oath for those living in publicly financed housing, and Los Angeles County's action of incorporating the oath into the standard tax forms so that, in effect, one had to sign the oath in order to pay the tax. The ROTC introduced an oath, not exactly required, but prerequisite to the issuance of textbooks or uniforms, and a non-signer had the obloquy of being forced to drill by himself!

It was possible also to have the best of all possible worlds, an all-encompassing loyalty oath program plus follow-up checking on memberships and associations. California added the Dilworth Act in 1953, instructing local school boards to interrogate teachers who were reported to have Communist-tainted memberships. Here, too, non-responsiveness was grounds for dismissal. The Los Angeles superintendent, after ten teachers had been dismissed, indicated that another 171 were to be interrogated as "suspected loyalty doubtfuls." The Luckel Act, also in 1953, exposed all other state employees to the same kind of questioning. It was interpreted as meaning that although a state employee might take refuge in the Fifth Amendment when questioned by a congressional committee, he would have no such privilege in Dilworth or Luckel-type questioning by state officials.

Many private universities found themselves in a twilight zone because of contracts for classified research, a situation also faced by many businesses because part of their production was for the armed services or the Atomic Energy Commission. The tendency was to broaden the base and apply a loyalty test to the entire personnel. If an aggressive or leftist union was in the picture or if a legislative investigator took an interest, such a response was all the more likely. McCarthy and the International Union of Electrical Workers share the credit for General Electric's decision late in 1953 to make its loyalty check comprehensive. At the time its employees numbered 280,000.

Loyalty tests by oath or by membership check spilled farther over into private employment, even where there was no relation to classified research or production. The American Bar Association adopted a test oath. Cedars of Lebanon Hospital in Los Angeles barred seven doctors as loyalty risks. On the less grim side, in Indiana no one could perform as a professional wrestler without taking a loyalty oath. The management of a Los Angeles radio station decided that its 200 employees should be under oath, a practice followed by many other companies.

Loyalty requirements had more ludicrous features. The Indiana oath was required of barbers and junk dealers. In California the oath had to be executed for an infant working as a model in an art class, which is reminiscent of the Texas requirement that loyalty affidavits be filed by or for every schoolbook author, the dead as well as the quick. The Texans had a grim logic in their argument; whoever writes the textbooks has a sensitive role, whereas many public employees do not.

Several months into their oath controversy, the regents of

the University of California discovered that they were not under oath. They immediately made a gala event of the sign-in, and the society pages soon reported oath-signing parties as the rage. The time would come when a novelty house offered a "loyalty oath kit." For a dollar you could make, sign, and seal your own oath!

Within a couple of years this apparatus of hyperpatriotism was elaborated and swinging. Herblock captured it as a complicated Rube Goldberg machine that screened "loyalty risks" out and "100 percent Americans" in. The apparatus was jerrybuilt and scattered unevenly over the country, with some states much more automated than others, but in spite of its irregularities this giant separator really worked.

With public sensitivity to Communist influence rubbed raw by the loyalty juggernaut, sooner than later the machine was bound to sweep up in its loyalty net those industries which bow to prevailing public moods.

The motion picture industry, living on box office receipts, saw itself as particularly vulnerable to charges of harboring Communists. The Hollywood Ten, the studios insisted, had violated the "morals clause" in their contracts by defying HUAC. These artists found themselves unemployed. The virus spread to the point that anyone named as a Communist or as Communist-inclined was off limits unless he purged himself of this taint.

Redemption sometimes required a "friendly" appearance before one of the legislative committees and the naming of past associates in the Communist Party or in alleged Communist fronts. Later a routine developed in which an affidavit of contrition and of detachment from such groups was submitted, copies of which might be sent to complaining groups such as the American Legion or to those in the lucrative business of checking Communist ties. To be successful, such an affidavit would have to explain away early indiscretions, such as a long-ago school editorial. The suspect would have to establish that he now had neutered out politically or, better still, that he had joined the hunt for pro-Communists. As of 1956, columnist George Sokolsky, an insider in the activity, estimated that some three hundred motion picture people had gone through this shattering form of "rehabilitation." Those who did not satisfy this requirement were dropped forthwith by the studios, and they were not re-employed.

Studio heads were skittish about admitting that such a thing as a blacklist existed, but the reality was that those who were publicized as Communist or pro-Communist ceased to be employable. To all intents and purposes they were either blacklisted or graylisted, the later designation describing what happened to persons dropped with little or no publicity. By the mid-fifties at least one hundred former movie-makers were in this second category. The American Legion and certain other patriotic groups hovering in the wings claimed credit, but the studios did not need much pushing.

Blacklisting or graylisting substantially injured the careers of creative artists and deprived the public of their talents. This practice took a long time to end, and for many the effects never wore off. Meanwhile the studios undertook to salvage some of the goods they had on hand. *The Las Vegas Story,* written and directed by Paul Jarrico, was released without a credit line. Blacklisting, as might have been expected, gave rise to a black market. Actors and directors did not profit from it; their participation did not lend itself to concealment. But writing could be sub rosa. To some of the unwelcome writers scripts or rewrites were commissioned at cut rates and used anonymously or under assumed names. Such a deal could be a generous and indeed a risky business for the man making the commission, or it could be most tawdry. In 1956 the Oscar for *The Brave One,* by Robert Rich, went begging because there was no Robert Rich. Much later it was verified that Dalton Trumbo, one of the Hollywood Ten, was the author.

Early in 1953 several of the blacklisted artists undertook to make a movie in association with the International Union of Mine, Mill, and Smelter Workers. They would do it on location in Grant County, New Mexico. For the first six weeks all went well, but on February 24 Congressman Jackson regaled the House of Representatives with a diatribe against what he charged was a Communist-made movie. It was intended, he said, as "a new weapon for Russia" and an inflamer of racial hatred. The papers in Silver City, New Mexico, and in nearby El Paso, Texas, played up his charges, as did the Silver City radio station, and the Immigration Service started deportation proceedings against Mexican actress Rosaura Revueltas, who had the leading role in the picture. Vigilante action at Central and Bayard, stirred by these outsiders, forced the crew to pack up and leave. Needless to say, *Salt of the Earth,* while finally made, was barred from all the regular theaters in the country.

The Broadway theater, partly because it was more sophisti-cated and partly because it was smaller, had much less of this pressure than Hollywood. The theatrical production of the musical *Guys and Dolls,* by Abe Burrows (suspect because of left-wing associations) stirred no sparks until Sam Goldwyn bought the movie rights. But in Greenwich, Connecticut, Paul Draper and Larry Adler were denounced and picketed; the repercussions drove these virtuosos of the dance and the har-monica to exile in England.

At the Philadelphia Playhouse in the Park in 1956 *Anastasia,* with Gale Sondergaard in the title role, ran the gauntlet of American Legion and United Veterans Council harassment. These groups had leverage because this was a municipally financed theater. HUAC came to stage a special hearing and Miss Sondergaard was asked if, following the appearance of her husband (director Herbert Biberman, one of the Holly-wood Ten) before that committee, her theatrical activities "were minimized." "Very definitely," she answered. But when the questioner went on to ask about membership in the Motion Picture Artists Committee or the League of Women Shoppers, she invoked the Fifth Amendment. Despite the hullabaloo, the play ran its scheduled two weeks.

Throughout the entertainment industry it was not easy to keep track of who was in and who was out, much less why. Judy Holliday, quite apart from the ideologically bold role she played in *Born Yesterday,* once had her clearance chal-lenged. She hired an investigator to find out what it was she was doing that made her suspect. And Walt Disney, a pillar of political respectability, found himself in trouble because he denounced the League of Women Voters as a Communist front. Called to account by outraged members, he hastened to make a correction. He had meant, he apologized, the League of Women Shoppers.

With the kind of tarbrush that was sweeping through film-making and, to a lesser extent, the theater and the concert halls, the advertising-consumer influenced field of radio and television inevitably received similar attention. Pressure groups such as the Syracuse post of the American Legion and the Houston Minute Women lent a hand, legislative committees cooperated, and the Hollywood blacklist and graylist over-lapped. In radio and television, however, the major thrust was by incorporated private informers such as the publishers of *Counterattack, Red Channels,* and *Aware.*

The technique was simple. Combing the reports of HUAC, the Internal Security Committee and the state "little Dies committees," and giving similar attention to such Communist newspapers as the *Daily Worker* and the *People's World,* these publications regurgitated a dossier of sorts for figure after figure in these media.

In June, 1950, an editor of *Red Channels* made the first test run. He organized a small-scale telephone campaign of protest against the casting of Jean Muir, a listee in *Red Channels,* for the radio serial "The Aldrich Family." The complaints went not to the station or the network but to the sponsor, General Foods, which immediately announced that Miss Muir would be replaced. "General Foods," it was proclaimed, "avoids the use of materials and personalities which in its judgment are controversial." In short, controversiality, not acts of real harm to the nation, was the benchmark for proving disloyalty, a pattern unfortunately followed in other similar cases.

The allegations against Miss Muir were nine associations ranging from membership in to appearances before organizations which *Red Channels* classified as Communist-oriented, on analysis a most flimsy indictment. But Miss Muir's explanations and denials got her nowhere; her career came to an abrupt end.

Thereafter, the industry was seldom so boldfaced in excluding a performer, writer, or producer. It was easy to terminate a contract at the end of a season or upon a change in sponsors, and still smoother to refrain from hiring anyone who had been listed. By that technique, as one sophisticate explained, Miss Muir would merely have been told that she was "too young for the part, too old, too fat, too thin."

Over the ensuing years the blacklisting method became institutionalized on the quieter basis of retaining persons who claimed expertise in running checks on the pro-Communist records of entertainment industry personnel. In this pre-computer age the technology was simple. All one needed was a file of HUAC and other committees' reports, a copy of the index HUAC had prepared, and files of the trade journals and the Communist papers.

On such a basis Vincent Hartnett of *Red Channels* and later of *Aware* made himself a card index of persons named in these publications. He then could quickly run down the records of a hundred persons on hold for a particular show. At five dollars a head and two dollars for repeats this soon was a profitable business. On occasion, for much higher fees, the same expertise might bring about a clearance. Without publicity, but inexorably, this mill ground industriously for the networks, for individual stations, and for certain sponsors.

In the summer of 1956, in the wake of a struggle for control of AFTRA, the television and radio artists' union, *Aware* put out a special issue attacking John Henry Faulk, an artist with a charisma reminiscent of Will Rogers'. The screed stopped short of saying he was a Communist but by innuendo conveyed the impression that by memberships and associations which it set forth he had faithfully served the interests of Communism.

Upon his return from vacation, Faulk was told that CBS had decided to drop his show. The reasons given were a decline in the ratings and defection by certain sponsors. An associate of Hartnett's in *Aware*, supermarket owner Lawrence Johnson, had pressured sponsors to demand Faulk's dismissal. Finding over the next two years that there was no place for him in radio or television or on Broadway, and convinced that *Aware* had procured his exclusion, Faulk decided to sue. Louis Nizer and his law firm agreed to represent him. The preliminaries stretched over several years. It took until 1962 for the damage suit against *Aware,* Hartnett, and Johnson to come to court. Faulk, meanwhile, had to scrounge for a living. There was none for him in New York, and even back home in Texas he had to switch to work unrelated to the media. Ed Murrow, Charles Collingwood, Myrna Loy, Garry Moore, David Susskind, among others, identified with the case and supported it financially or as witnesses.

In the pre-trial interrogations and other preparatory work Nizer and his associates laid a thorough foundation, and in court they developed convincing proof of libel and conspiracy. So effectively was this done that the judge instructed the jury that its task was merely to determine what mitigating circumstances there were, if any, and what damages should be awarded. The jury, after coming into court to ask if it could award a larger sum than Faulk had asked, found for Faulk and awarded $3.5 million in damages. Even when the appellate court reduced the amount to $550,000, the award was still exemplary and potentially a caution to others.

Theoretically Faulk was "made whole," that is, compensated for all that he had lost. But Johnson, the only defendant with substantial wealth, died the day before the verdict was rendered and left an estate of only $250,000. Furthermore, Faulk's post-trial opportunities never measured up to his pre-dismissal prospects, estimated by experts at from $150,000 or $200,000 to as much as $1 million a year. Except for a couple of token appearances the networks did nothing for him. A tip-off had been that CBS executives took the stand for the defendants, but on top of that were the short memories of radio and television audiences and an ingrained timidity in the industry about using persons who are controversial. Faulk's going to court stamped him indelibly as controversial. In 1967, five years after the victory, Faulk, still an exile from the media, was earning a much more arduous living on the lecture circuit.

His challenge had broken the back of *Aware* and had shown up the tawdry business of dossier-peddling. Just as clearly, the cravenness of the industry was exposed. That did not mean that the media's blacklist or graylist was torn up or even that Faulk's own name was expunged from it.

In the early and mid-fifties the most resounding question in American education was the rhetorical "You don't want a Communist teaching your children, do you?" It was an argument-clincher all the way from kindergarten to the graduate schools. It implied that Communists were all of a sort, every one completely dedicated to the Party line and to indoctrination, and that American students from the youngest to the oldest were gullible to any preachment.

One could argue to the contrary that Communists were still people and had the common human frailties, that not all were overwhelmingly committed, and that in teaching mathematics or brain surgery politics would not intrude. At a time when half the voters in France were Communists, it seemed certain that among them were schoolteachers as well as university professors who would be valuable in any American school. One could argue that the constitutional guarantees of freedom of speech, the press, and political assembly, the right to due process, and protection against forced self-incrimination applied to Communists as well as non-Communists and that guilt should be assessed individually rather than on Communists en masse.

One could argue, but not with much effect. Although the ACLU took the position that a political association—even being a Communist Party member—and functioning as a teacher were not incompatible, the machinery for eliminating Communists from schoolrooms and college campuses was quickly installed and set in motion. Resistance became futile. It also became academic, because after 1949 or 1950 there were very few Communists left to fire. Indeed, the reason for firing came to be the subsidiary one of insubordination in refusal to sign a "loyalty" oath or in some other form to respond to loyalty-related questions.

In 1953 the American Association of Universities, which more honestly should have called itself the American Association of University Presidents, proclaimed that membership in the Communist Party "extinguishes the right to a university position" and that an instructor who becomes a propagandist or follows the Party line "forfeits his right to membership in the faculty." As to pleading the Fifth Amendment, these thirty-seven presidents maintained that a professional obligation to candor outweighed that privilege.

At that very time the forty thousand members of the American Association of University Professors wrestled with this same double-barbed problem. In practice, the crux was guilt by silence or the requirement to respond. There was no disposition to say that professors do not have the protection of the Fifth Amendment or that "loyalty" oaths are permissible. But were a professor's colleagues entitled to answers to these same questions, to help them determine fitness to teach? Some said yes; others saw an intolerable inconsistency. One who refused to answer the regents on Communist Party membership felt constrained not to say to anyone else, "I am not and never have been a Communist." And the logic of resistance at any of these levels was seriously undercut if proscription of Communists as a group was conceded.

The California faculty had found itself discredited in 1950 when it adopted a delphic position statement, "No person whose commitments or obligations to any organization, Communist or other, prejudice impartial scholarship and the free pursuit of truth will be employed by the University. Proved members of the Communist Party having such commitment are not acceptable as members of the faculty."

The ice admittedly was paper-thin. Only the absence of commas around the clause "having such commitment" saved this resolution from being an absolute endorsement of the instant firing of Communists. If that was granted, the niceties of method of detection were reduced almost to absurdity.

The doctrine which the university presidents asserted and which the professors came within a hair of endorsing was put into the vernacular by Senator McCarthy. In the course of the Army-McCarthy hearings he was asked what was the best thing that each American—man, woman, or child—could do to liquidate Communism. "The thing that the American people can do," he answered, "is to be vigilant day and night to make sure they don't have Communists teaching the sons and daughters of America." Anticipating the "phony cry" that he was interfering with academic freedom, McCarthy elaborated that he did not worry about "screwball or crackpot professors" but that we must protect against a "network of professors and teachers getting orders from Moscow and intent on destroying this nation and corrupting the minds of youth."

At the time of McCarthy's pronouncement the AAUP was in disarray. An association rather than a union, and without the muscle that a union might have had, this organization had developed a technique of intervening on behalf of procedures supportive of academic freedom. The AAUP tried to persuade college and university administrators to follow these sound procedures. The AAUP stood ready to investigate complaints and, if the evidence justified, would censure the school administration involved, sometimes with salutary effect.

In the climate of the early fifties, with "loyalty" tests and screenings rampant, the AAUP was deluged with cases of this sort, many more than it could effectively handle, and some of them from institutions as large as the state universities of Washington, California, Michigan, and Ohio. Such institutions, it appeared to many, were too strong to be budged by AAUP censure. Furthermore, there was the certainty that any such action would be read as being "soft on Communism" or as playing into the hands of the Communists.

The AAUP fell into paralysis. Its staff had its hands full, seeking by intervention to prevent firings rather than making historical appraisal of firings that had already taken place. The AAUP council was absorbed in trying to formulate a policy combining opposition to Communism and rejection of the methods of anti-Communism which ran roughshod over freedom of scholarly research and the right to learn.

Not until 1955, after the Korean fighting stopped and after the downfall of McCarthy, did the AAUP find a way to cut through its log-jam. It set up a special committee to deal with the accumulated cases and authorized that committee to evaluate them on the basis of the public record rather than by the time-consuming method of visitations, interviews, and assembling of evidence. For several of the cases, those of the Universities of Washington and California, for instance, the public record was voluminous and more than sufficient.

Early in 1956, on the recommendation of this committee, the AAUP voted that the University of Washington should have been censured in 1950, that the seven-year record of the

University of California extending up to 1956 called for censure, and that several other college and university administrations should also be listed. In addition to producing favorable results on several campuses, this action regenerated the AAUP. Membership picked up, efficiency improved in intervening before drastic disciplinary action was taken, and by the end of the decade the AAUP once more was an effective defender of academic freedom and of scholarship.

The Korean War and the cataclysmic events of the McCarthy era which left their indelible imprint on the fabric of free speech, free association, and due process tended throughout the early fifties to overshadow the civil rights sector of civil liberties. The slumbering giant of non-discrimination which had taken some awakening stretches in the forties was still pinned down by broad-based, ingrained racism. True, a few positive gains were noted, but the record was spotty. Tuskegee Institute could report that in 1952, for the first time in seventy-one years, there had been no lynchings. But in many categories of our national life, including unions, public accomodations, and housing, gross discrimination continued. At Cicero, Illinois, in July, 1951, a mob of three thousand turned back a black family attempting to move in. On Christmas Day the Florida field secretary of the NAACP was killed by a bomb. Local prosecutors, loyal to southern custom, failed to act in outbreaks of violence against Negroes. Southern rape cases, resembling the celebrated Scottsboro case of the thirties, all too often had discriminatory trials and sentencing.

In the early fifties the most spectacular advance in integration was scored in, of all places, the U.S. Army. In 1948 President Truman had issued an executive order against discriminatory placement in the armed services and two years later Secretary of the Army Gordon Gray circulated a directive that made this order somewhat more explicit. Nothing much happened until the emergency of the crash program to induct and train draftees for the Korean War.

At Fort Jackson, South Carolina, General Frank McConnell saw that the work would go forward much more expeditiously if the sorting of whites and blacks into dual programs was bypassed. He decided to conform to Gray's order. Everything went smoothly. The recruits accepted integration as the Army routine. Integration spread offbase to erode some other bastions of Jim Crow, and the practice soon spread to other training camps.

In Korea, somewhat similarly, a field decision initiated integration. Colonel John G. Hill commanded two white combat battalions and a Negro battalion which, as customary, was left at guard duty in the rear. Suffering heavy casualties, Hill moved Negro soldiers in as replacements. They fought unexpectedly well. The practice spread, and soon this war was being waged by an integrated army. The demonstration was the more encouraging because integration was introduced for efficiency and the general betterment of performance.

Back home in Sioux City, Iowa, however, a graveside protest interrupted the burial of a soldier killed in Korea, a Winnebago Indian. President Truman and many others, including representatives of veterans' organizations, expressed indignation. The issue was sidestepped when the widow chose burial in the National Cemetery in Arlington. In Tucson, Arizona, burial of another soldier killed in Korea, in this instance a Negro, was postponed pending notarized clearances from three veterans' organizations.

The courts voided certain discriminations. In 1950 the Supreme Court had struck down "the curtains, partitions, and signs" used to wall off Negro dining car patrons and in two parallel rulings held that a separate law school for Negroes could not measure up to the one for whites. In 1953 the Supreme Court closed a loophole for eluding the ban on restrictive housing covenants. That same year it supported enforcement of an 1873 statute forbidding racial discrimination in restaurants in the District of Columbia, and in 1954, on the basis of due process, it outlawed school segregation in the District.

Encouraged by such rulings, the National Association for the Advancement of Colored People extended its challenge to the separateness of the "separate but equal" school. For some years the challenge had centered on inferior buildings and equipment, for which the Southern Regional Council estimated that half a billion dollars would be required to bring them up to par. Now the NAACP struck at the essential fallacy by asserting that segregation in and of itself has adverse effect on minority students and their opportunity to learn. Counsel buttressed this argument with testimony by experts in education, psychology, and sociology, among them Kenneth Clark and Gunnar Myrdal. The lower courts having disagreed, the Supreme Court consolidated several cases on appeal and, in the 1952–53 term, heard extended argument and received *amicus curiae* ("friend of the court") briefs. In June, 1953, the Court requested additional briefs.

Georgia and South Carolina were worried enough to prepare a second line of defense for the segregated school. Georgia enacted a law denying state funds to any school admitting a Negro student under court order. South Carolina amended its constitution to eliminate the requirement of state-supported public schools.

The nation at large was much less attentive, which added to the drama on May 17, 1954, when Chief Justice Earl Warren, speaking for a unanimous Court, read the opinion and decision in *Brown* v. *Board of Education of Topeka*. In unmistakable terms the Court ruled "that separate educational facilities are inherently unequal" and that minority children, "by reason of the segregation," are "deprived of the equal protection of the laws guaranteed by the Fourteenth Amendment." The Court thereby turned its back on the discredited doctrine of "separate but equal." The Court softened the impact by remanding the cases to the courts of origin for determination of the appropriate orders and a year later further cushioned the order with the equivocal phrase "with all deliberate speed."

Brown spoke directly to the seventeen states in or peripheral to the South that had laws requiring school segregation. Its impact thus was sectional. Some southerners saw merit in the decision and some northerners did not. Other southerners were ready to accept the order as the law of the land. In press and pulpit and in political oratory the North praised the decision as a great step forward and the South, much more vehemently, denounced it as an invasion of states' rights, judge-made law, and a Yankee attack on the southern way of life.

Although Baltimore, Washington, and a number of other school systems moved to comply, an angry resentment flared. White Citizens Councils, first at Indianola, Mississippi, and then by contagion throughout the South, sprang up to rouse a massive resistance, pressure officeholders, and keep the federal authorities and the Negroes in their place.

Moderate voices such as Ralph McGill's in Atlanta and Jonathan Daniels's in Raleigh were outshouted. In *Black Monday* (the Monday of the decision in *Brown*), Judge Tom Brady of Mississippi attacked the Supreme Court's "plot" to promote miscegenation and racial hate. Southerners had died for their sacred principles; they were ready, he said, to die again. Journalist James J. Kirkpatrick of Virginia told the South that the Fourteenth Amendment was fraudulently enacted. Citing statistics on illegitimate births, homicides, and I.Q. scores, he asserted an innate deficiency in the Negro which justified the dual society of the South. He saw segregated schools as the most essential defense of white supremacy.

In March, 1956, ninety-six members of Congress put their names on a Southern Manifesto commending in more restrained language state actions "to resist forced integration by any lawful means." Some of these senators and congressmen may have exceeded their own enthusiasm but not that of their constituents. Resistance hardened, especially in a belt stretching from Virginia through the Old South and the Deep South.

The pervasive and deep hold McCarthy had on the nation's anti-Communist emotions seemingly raised him to a pinnacle of unsurmountable political power. On February 24, 1954, with Secretary of the Army Stevens's memorandum of capitulation in hand, McCarthy appeared to be invincible. But the news generated shock waves. Adlai Stevenson commented that the Republican Party had come to be "half McCarthy and half Eisenhower." Senator Ralph Flanders, Republican from Vermont, gave McCarthy a scornful upbraiding on the floor of the Senate. Others expressed outrage. Indeed, the Madison *Capitol Times*, the Milwaukee *Journal*, the *Progressive*, all in Wisconsin, and papers elsewhere had systematically exposed his tactics. The most telling attack was a televised Edward R.

Murrow documentary sharply critical of McCarthy. The public indignation it catalyzed roused the Eisenhower administration.

On March 11 the administration publicized charges that McCarthy and his chief counsel, Roy Cohn, had repeatedly sought preferential treatment for David Schine, draftee and now a buck private. The McCarthy riposte was a counter-charge that the Army had pressured him to stop his Fort Monmouth hearings and had used Schine as a hostage.

The issues could conceivably have been taken to court, or a special inquiry might have been set up. Instead, the most unlikely of tribunals took charge. On April 24 the McCarthy subcommittee, with Senator Karl Mundt of South Dakota presiding, opened hearings on these contrary charges. This television attraction ran for thirty-five days, exposing at times more than twenty million viewers to the installments of this 187-hour show.

The tone was set immediately when Chairman Mundt called on the committee's special counsel to begin the questioning. McCarthy interrupted with an insistent "Point of order, point of order." He then seized the initiative and, with a few discomfitures, held it throughout the trial-like hearings. On the fourth day, Joseph Welch, counsel for the Army, won an admission that an exhibit purportedly showing Schine and Secretary Stevens standing agreeably together was in actuality cropped from a larger group picture and as used was a falsification. Back in 1952, when he was campaigning for the defeat of Tydings as Senator, McCarthy had made devastating use of a spliced photograph purporting to show Tydings and Communist leader Earl Browder in affable conversation.

Later in the hearings McCarthy resolutely "protected his source" for a purloined letter from J. Edgar Hoover. That was consistent with his urging to those who had classified information against Communists to give it to his committee. Although Welch pressed him for an answer, McCarthy's unwillingness to name names was as staunch as that of any "Fifth Amendment Communist."

Near the end of the hearings, at a time when Welch was giving Cohn a hard time, McCarthy undertook to come to the rescue by taxing Welch with having brought to Washington as prospective assistant in the hearings a young man in his firm, Fred Fisher, who once had been a member of the National Lawyers' Guild, which McCarthy said HUAC had identified as a bulwark of the Communist Party. McCarthy's transparent intention was to embarrass Welch, but McCarthyism had helped to see to it that such an accusation was a species of character assassination. Welch's concern was for Fisher. He said, in part: "Until this moment, Senator, I think I never really gauged your cruelty or your recklessness. . . . Little did I dream you could be so reckless and so cruel as to do an injury to that lad. . . . I fear he shall always bear a scar needlessly inflicted by you. . . . Have you no sense of decency, sir? At long last, have you no sense of decency?"

Except for Welch, no one gained stature in the hearings. Certainly not Stevens, though sympathy for him was aroused, and certainly not Cohn, whose usefulness to the committee came to an end. McCarthy had kept the spotlight on himself, and it was he who was most damagingly revealed. Not to his committed supporters; they liked what they saw. Not to his dedicated opponents; their conclusion was already clear. But many of the undecided, those viewers whose minds had not been made up, were turned off by the cumulative demonstration of McCarthyan malevolence.

On the issues as stated the hearings ended in a sort of draw, with the allegations and counter-allegations both proved. The committee report would be split four ways, but before it came in Senator Flanders introduced a pithy resolution of censure which the Senate referred to a special committee headed by Senator Arthur V. Watkins, Republican of Utah. This committee recommended rebuke of McCarthy for contempt of another Senate committee in 1951–52 and for his abuse of General Zwicker. The Senate changed the second count to contempt of the Watkins committee and on December 2, 1954, so voted censure, 67–22. The condemnation was merely for embarrassing conduct against the Senate, the least of McCarthy's onslaughts.

Although to many that seemed like a glossing over of sterner findings that could have been made, the hearings broke Mc-

Carthy. Even before the hearings adjourned it was clear that
he had lost his subcommittee and the assistant on whom he
had relied most heavily, Roy Cohn. He also lost his tremendous momentum. Suddenly he was unable to frighten senators
or anyone else. The newsmen ceased maintaining a watch for
the stories he would break. He made a few efforts to exercise
his old magic, but without success. He still had hosts of ad-
mirers for his five years of labor as the tribune of anti-Communism, but a segment of the population and the leadership
that had quailed before him now plucked up.

Perhaps if ill health had not plagued him he could have
rallied from this setback and resumed his tempestuous attacking. Two years and more went by with no indications of such
a comeback. On May 2, 1957, he died.

McCarthyism, in contrast, carried sturdily on. Even the
sharpest critics in McCarthy's subcommittee saw the need to
underscore their anti-Communism. "I can be as hard as anyone in rooting out Communism," Senator McClellan had insisted. Nor was Counsel Welch immune. Questioning Cohn on
130 alleged Communists at work in defense plants, he wanted
to know why they were not reported at once to the Secretary
of Defense so that "before the sun goes down" they could be
put out. Welch seemingly took for granted that shortcuts
through due process were acceptable when it came to eliminating alleged Communists.

An illustration of how ingrained McCarthyism became is
volunteered by Richard Rovere, one of McCarthy's harsher
critics. Rovere, listening from the press gallery as the senator
was describing a new case, had recognized the suspect as
someone he had reason to believe was actually an unconfessed
former Communist. "I had the feeling, sitting there and
listening to McCarthy harangue a practically nonexistent audience, that he might be on the point of enjoying his first real
success."

It occurred to Rovere that McCarthy might be prevented
from scoring a victory. As Rovere relates,

Reluctantly—for it involved an intervention in politics,
which is something that, as a correspondent, I had always

sought to avoid—I took it upon myself to go to an official of X's agency and tell him my story. . . . I made my point. And it turned out that X, in the course of the various security and loyalty checks he had been through, had chosen to conceal his Communist past—a choice that might allow of any one of several moral judgments, but one that, to his misfortune, exposed him to charges of perjury. He was advised that it would be necessary to reopen the case. Within a few days, he quit the government.

How does one explain a man, much opposed to McCarthy, acting to deny the senator a possible triumph but taking in stride that the means employed were pure McCarthyism?

The king was dead, but his kingdom was well institutionalized on the conscious and unconscious levels. McCarthyism marched on.

In the six-month period beginning in December, 1953, at the intersection of the federal employee security programs and of loyalty inspection of intellectuals, a cause celebre arose. President Eisenhower signaled it by ordering "a blank wall" erected between J. Robert Oppenheimer and the nation's atomic secrets.

As the directing genius in fashioning the atomic device exploded at White Sands, New Mexico, and the bombs dropped on Hiroshima and Nagasaki, Oppenheimer symbolized the applied physics that had terminated the war in the Pacific and in 1953 had enabled Eisenhower to force a halt to the hostilities in Korea. Oppenheimer also represented the new breed of scientists sensitive and concerned about the relationship of science to human beings and of human beings to one another. Before the war a professor and researcher in California and since 1947 the director of the Institute for Advanced Study in Princeton, he was a top-level representative of the scholarly profession.

When he was chosen to head the atomic research project at Los Alamos, Oppenheimer's security qualifications were thoroughly evaluated. At intervals thereafter there were further inspections. In fact, just a month before the Eisenhower order, the retiring chairman of the Atomic Energy Commission had reviewed Oppenheimer's dossier and endorsed continued clearance. It was the new chairman, Lewis L. Strauss, who challenged his fitness.

Strauss offered Oppenheimer the option of quietly resigning his appointment as consultant to the AEC. Rather than go out under such a cloud, Oppenheimer asked for a weighing of the evidence by a security board, which the AEC thereupon set up.

In routine security procedures many federal employees were dismissed without notice or explanation, or at most there was a closed-door hearing with limited disclosure of charges and limited opportunity for rebuttal. In the academic world, too, many a dismissal was on minimal evidence and with much less than due process. Oppenheimer was too prominent a personage to be disposed of in that fashion. He was not shown his dossier or the reports of the FBI and of military intelligence. But he was shown a voluminous bill of particulars and was allowed to respond, to be represented by counsel, to introduce witnesses, through counsel to cross-examine other witnesses, and through counsel to file a closing brief.

The inquiry by the AEC security board had many of the characteristics of a trial. The derogatory allegations, Oppenheimer's answer, most of the transcript of the hearing, the majority and minority opinions of the Board, and the divided opinions of the Commission were promptly published. Consequently the Oppenheimer trial became the showcase in its genre. As observed during the hearing, in the handling of Oppenheimer the whole federal security system was on trial, as was by implication the loyalty-testing program pervasive through the nation's colleges and universities.

The two-man majority of the board, a lawyer and a corporation president, held against Oppenheimer. Conceding that his actions had been "unswervingly loyal," they thought that enthusiasm on his part would have hastened the hydrogen bomb research. But their adverse ruling was essentially on two points. Their confidence was shaken by Oppenheimer's early record of association, intimacy, and involvement with Communists and allegedly Communist causes. They also faulted his remorse for having brought into being so monstrous a weapon as the atomic bomb and his, as they saw it, undue sensitivity. These two board members invoked what they called "the jurisprudence of security," a doctrine that doubt must be resolved in favor of the national interest.

Physicist Ward V. Evans, more impressed with Oppenheimer's loyalty and his safeguarding of all secrets, many and great, that had been entrusted to him, and with the overall evidence as to his character, endorsed his clearance.

The AEC divided 4–1. Physicist Henry DeWolf Smyth agreed with the security board's unanimous evaluation of Oppenheimer's complete loyalty and with physicist Evans's endorsement. By this inner jury of his peers Oppenheimer was upheld. But Strauss and the other three commissioners turned thumbs down. They saw "fundamental defects in character" and Communist associations extending "far beyond the tolerable limits." Amplifying the "jurisprudence of security," Joseph Campbell pointed out that because of the abundance of atomic physicists Oppenheimer had become expendable. Thomas E. Murray added the *coup de grâce*. To him Oppenheimer's lack of "exact fidelity" to established security regulations demonstrated disloyalty.

After the decision Oppenheimer could go back to his private employment in the Institute; he had lost only honor and his eligibility to advise the government on anything confidential. What happened has not stood up under careful scrutiny of the record, and at the time it was most disquieting that the two examiners most habituated to coldly scientific appraisal were in categorical disagreement with the action taken.

Yet what happened in this much-publicized microcosm ran true to the nature of the loyalty-security program. Circumstantial evidence of associations, the bits and pieces of stray words and actions of which dossiers are built, occasional unresponsiveness, instances of insubordination, and independence of opinion—these, as they had been in most other loyalty or security dismissals, were the basis for excommunicating Oppenheimer.

The relating of these major episodes of the McCarthy era makes it abundantly clear that the lives of Americans were severely affected. But because in the fifties anti-Communism functioned in many disguises and so much of the screening out of alleged pro-Communists was *sub rosa,* exact quantification is difficult. In the course of his meticulous study *Loyalty and Security,* Ralph S. Brown, Jr., concluded in 1958 that loyalty oaths and checks had been applied to some 13,500,000 persons—a fifth of the nation's work force—as a condition of their employment. Other millions encountered such tests in relation to tax exemptions or payments or applications for various government services. The civil liberties violations were compounded especially in the more fear-ridden states, where it was commonplace to be confronted with the oath over and over again.

How many persons actually were fired as a consequence of the loyalty-security checks or in the routines thus set up? Brown's calculations bring him to a figure of 10,000 by 1958. With the Eisenhower administration three years earlier claiming 8,008 civil servants ejected in the federal program alone, Brown's figure seems exceedingly conservative.

Brown's subtotal of 500 dismissed from schools and colleges is manifestly too small. In June, 1950, the University of California terminated 175 of its staff for non-compliance with its "loyalty" requirements and in the next two months dismissed another 32. R. E. Combs, factotum for the California Un-American Activities Committee, subsequently claimed another 100 rejected from college and university faculties at his instance. Dismissals under the Levering, Dilworth, and Luckel Acts easily brought this one-state total to two-thirds of Brown's estimate for the forty-eight states.

To be an "unfriendly" witness before an investigating committee was an invitation to dismissal from private as well as public employment. In 1953, when two Bethlehem Steel employees took the Fifth Amendment before his subcommittee, Senator Mundt wrote a letter to the company and they were fired. Ordinarily no such notification was needed. That same year, when a subcommittee of the Internal Security Committee held hearings in New York, some thirty schoolteachers were dismissed. The toll that McCarthy generated at Fort Monmouth has been mentioned. In 1956 Senator Eastland took a subcommittee to New York with sights trained on the *New*

York Times. By the time they departed, five newsmen were fired by the *Times* and other newspapers, ten or twelve were placed in hazard of prosecution for contempt, and four "friendly" witnesses were pushed into humiliating disclosures that might blight their careers.

An uncalculated number of persons lost their jobs through the operation of the loyalty-security testing apparatus without being told that that was the reason. A much larger number were refused employment on this basis, but in many instances without the reason being asserted. At the time he posted his claim that he had procured dismissal of a hundred professors in California, agent Combs also boasted of twice that many new appointments intercepted and prevented.

Brown notes still another category, the "walking wounded," persons allowed to go on working or reinstated after a loyalty or security question had been raised, but under a cloud, retained on sufferance, passed over for promotion or salary increases, and in other respects second-class employees. The number of persons thus affected was considerable.

Among the major casualties in this purge, the ten thousand or probably more persons who were put out of work by the loyalty-security procedures in the fifties, the pain and obloquy and the shutting off of income stand out. Some of these people survived by shifting to much less rewarding and less challenging jobs, as with a teacher who became a night-shift janitor in a supermarket. A fortunate few landed on their feet.

Although some were embittered, a more characteristic reaction was to become more committed to civil liberties, indeed to choose that as the new career. Lawrence Speiser, litigant against California's veterans' oath, became the director of the ACLU's Washington office. Frank Wilkinson, former administrator in the public housing office in Los Angeles, became head of the National Committee to Abolish HUAC after serving his sentence for contempt of HUAC for refusing, on First Amendment grounds, to answer the Committee's questions. Eason Monroe, after his professorship of English at San Francisco State College was interrupted by the Levering oath, became the director of the large and active southern California branch of ACLU. He gave it dynamic leadership on such issues as the determined effort to make the school integration principle of *Brown* operative in the Los Angeles school system and to have capital punishment ruled out as violative of the Eighth Amendment ban on "cruel and unusual punishment." In 1972, backed by an order from the state supreme court, which had retracted its approval of the Levering oath, Monroe could return to his career as a professor at what now was San Francisco State University.

A highly pervasive consequence of the nationwide panic about security was widespread intimidation. McCarthy intimidated two presidents and, for a time, most members of the Senate. As federal and state committees conducted loyalty probes and other government programs sought to flush out "subversives," a vast number of persons less advantageously placed were made cautious or silent. Jobs, careers, community standing were on the line. An index to the impact was that Americans of all political persuasions felt constrained periodically to announce "I am not a Communist." Such a disclaimer was the normal and therefore necessary introduction to any statement of fact or opinion, even comments attacking the loyalty investigations and their far-reaching excesses. This ingrained compulsion carried over to organizations.

Americans for Democratic Action, whose very name accentuated the positive, made a great point of stressing that the absolute condition of membership in ADA was to *not* be a Communist. The American Association of University Professors, as mentioned previously, anguished over this problem.

The virus even infected the American Civil Liberties Union, then as now the organization most centrally committed to upholding the freedoms guaranteed in the Bill of Rights. In 1940, as described in the essay by Jerold S. Auerbach, above, the ACLU barred supporters of totalitarianism, whether Communist, Fascist, or Ku Klux Klan, from serving on its governing councils and staff. In 1954, when McCarthy was in his heyday, ACLU reaffirmed this policy and extended it. Membership forms carried this notice: "The ACLU needs and welcomes the support of all those—and only those—whose devotion to civil liberties is not qualified by adherence to Communist, Fascist, KKK, or other totalitarian doctrine."

In the late fifties and more vigorously in the sixties a number of ACLU branches pointed out the glaring inconsistency that the organization most active in protesting "loyalty" oaths and other such applications of guilt by association should apply just such a blanket disclaimer in its own operations. They also noted that the example the ACLU was setting made it much more difficult for individuals and other organizations to stand against this trespass on constitutionally guaranteed rights. As qualification for membership and office these critics recommended merely support of civil liberties as guaranteed in the Constitution.

This proposal drew fire from Norman Thomas, Roger Baldwin and others who had been leaders in the adoption of the 1940 requirement. Quite apart from desiring to reaffirm their earlier philosophical stand, they were concerned that the Union's defense of liberty for all, including Communists, would be discounted by courts and legislatures unless a clear-cut position was taken. Others insisted that without an express disavowal of Communism, many staunch civil libertarians could not continue their membership in the Union. The battle raged for three years. At length, in 1967, the sentence objected to was deleted from the membership form, and the ACLU constitution was amended to eliminate the reference to service on boards, committees, and staff conditioned on non-membership in proscribed organizations. Instead, the constitution was changed to state that all members of boards, committees, and staff "shall be unequivocally committed to the objects of the Union and to the concept of democratic government and civil liberties for all people."

Yet, convinced that the ACLU's effectiveness would be blunted by elimination of the controversial section, or for face-saving or as anchor to windward, the opposition insisted on a separate policy statement that "leadership and staff should be composed of those—and only those—whose devotion to civil liberties is not qualified by the advocacy of those Communist, Fascist, racist, or other doctrines which reject the concept of democratic government and of civil liberties. . . ." The clause was merely an admonition, but it enshrined this reminder of the time when ACLU did not feel safe without a rock-ribbed disclaimer of Communism.

This bit of institutional history indicates how deep-seated

the habit of "loyalty" through test oaths and security through checks of membership and association had become during the fifties. Through that and the next decade the nation carried on with a heavy incubus of such procedures.

Late in 1967 the California Supreme Court saw the light and reversed its 1952 endorsement of the statewide "loyalty" oath. Nevertheless, notaries at various desks throughout the state kept on using the old forms and the momentum of oath-signing continued, as did much of the Luckel and Dilworth Acts and other such laws. These old oath forms, paralleling the State Department's procedure with passport applications, were continued out of ignorance or for the economy of using them up. That was poetic justice, because the California suit that upset this oath requirement was brought by a taxpayer objecting to the cost of printing and filing these oaths. There may have been administrators who took a sardonic pleasure in collecting more signatures. Many an unsuspecting citizen signed the oath, "just because it was there." There also were the cautious who knew that the requirement had been found unconstitutional but signed rather than raise a fuss.

It was the strange paradox of the 1950s that as the tight, re-strictive blanket of security, fear, and caution fell over the country, repeated demonstrations of personal courage and as-sertion of rights in another area uncovered new avenues for advancing freedom. The beginning steps were taken in Mont-gomery, Alabama. On December 1, 1955, Mrs. Rosa Parks, on her way home from work, refused to give up her seat and move to the back of the bus. Her reason, as she recalled, was simply that she was tired and her feet hurt. Her arrest and conviction prompted a one-day bus boycott, so enthusiastically supported that the Montgomery Negroes decided to continue it. For 382 days they trudged to work, to the stores, to church.

In addition to the encouragement lent by the Supreme Court's school integration decision, they were motivated by a particularly revolting lynching a few months earlier in Mis-sissippi which touched a raw nerve in race relations. Emmett Till, a fourteen-year-old visitor from Chicago, had committed the indiscretion of whistling at a white woman and for that was kidnapped and killed. But the bus boycott also had inspiring leadership. The Negro clergy supported it vigorously in person and through the Montgomery Improvement Association, which arranged private transportation where necessary and gave other assistance. The Association made the ideal choice for its president, Dr. Martin Luther King, Jr. His energy and example, his spellbinding, and his preaching of non-violence kept the boycott going and on target. Assisted by a Supreme Court ruling against back-of-the-bus segregation, victory came just before Christmas in 1956.

The Montgomery bus boycott changed the face and heart of Negro America. It was a great builder of Negro morale everywhere. It encouraged similar efforts in other cities. It was fundamental to the establishment of the Southern Christian Leadership Conference, coordinator of the Negro-led campaign for civil rights. The boycott also gave Martin Luther King his springboard to fame.

In the course of the boycott King refined his philosophy of non-violence. Suddenly he was in demand as a speaker, stumping the South and making many appearances elsewhere. He put himself on the firing line, braving arrest and jailing. The NAACP honored him, as did several universities and the new African nation of Ghana. In 1959 he found time to make a pilgrimage to India, the birthplace of non-violent leader Mohandas Gandhi. By the end of the decade he was the high priest of the Negro drive for equal rights through non-violence, though to that time he continued as the minister of the Drexel Avenue Baptist Church in Montgomery and only thereafter devoted himself full-time to the crusade for reform.

In February, 1956, Autherine Lucey attempted to integrate the University of Alabama by registering as a student. A riot erupted; within four days she was suspended and within a fortnight expelled. Her experience was a portent of what might come in September, when by school board decision, court order, or Negro initiative many southern schools districts would face integration. In Louisville, the largest city in Kentucky, integration came smoothly, but at Sturgis and Clay, in the same state, angry whites were out in force and Negro elementary pupils could enter only under escort by the National

Guard. At Clay the two mothers involved decided to put their children in the Negro school for one more year. Guardsmen were needed at Clinton, Tennessee, where an "outside agitator" was blamed for inciting a mob. In Mansfield, Texas, roused whites massed at the high school and prevented entrance by the Negroes.

The author of *Black Monday* had correctly predicted that enforcement of school integration would lead to strife and bloodshed. Singer Nat King Cole was attacked on stage in a Birmingham theater and the homes of Martin Luther King and the Reverend F. L. Shuttlesworth were bombed. On September 9, 1957, an elementary school in Nashville, where one Negro had joined 388 white pupils, was blown up and destroyed, and in Birmingham a mob beat Shuttlesworth when he attempted to enroll his daughters in a white school.

Incidents such as these were eclipsed by the commotion at Central High School in Little Rock, Arkansas. By court order nine Negroes were to be admitted. Although the mayor was confident that nothing would happen that the city police could not handle, Governor Orval Faubus appealed to "the mob that wasn't there." He sent the National Guard to preserve the peace by barring the nine Negro boys and girls. This gesture rallied angry segregationists. President Eisenhower had studiously refrained from any favorable comment on the Supreme Court decision in *Brown*. He continued to maintain that silence, but defiance of a federal court order was more than he would tolerate. He sent a detachment of the 101st Airborne Division and under this escort the nine plucky Negro students were enrolled.

Although Faubus lost this round, he kept on denouncing the forced integration. White student activists took up where the adult mob had been foiled. By physical and psychological assault they made life miserable for their unwelcome fellow students. The nine might have given up, except that Daisy Bates, the state president of the NAACP, went all out to encourage and support them. Because of the nationwide publicity much more than Central High was at stake. The NAACP conferred on Daisy Bates and these nine students the Spingarn Award and rejoiced further at commencement time, when one of the nine was one of Central High's six hundred graduating seniors.

By the end of the decade, five years and seven and a half months after the *Brown* decision, some advances in schools integration were observable. As of June, 1959, the *Southern School News* reported that in an eighteen-state area close to a quarter of the white children and a sixth of the Negro children were in desegregated schools. A desegregated school, however, was defined as a school with as few as one pupil of the other race. The tragedy was that 77 percent of the whites and 85 percent of the Negroes were in all-white or all-Negro schools. Six states—South Carolina, Georgia, Florida, Alabama, Mississippi, and Louisiana—had no desegregated public schools. Several other states had thrown up formidable roadblocks, and Prince Edward County in Virginia had just closed its public schools rather than submit to integration. The Supreme Court's dictum "with all deliberate speed" had been narrowed to simply "deliberate."

In a bid for national support, Negroes in 1957 made a prayer pilgrimage that brought fifty thousand persons to Washington. A year later they called a summit conference, which President Eisenhower dampened at the outset by counseling "patience and forebearance."

Negro leadership, furthermore, was painfully divided. The Urban League and the NAACP advocated persuasion and litigation, while the new leaders favored aggressive non-violent action, employing pressure and demands. The resurgent white resistance in the South was not that discerning. It made the NAACP a particular target; several states moved to force that organization to file as a "foreign agency" and publish its membership rolls. That was something the NAACP had no intention of doing, among other reasons because of the retaliation to which its members might have been exposed. In decisions stretched out over several years the Supreme Court belatedly scotched this effort.

At the close of the fifties Negro insistence on civil rights was strong and certain victories had been won, but they were more on paper than in actual realization. The struggle to achieve real freedom still had to go on.

Day-to-day life has a way of going on in the face of what would seem overwhelming interference by war, pestilence, or madness. It did in the United States during the Civil War and in the London blitz. During World War II, even as we spoke of total commitment, the so-called substitute for war, football, continued, though with such concessions to rationing as local teams which played each other twice instead of once a season.

Similarly, on the civil liberties front in the fifties the great flare-up of the security-loyalty syndrome occasioned by anti-Communism did not relieve civil libertarians of the need to exercise across the board the "eternal vigilance" that Thomas Jefferson had warned was essential to preserve freedoms. The normal agenda of threatened or attempted violations ran on, and the champions of these rights had to run hard to stay even. Hundreds of violations occurred every year, on many of which the ACLU or a kindred organization lodged a protest, filed an *amicus curiae* brief, or interposed as litigant.

Experiments with "released time" for public school pupils to receive religious instruction and state aid to parochial schools impinged on separation of church and state. School prayers were challenged in New York, as was the wearing of religious habits by public school teachers in New Mexico.

Speaker bans in colleges and some of the leading universities diminished freedom to hear, while overt censorship of campus newspapers curtailed freedom to read. Presaging the academic freedom struggles of the decades to come, the ACLU issued its first pamphlets delineating rules and procedures for handling academic freedom cases and defining student rights.

Off-campus, volunteer and official censors pressed ahead with censorship plans. One serious suggestion was federal censorship of comic books. Boycotts based on a Roman Catholic list struck at the writings of Dos Passos, Hemingway, Faulkner, and Steinbeck. In mid-decade the Association of the Bar of the City of New York, after a study of ninety cases in a single year, decried private censorship as more insidious than that by the state. Yet, according to writer John Lardner, Detroit had twelve policemen on assignment to read and censor books, and their list was available to any police department on request.

In one instance, at least, the censors must be applauded; the Georgia board of education rejected a school songbook which had changed Stephen Foster's "darkies" to "young folks." And the Post Office beat an embarrassed retreat after impounding a rare edition of Aristophanes' *Lysistrata,* but was not deterred from its accustomed rounds of intercepting what it defined as obscene.

Another area of censorship, denial of access to government information, was sharply brought to public attention in the fifties. The growth of government agencies, necessitated by the number and complexity of societal problems, accentuated the natural tendency of government officials to cover up policy mistakes or restrict release of embarrassing information. Although no major overhaul of the system was achieved, the constant exposure given to the problem by the press and civil liberties groups laid the legislative and educational foundation for better protecting the "public's right to know" when the issue reached full flower in later decades.

Private, provincial, and, in some instances, state censorship was applied to *The Moon Is Blue* and other movies regarded as obscene, to the touring company of *Tobacco Road,* and to Chicago showings of *The Miracle.* This Rossellini film, regarded as sacrilegious because of its treatment of the Nativity, led to a victorious test in the United States Supreme Court. A New York City prosecution was voided on the ground that the standard of sacrilege was too vague. The decision, which warned against censorship and "powerful orthodoxy," was the opening wedge for further Supreme Court decisions later in the decade limiting state and local censors. The motion picture industry sought protective coloring in a code of its own enforcement, which ACLU criticized as too restrictive of the creative artist's right of expression and the public's right to see films of a controversial nature.

In police practices and the criminal justice system a miscellany of abuses occurred. Some were well known to be contrary to law and could be abated. Others, more novel, required special proofs and pleadings. Early in the fifties ACLU counsel A. L. Wirin successfully argued that wiretapping the home of gambler Mickey Cohen was an invasion of privacy. The same objection to improper police procedures held in mid-decade in the equally successful effort to bar evidence the police had seized by stomach-pump. A particular concentration of police and justice abuses arose in the South as repercussions of the school integration decision. With or without racial discrimination, similar instances of false arrest, brutality, and illegal detention occurred throughout the nation. The civil liberties gains scored were nominal.

As to equality under the law, the most impressive gains of the decade were those for which the NAACP was laboring and which climaxed in the 1954 school decision. The basis was laid in discrimination against Negro children, but the principle enunciated applied to all minorities. Certain claims were pushed for Indian voting and treaty rights and on discrimination against women, but again with slight success. The government made some moves to redress the gross miscarriage of justice of the war years, when thousands of Japanese-Americans were held in detention camps and renounced their citizenship. Citizenship was restored and some financial settlements were worked out for land taken during the evacuation.[1]

The Korean War gave new intensity to the plight of conscientious objectors. The draft quotas were much increased and the prospect was to engage not just in military training but in killing. ACLU interceded for objectors who were redrafted and resentenced. It objected, for instance, to the discriminatory reconvicting and resentencing of a Quaker to two five-year terms. And it spoke up for the right of conscience based on reason or ethics rather than theistic religion.

Many ramifications arose: Was every Jehovah's Witness a

[1] In the stockaded camps to which they were removed during the Second World War several thousand Japanese-Americans renounced American citizenship. For most of them this action was obviously taken under pressure, as the federal district and circuit courts recognized. Although the illegality was not firmly established, by 1951 the federal authorities dropped further proceedings for expatriation. No inmate of these camps was paid a cent for inconvenience, hardships, or suffering, or for income that might have been earned during the period of confinement. After the war some 26,560 people entered claims for property losses incurred. The Federal Reserve Bank, custodian of the property necessarily left behind, estimated the total loss at $400 million. Processing of the claims stretched out through the fifties and was not concluded until October, 1965. The authorized payments eventually reached $38 million, against which there were offsets for court costs and attorneys' fees. The payments can be construed as admission of a wrong done; they mitigated only slightly the economic penalty inflicted by removal.

minister, as contended by that church? Were C.O. defendants entitled to see FBI evidence used against them? Was it pertinent to cite arrests for speeding and for drunkenness to impugn the genuineness of religious conviction? Were a C.O.'s arrest and imprisonment to be allowed to wall off subsequent employment? These civil liberties issues were pressed, seldom conclusively.

The treatment of labor unions, generally a good bellwether for testing the civil liberties atmosphere, underwent change after the Taft-Hartley Act was adopted in the late forties. The Supreme Court placed limits on the right to strike, including, in a Wisconsin public utility case, the barring of strikes by public employees. President Truman stirred memories of anti-union government controls by seizing the steel mills during a Korean War controversy over wages. Although the argument was made that the Constitution granted residual powers to the chief executive, the president's position was not upheld by the Supreme Court.

If unions were confronted by moves to curb their power, they also began to come face to face with complaints that they were denying rights to their own members. Union violations of internal democracy were exposed, especially in the areas of open and free participation in the unions' organizational and political structure and of due process in internal disciplinary matters. Late in the decade federal legislation was passed to protect the millions of dollars of union dues from being squandered and to insure members' democratic rights.

In the government's McCarthyite assaults upon individuals and institutions, especially vitriolic attacks were mounted against unions alleged to be Communist-controlled. Certain unions also were strong practitioners of McCarthyism, requiring oaths for officers and hounding members because of suspect beliefs and associations.

Historically, the United States had been the greatest welcomer of aliens. In law, however, the alien is at a distinct disadvantage; his claim to due process is much diluted; his rights often are passed on by a bureaucratic functionary; and his claims are subject to discount on evidence that would not stand up in court.

In 1952 the McCarran-Walter Act revised immigration

quotas and permitted a trickle of Asian immigrants. On the other hand, the law "opened an Ellis Island of ideas" and politicized the tests for entrance and citizenship. Inspectors barred a broad assortment of applicants, mostly on guilt by association, taken right out of McCarthyism. War brides, scholars, and defectors from Communism could be stopped. In 1956, when an emergency measure admitted fifty thousand refugees from the Communist takeover of Hungary, Congressman Francis Walter bemoaned that, for all that anyone knew, they might all be Communists.

These restrictions made it very difficult to convene an international scholarly meeting in the United States. In the case of several scholars who, after completing their studies in the United States, applied for permission to return to mainland China, permission was not given because it did not serve the interest of the United States to have their scientific know-how available to a Communist power. On the other hand, certain residents denounced as pro-Communists were deported, among them a history professor brought to America from Russia as a boy. He had served as an American soldier in the First World War and was for many years a registered voter. On these grounds he assumed that he was a citizen. Anonymous complaints were made on the basis of his lectures in labor history. Unable to provide proof of citizenship, he was deported, by his choice to Israel, where his American wife followed him.

In the Department of State the passport controller ran a tight ship on who should be approved for travel and where. Here, too, the criterion was political and the decisions awkward to appeal. When a distinguished American historian was invited to a Fulbright professorship in Europe but denied clearance for the appointment, the two most prestigious associations of historians interceded for him but won only a slight modification for future appointees.

The foregoing particulars suggest the great number of areas requiring defense and championing of civil liberties in the fifties. What might be called traditional threats to freedom occurred on many fronts: in censorship, academic freedom, church-state relations, and in police practices. But again and again the overall problem of protecting liberty was exacerbated because it was envenomed with anti-Communism.

Any discussion of civil liberties in the fifties must center on the fact that this decade was a time of great fear of Russia, panic about security, and paranoid reaction against anything with a Communist touch. Although that Cold War-engendered hysteria does not explain all the violations of civil liberties, it was basic to the major onslaughts.

The fever chart for the decade has to be a composite of readings of many different issues and actions. Clearly the fever rose to climax toward the middle of the decade, or more precisely in the second quarter of 1954. That was the time of three spectacular occurrences. Two suggested a turning of the tide: the Army-McCarthy hearings, which severely discredited McCarthy, and the Supreme Court's discrediting of the notion of "separate but equal." But as a most forceful warning that the purge of nonconformists would go right on, the AEC approved the walling off of the foremost of the atomic scientists. In 1954 the fever may have stopped rising, but it remained high through the rest of the decade as the stubborn infection was still locked in the nation's entire system.

All through his presidency Eisenhower was most reticent about active championing of the endangered freedoms. The successive Congresses with comparable consistency enacted no laws supportive of the Bill of Rights promises and enacted measures curtailing personal liberty. The Supreme Court, except in its great corrective action on segregated schooling, especially in the first part of the decade, also moved cautiously. The furor that arose over the decision in *Brown* may suggest that the Court was ready to move far out in front of public opinion. But this was true only of governmentally imposed racial segregation. The Court's overall record was much more in step with the public's mood of anxiety over national security and of general conservatism.

Thus in the course of the decade the Court's decisions accepted search without a warrant (*Rabinowitz*), extracted confessions (*Stein*), and bugging (*Irvine*). The Court upheld imprisonment for unpopular speech (*Feiner* and *Beauharnais*), contempt sentences by the offended judge (*Sacher* and *Nilva*), and double jeopardy (*Bartkus*). The Court approved deportation or imprisonment of aliens without due process (*Mezsi* and *Galvan*), divesting of citizenship (*Trop*), arbitrary suspension on political grounds of a license to practice medicine (*Barsky*), and comparable disbarment of lawyers (*Isserman* and *Konigsberg*). It let stand most of the Communist-hunt procedures such as loyalty oaths, association checks, and assessment of group guilt (*Douds, Garner, Adler,* and *Dennis*). Through most of this decade judicial encouragement to civil liberties came mainly in the eloquent dissents by Justices Hugo Black, William O. Douglas, and Earl Warren. These dissents began early, continued right through the decade, and laid the groundwork for some change in the Supreme Court's direction in later years.

Here and there, to be sure, the courts strengthened particular liberties in the early fifties. The California supreme court did so in 1952 when it struck down the forty-year-old Alien Land Act, an anti-Japanese measure, and the Supreme Court in 1951 when it saw the quality of a bill of attainder in the listing of the Anti-Fascist Refugee Committee as subversive.

A definite change occurred in the later portion of the decade, sparked by the courage of the Supreme Court and the growing public sensitivity to—if not full understanding of—the deep rents McCarthyism was making in the social fabric.

In June, 1957, in a cluster of decisions the Supreme Court cut back on several of the prevailing violations. Following up on its 1956 *Young* decision limiting the federal loyalty-security program only to sensitive positions, the high court held in *Service* that a dismissal through the program had been in violation of the substantive and procedural rules laid down by the department concerned. In *Yates* the Court reversed the Smith Act conspiracy convictions of several Communists. Along with throwing out the conspiracy charge, the court, in an alteration of *Dennis*, asserted that whereas advocacy of action to overthrow the government by force and violence would have justified conviction, advocacy of mere belief did not. In their opinions Black and Douglas spoke against conviction for either variety of advocacy. In *Sweezy* the Court struck a blow for academic freedom by invalidating a subletting by the New Hampshire legislature of interrogatory authority to a state official. In *Watkins* it rebuked the House-Un-American Activities Committee for practicing "exposure for the sake of exposure."

A year later the Supreme Court held unconstitutional the most vulnerable part of the California apparatus for testing "loyalty," the oath of denial demanded of churches and veterans claiming tax exemptions. Justices Black and Douglas were of the opinion that the requirement was a palpable violation of First Amendment rights, including that of freedom of religion. That was of weight in the argument, but the majority found more narrowly in terms of denial of due process in the setting up of "taxation on advocacy."

These decisions made in 1957 and 1958 may be interpreted as the beginning of a rollback of the anti-Communist security blanket spread rather unevenly over the American people and stifling First Amendment freedoms of speech, press, religion, petition, and assembly. But the disease of McCarthyism was not cured by the court decisions. The virus was buried too deep; most of the oath requirements remained intact, as did most checks on government employees. HUAC and its counterparts, though having to assert a legislative purpose, kept on inflicting punishment by exposure. Unfortunately, in *Barenblatt* in 1959 the Supreme Court retracted much of what it had advanced in *Watkins* and upheld the congressional mandate given to HUAC to investigate "un-American" propaganda.

At a time such as this, when many were being punished for their opinions or the opinions of their associates, when millions demeaned themselves under pressure, when college students fell silent and many of their elders turned timorous, special honor attaches to those who stood against the tide.

Civil liberties had a limited amount of organizational backing, as in the Presbyterian encyclical and the American Library Association and the Association of American Publishers joint resolution supporting freedom to read. The most resplendent champion was the Fund for the Republic, a $15 million spin-off from the Ford Foundation headed by Robert M. Hutch-

ins. It operated mostly in the realm of theory but drew fire
from several congressional investigators for aiding victims of
McCarthyism and funding studies showing the incursions into
civil liberties. The AAUP, as indicated, suffered a shattering
breakdown but rallied to resume its work for academic freedom. The scholarly professional organizations were not towers
of strength, but they were much more alert than the bar associations or the American Medical Association. The NAACP
persisted doggedly in its fight for equal rights and in the face
of bitter opposition, as in the demands for release of its southern membership rolls.

Other organizations took part, but none more consistently
than the American Civil Liberties Union, idealized as a volunteer fire brigade ready to rush to the defense of denials of
freedoms. From its national office and its branches spread
coast to coast ACLU spoke up for civil liberties, found or provided counsel for many interventions at court, and on occasion carried key cases. On this regimen of strenuous activity
ACLU flourished. It began the decade with 9,355 members, 16
branches, and $82,000 to spend in 1950. In 1959 it had 45,935
members, 28 branches, and a budget of $531,000.

Scattered as they were in a population of many millions, the
defenders of civil liberties in this decade often had a very
lonesome feeling. Nevertheless, hundreds, indeed thousands,
made a stand, braving oaths, subpoenas, false accusations,
smears, citations, blacklists, fines, imprisonment, or disgrace.
A few had wide publicity, but many scattered and solitary defenders of freedom were soon forgotten or perhaps were never
known.

In a campaign speech in 1952, Adlai Stevenson made this
considered observation:

> Disturbing things have taken place in our land. The
> pillorying of the innocent has caused the wise to stammer
> and the timid to retreat. I would shudder for this country
> if I thought that we too must surrender to the sinister fig-
> ure of the Inquisitor, of the great accuser. I hope that the
> time will never come in America when charges are taken
> as the equivalent of facts, when suspicions are confused

with certainties, and when the voice of the accuser stills every other voice in the land.

By 1960 most Americans may have been willing to retire the chief advocate of brinksmanship diplomacy, but they were still committed to the Cold War policy of holding the line against the spread of Communism. Only years later, with the realization of the monumental tragedy and futility of the war in Vietnam and its neighboring states, did the nation turn toward a more realistic foreign policy. Long before that, in fact with the close of the decade of the fifties, historians approached consensus that anti-Communism as it was practiced did heavy damage to the American guarantees of freedom, set most dangerous precedents, and had not been necessary for saving the nation from Communist takeover. A recognized corollary was that the American people had a long way to go to revive the Bill of Rights and recharge their faith in its principles.

Bibliographical Note

On the state of civil liberties in the fifties the files of the *Nation, New Republic, Progressive, Reporter,* and *Frontier,* and the *Annual Reports* of the American Civil Liberties Union are helpful. For the broader background see John P. Roche, *The Quest for the Dream* (New York, 1963) and Carey McWilliams, *Witch Hunt* (Boston, 1950). Multiple-topic attention is given in John W. Caughey, *In Clear and Present Danger: The Crucial State of Our Freedoms* (Chicago, 1958); Eric F. Goldman, *The Crucial Decade, 1945–1955* (New York, 1956); Corliss Lamont, *Freedom Is as Freedom Does* (New York, 1956); Walter Gellhorn, *American Rights: The Constitution in Action* (New York, 1960); and Fred J. Cook, *Nightmare Decade* (1971). Alan Barth, *The Loyalty of Free Men* (New York, 1951); John W. Wahlke, ed., *Loyalty in a Democratic State* (Boston, 1952); and Elmer Davis, *But We Were Born Free* (Indianapolis, 1954) report vividly on the tensions of the early fifties.

Jack Anderson and Ronald W. May, *McCarthy* (Boston, 1952) is a detailed account of McCarthy's road to the Senate and his first couple of years of concentration on Communism. See also the special issue of the *Progressive* for April, 1954; James Rorty and Moshe Decter, *McCarthy and the Communists* (Boston, 1954); and Sherman Ford, Jr., *The McCarthy Menace* (New York, 1954). Owen Lattimore, *Ordeal by Slander* (Boston, 1951); James A. Wechsler, *The Age of Suspicion* (New York, 1953); and Martin Merson, *The Private Diary of a Public Servant* (New York, 1955) are responses by persons attacked by McCarthy. Richard H. Rovere, *Senator Joe McCarthy* (New York, 1959) is an admirable biography. Earl Latham, ed., *The Meaning of McCarthyism* (Boston, 1965) is a symposium, and Michael Paul Rogin, *The Intellectuals and Mc-Carthy* (Cambridge, Mass., 1967) revises earlier speculations on the nature of the support for McCarthy.

Michael Straight, *Trial by Television* (Boston, 1954) and Emile de Antonio and Daniel Talbot, *Point of Order!* (New York, 1964) are dramatic excerpts from the Army-McCarthy hearings, well covered also in Rovere's *Senator Joe McCarthy*. In *Communism, Conformity, and Civil Liberties* (Garden City, N.Y., 1955), Samuel A. Stouffer reports on a scientific sampling of the American mind on those hearings, the decision in *Brown*, and the Oppenheimer trial.

In the Matter of J. Robert Oppenheimer (Washington, D.C., 1954) is the Atomic Energy Commission release on the proceedings. *We Accuse* (New York, 1955) by Joseph and Stewart Alsop denounces the procedure. Charles P. Curtis, *The Oppenheimer Case* (New York, 1955) also is highly critical.

Eleanor Bontecou, *The Federal Loyalty-Security Program* (Ithaca, N.Y., 1953), on the Truman years, has a sequel by the Association of the Bar of the City of New York (New York, 1956) on the Eisenhower program. Ralph S. Brown, Jr., *Loyalty and Security* (New Haven, Conn., 1958) takes stock of the multitude of loyalty-security tests.

Frank J. Donner, *The Un-Americans* (New York, 1960) is a documented exposé of abuses of power by HUAC. For specific examples see Adam Yarmolinsky, *Case Studies in Personnel Security* (Washington, D.C., 1955).

Telford Taylor, *Grand Inquest* (New York, 1955) appraises the investigative power vis-à-vis the privilege against self-incrimination. In *Heresy, Yes, Conspiracy, No* (New York, 1953) and *Common Sense and the Fifth Amendment* (New York, 1956) Sidney Hook argues that Communists did not qualify for the full protection of that part of the Bill of Rights. Equal dispensation is argued in John W. Caughey, "The Decline and Fall of the Fifth Amendment," *Frontier*, August, 1953, and "How to Fire a Communist,"

Frontier, May, 1956; Erwin N. Griswold, *The Fifth Amendment Today* (Cambridge, Mass., 1955); and Alexander Meikeljohn, *Political Freedom: The Constitutional Powers of the People* (New York, 1960). Dan Gilmor, *Fear, The Accuser* (New York, 1954) quotes extensively from the records of several legislative committees. Mark H. Hennessey, "Saving Los Angeles from the U.N.," *Reporter*, Nov. 11, 1952, tells of one grass-roots exercise. On much more robust action in Houston, see Ralph S. O'Leary, "Minute Women: Daughters of Vigilantism," *Nation*, January 9, 1954.

John G. Cogley, *Report on Blacklisting* (New York, 1956) consists of one volume on the movies and a second on radio and television. Elizabeth Poe, "The Hollywood Story," *Frontier*, May, 1954, adds specifics on the Hollywood blacklist. Her "Violence in Silver City," *Frontier*, May, 1953, relates the attack on *Salt of the Earth*. Alvah Bessie, *The Un-Americans* (New York, 1957) and several of Dalton Trumbo's letters in *Additional Dialogue* (New York, 1970) report the experience of being blacklisted. Merle Miller, *The Judges and the Judged* (New York, 1952) reconstructs the Jean Muir case. John Henry Faulk's epic experience is recited in his book, *Fear on Trial* (New York, 1964).

Robert M. MacIver, *Academic Freedom in Our Time* (New York, 1955) is supplemented by Robert M. Hutchins, *The University in Utopia* (Chicago, 1953). On the impact of the University of California oath see George R. Stewart, *Year of the Oath* (Garden City, N.Y., 1950); John W. Caughey, "A University in Jeopardy," *Harper's*, November, 1950; and David P. Gardner, *The California Oath Controversy* (Berkeley, Calif., 1967). The AAUP *Bulletin*, Spring, 1956, contains reports on several academic freedom violations.

The role of the courts is assessed in C. Herman Pritchett, *Civil Liberties and the Vinson Court* (Chicago, 1954) and *The Political Offender and the Warren Court* (Boston, 1958). Many of the pertinent decisions are reproduced or excerpted in James Morton Smith and Paul L. Murphy, *Liberty and Justice: A Historical Record of American Constitutional Development* (New York, 1958). Irving Dilliard, ed., *One Man's Stand for Freedom* (New York, 1963) presents Justice Hugo Black's opinions, many of the most eloquent in dissent.

Biographies of those who exposed themselves to the penalties of the anti-Communism of the fifties are almost nonexistent, though Wechsler, Oxnam, Lamont, and Faulk wrote about their experiences. Philip Wittenberg, *The Lamont Case* (New York, 1957) is the history of a successful defense against a congressional investigation. Novelists also report, as in May Sarton, *Faithful Are the Wounds* (New York, 1955); Martha Dodd, *The Searching Light* (New York, 1955); and Abraham Polonsky, *A Season of Fear* (New York, 1956).

Lerone Bennett, *Before the Mayflower* (Chicago, 1962) summarizes the history of the Negro in America and is equipped with a convenient chronology. On the southern response to the integration order see Thomas D. Clark, *The Emerging South* (New York, 1961). John W. Caughey, *Their Majesties the Mob* (Chicago, 1960) contains reports on the southern resistance in 1956 and 1957. For Martin Luther King's entry into leadership of the movement of non-violence see Lerone Bennett, *What Manner of Man* (Chicago, 1964).

THE FLOWER AND
THE THORN

MILTON R. KONVITZ

A look at the United States in the 1960s immediately brings to mind two situations which dominated the scene: the war in Indochina and the enlargement of equality among the different components of the American people. Both had deep and significant meaning for civil liberties, leaving negative and positive imprints on the guarantees proclaimed in the Bill of Rights.

While much that has been said and written about the Vietnam war bears heavily on civil liberties values, the following comments on that conflict will concentrate on the constitutional issue.

The war, which began in 1961 and involved Cambodia, Laos, and North Vietnam as well as South Vietnam, took on major proportions as the United States began to bomb North Vietnam in 1965. By the end of the war in 1973, nearly 46,000 Americans had been killed, and over 300,000 men had been wounded.[1] If the American Revolution lasted six and a half years, as is generally assumed, then by June, 1968, the Vietnam

[1] *New York Times,* January 24, 1973.

war had become the longest war in American history. In February, 1969, our troop strength reached its peak with 534,400 men. American defense expenditures almost doubled in the decade, reaching $85.5 billion in 1969.

Despite its length and other dimensions the war was an undeclared one, and for this reason its constitutionality was repeatedly challenged. For Article I of the Constitution provides that Congress shall have power "to declare war," "to raise and support armies," "to suppress insurrections and repel invasions." At the Constitutional Convention in 1787 it was originally proposed that Congress should have power "to make war," but this was opposed because, it was argued, legislative proceedings may be too slow for so momentous and necessary a power as that "to make war." So it was then decided to substitute the phrase "to declare war"—the idea being to leave the president free to repel any sudden attacks.

The most direct challenge to the constitutionality of the Vietnam war could, of course, come from a young man who was subject to compulsory military service. There were no direct precedents, however. The Selective Draft Act of 1917 was the first conscription act in American history,[2] and that act was not challenged. The Selective Service Act of 1940 provided for conscription, but there was a declaration of war by Congress on December 8, 1941. The 1940 law was superseded by continuing legislation in 1948 and 1967. Several cases came up involving the 1948 act as it was used in the Korean War, which had not been declared. But the cases involved induction before the state of war with Germany and Japan had ended,[3] so the courts held that the men were subject to a war-time, not a peace-time, draft.

A war, said the courts, does not end with a cease-fire order, for there may be a renewal of conflict; war powers continue

---

[2] In the Civil War, the draft act of 1863 was a draft on paper only, for a man could procure a substitute, or buy his way out by paying three hundred dollars. As a result, the North had only 46,000 conscripts and 118,000 substitutes. The act was not attacked in the courts.

[3] The state of war with Germany ended on October 19, 1951; with Japan, on April 28, 1952. In the Korean War armistice talks began in July, 1951, but an armistice was not signed until July 27, 1953.

unabated until a treaty of peace comes into effect. For World War II, seven years passed between the cessation of hostilities and peace. For the Korean War there was, then, first, the claim that the draft was covered by our World War II declaration of war by Congress. In addition it was claimed that the president acted on the basis of our obligations under a treaty; for the United Nations Security Council, acting under the UN Charter, which is a treaty, asked for assistance to South Korea against Communist-armed attack.[4] Responding to this request, President Truman ordered the general of the army, Douglas MacArthur, to aid South Korea, and General Mac-Arthur was later named commander only after the UN had asked the president to appoint one. The United States force was, then, under the UN command.

One of the arguments used by the Department of State in support of its claim of legality of United States defense of South Vietnam was that American participation in the war was grounded in its treaty obligations. In 1954 the United States joined other nations in signing the Southeast Asia Collective Defense Treaty (SEATO), in which each party agreed that it would respond to armed aggression against Cambodia, Laos, and South Asia, as well as other designated countries.[5] Another argument was that our military involvement in Vietnam was constitutional under the terms of the Geneva accords of 1954, and under the joint resolution of Congress, on August 19, 1964. The latter, referred to as the Gulf of Tonkin Resolution, allowed the president to take "all necessary steps, including the use of armed forces," to aid South Vietnam and other allies in Indochina and to protect American forces.[6] In addition, the government has argued that congressional approval of appro-

[4] The Communist invasion of South Korea began on June 25, 1950. The Security Council action, asking member states to halt the aggression, came two days later, and President Truman responded on the same day.

[5] The treaty, however, states that the measures each country is to take against aggression shall be "in accordance with its constitutional processes."

[6] The Gulf of Tonkin Resolution was repealed on January 14, 1971, when President Nixon signed the repeal measure. Nixon had previously said that he had no need of the resolution, since he had authority as commander-in-chief to protect United States forces in Indochina.

priations to meet the expenses of military requirements in Vietnam constituted congressional endorsement and approval of the actions taken by the president.[7]

In a number of cases which the Supreme Court refused to review, Justices William O. Douglas and Potter Stewart, in memoranda or dissenting opinions, stated their view that the Court should pass on the question of the constitutionality of peace-time conscription or of a war that was not expressly declared by Congress. Without passing on the merits of this question, Justice Douglas in one case said: "But there is a weighty view that what has transpired respecting Vietnam is unconstitutional absent a declaration of war; that the Tonkin Gulf Resolution is no constitutional substitute for a declaration of war; that the making of appropriations was not an adequate substitute; and that 'executive war-making is illegal.'"[8]

In the spring of 1970, nine state legislatures considered bills to lend support to draftees in the absence of a declaration of war by Congress. Only Massachusetts, however, actually enacted such a measure, which was signed by Governor Francis W. Sargent on April 2, 1970. The statute provided that servicemen from that state, in the absence of a declaration of war by Congress, may refuse to take part in "armed hostilities" outside the United States that are not "an emergency and not otherwise authorized in the powers granted to the president . . . as the commander in chief." The measure required the state's attorney general to defend the rights of such servicemen in all United States courts if necessary.

Proceeding on the basis of this act, the Massachusetts attorney general filed a motion in the United States Supreme Court requesting permission to file a complaint to secure judicial determination of whether United States participation

---

[7] See Legal Memorandum by Legal Adviser of the Department of State, on "The Legality of U.S. Participation in the Defense of Vietnam," in *Dept. of State Bulletin*, March 28, 1966.

[8] *Mora* v. *McNamara*, 389 U.S. 934 (1937); *Holmes* v. *U.S.*, 391 U.S. 936 (1968). See also *Drifka* v. *Brainard*, 21 L. Ed. 2d 427, 89 S. Ct. 434 (1968); *McArthur* v. *Clifford*, 393 U.S. 1002 (1968); *Morse* v. *Boswell*, 21 L. Ed. 2d 430, 89 S. Ct. 709 (1968).

in the Vietnam war was constitutional. By a 6–3 vote the motion was denied, without an opinion. Two dissents, by Justices John Harlan and Potter Stewart, stated only that they would set the motion for argument on the questions of standing and justiciability. Justice Douglas wrote a substantial dissenting opinion in which he contended that Massachusetts had standing to challenge the conscription of any of its citizens in the absence of a congressional declaration of war. On the question of justiciability, Justice Douglas argued that Massachusetts could meet all the tests that were laid down by the Court in the case of *Baker* v. *Carr*,[9] the 1962 one man, one vote case, in which the Court faced and answered the argument that the issue in that case was "political" and therefore non-justiciable. In any case, said Justice Douglas, these questions should be decided on the merits only after hearing full argument.

In its brief supporting the motion of the attorney general of Massachusetts, the American Civil Liberties Union argued that Massachusetts had standing to sue on behalf of its citizens who were subject to conscription; that the issue of the constitutionality of the Vietnam war did not present a non-justiciable "political" question; that it was possible to propose a standard whereby the president may constitutionally commit the military forces of the nation to armed hostilities abroad without congressional authorization, and a standard whereby congressional action was necessary; that our participation in the Vietnam war was unconstitutional without congressional authorization; that the Gulf of Tonkin Resolution was not equivalent to a declaration of war; and that war appropriation measures were not a constitutional substitute for express congressional authorization of the war.[10]

Regardless of contentious claims and counter-claims involving the wisdom or morality of the war, and regardless of how the issue of constitutionality might be finally answered on its merits, it is strange that the Supreme Court shunned

[9] *Baker* v. *Carr*, 369 U.S. 186 (1962).

[10] The ACLU also argued the constitutional question regarding the war in other cases, including *Berk* v. *Laird*, 429 F. 2d 302 (C.C.A. 2d 1970).

the question of constitutionality without even hearing full argument on this crucial matter. The war powers of government, like any other powers, are subject to constitutional limitations. These powers, challenged by draftees, by men in actual service, and by Massachusetts, are subject to judicial interpretation, just as are any other powers enumerated in the Constitution. The ideal of the rule of law was hardly advanced by the persistent and enigmatic refusal of the Court to entertain any action that would allow for an objective airing of the constitutional question. While this issue has been debated endlessly in the halls of Congress, in the press and legal literature, and in schools and homes, it is odd, indeed, that it has been effectively shut out from the one forum where it preeminently belongs. At a time when we try to teach young people the meaning and importance of the rule of law, it was distressing, to say the least, to have the Supreme Court simply refuse, without explanation, without an opinion explicating the constitutional basis for its decision, to consider the constitutional issue on its merits, or even to allow Massachusetts to file its bill of complaint.

Wars have often been used as excuses for denying or delaying necessary reforms, and even for curtailing essential democratic freedoms. This, however, was not true of the Indochina war in the 1960s. During no previous war was there in the United States so much freedom of speech and the press, so much freedom to criticize or even attack the war itself. For parallel to the war, and receiving no less public attention than the war itself, were speeches, demonstrations, anti-war rallies, symbolic acts, anti-war committees, and "declarations" —countless attacks on the war, on its conduct and objectives.

It is doubtful that such a spectacle would have been tolerated in any other country in the world. In part, this toleration of anti-war sentiments and forces may have been due to the fact that the United States was involved in an undeclared war: the constitutional, political, and moral ambiguity of the war, undeclared by Congress, could not be swept under the rug. Another reason for the unprecedented margin of freedom was that opposition to the war was too widespread and too deeply felt to be dealt with as simply criminal acts. Still another reason was that the anti-war opinion could not be merely identified with Communists or radicals; millions of young people in high schools and colleges, leading clergymen and professors, prominent members of both houses of Congress, countless professional and business people everywhere, newspaper editors, and entertainers were outspoken opponents of the war. It just would not have done to claim that antagonism to the war was a Communist conspiracy. No easy scapegoat was available.

However, the mere existence of opposition to the war did not imply that it was welcomed by the government. On the contrary, government, on all levels, often responded with criminal prosecutions and other exercises of police power to crack down on dissent, even punishing various forms of peaceful expression and symbolic speech such as flag offenses and draft-card burning.

Both formal and informal methods were employed by public officials to intimidate or stifle opposition. The American Civil Liberties Union catalogued some of these episodes in a June 4, 1967, statement warning that clear and discernible pressures were rising for restraints on unpopular expression.

The White House statement that the FBI is making reports on the "Communist influence" in the Spring Mobilization for peace march (conveniently disclosed for the press on the day of the April 15 march);

demands by congressmen for the jailing of those who, by speech, urge resistance to the draft, despite Assistant Attorney General Vinson's calm comment that the Constitution forbids it;

the widespread practice by city police of photographing and checking license plates of those participating in anti–Vietnam war meetings (and who reserve this technique for use against those with whom they disagree);

the penalization of professors who publicly advocate an end to the war;

the overnight stripping of Muhammad Ali of his boxing title by the New York, Texas, and Kentucky boxing commissions when the heavyweight champion, on grounds of conscience and erroneous classification, refused to be inducted.

When these incidents were paralleled by Vice President Spiro Agnew's attacks on the press for featuring anti-war commentary, the coupling of war critics with treason, and the disclosure of FBI and Army dossiers and other methods for surveillance of peaceful, constitutionally protected activities of war foes, it was readily seen why the ACLU in an unprecedented resolution on June 3, 1970, called for the war's termination because in part its continuation "so pervasively jeopardizes the exercise of civil liberties in our country."

But, as often as not, repression proved to be counter-productive, and what was vindicated was not the war but the constitutional legitimacy of the outcry against the war. Fundamental American values that had been unquestioned for generations were shaken by the war, and it may take generations for the nation to purge itself of the poisons that the war brought as unwanted side-effects. But the war failed to curtail in any essential way the fundamental liberties of the American people. And this by itself was no mean achievement.

The Vietnam war, and the great forces of opposition to it, together with the civil rights movement, stimulated many groups in American society to assert their claims for recognition, for equal dignity, and for equal rights. The result was an unprecedented period of progress toward equality within the nation. In the 1960s the constituency of the American people became greatly enlarged, not by the influx of immigrants from foreign countries, but by various classes and groups surfacing and becoming at last visible and audible: millions of non-persons gained legal personality and made a notable start, for the first time in our history, on enjoyment of legal stature and dignity.

The Preamble to the Constitution begins with the words, "We the people of the United States. . . ." In 1789 those who formed the sovereignty of the United States, held the power, and conducted the government consisted of no more than one-fourth of the white adult males. Indians, Negroes, women, and minors were outside the civil polity, and onerous property qualifications for voting were a further serious restriction on citizenship and its rights. The majority of the American people also lacked effective access to courts and legal protection of their putative interests. They could not claim the right of equal protection of the law,[11] and they could only barely be said to have the liberties that are guaranteed by the First Amendment.[12]

Some changes in the composition of our peoplehood we now take for granted as if they happened centuries ago. By adoption of the Fourteenth Amendment in 1868, Negroes born in the United States were declared citizens of the United States and of the states wherein they reside; but this provision was more honored in the breach than in the observance. Indians had to wait for an act of Congress in 1924 to be recognized as citizens of the United States. Chinese immigrants were not eligible for citizenship until 1943. Filipinos were not granted such status until 1946, and Japanese until 1952. These developments remind us that American democracy has had a gradual, and a painfully and embarrassingly slow, evolution.

In the 1960s, however, a revolution took place that brought to the foreground of our society and our consciousness groups of millions of individuals, who quite suddenly became persons with constitutional and legal rights. They burst with dramatic suddenness onto the American scene, spurred by emerging feelings of moral and social justice, of rights hitherto denied. Using such effective ways of protest as sit-ins, marches, demonstrations, and litigation, and aided by innovative gov-

[11] There was no equal protection clause in the Fifth Amendment. The phrase appears for the first time in the Fourteenth Amendment, ratified in 1868.

[12] The First Amendment was a limitation only on the federal government. It was not until the 1920s and 1930s that the Supreme Court began to read the First Amendment guarantees into the Fourteenth Amendment as a limit on the power of the states. See Milton R. Konvitz, *Fundamental Liberties of a Free People* (Ithaca, N.Y., 1957), p. 35.

ernment programs, they began to vindicate their asserted claims and interests.

The new additions embraced by the constitutional phrase "We the people of the United States" include:

Youth in secondary schools and in colleges and universities, to whom have been extended the guarantees of the First and Fourteenth Amendments;

women, whose claims to full equality began to be vindicated by judicial decision, legislation, and administrative action;

men in the armed forces, who were beneficiaries of a new spirit that began to make itself felt in the administration of military justice;

inmates of prisons, jails, and mental hospitals, who have been brought under the guarantees of the Constitution and the rule of law;

the poor, whose rights to equal justice and due process of law have been affirmed;

negroes, who have at last won freedom from discrimination in all places of public accommodation everywhere, and whose rights of suffrage have the firm support of federal law;

other ethnic groups, especially the American Indians, Mexican-Americans, Americans of Oriental origin, and Puerto Ricans, who have asserted their claims to full rights and privileges as American citizens.

The adoption of the new Immigration Act of 1965 at last brought to an end the notorious national quota origins system in immigration laws that had been on the statute books since the early 1920s. These laws discriminated against would-be immigrants from Eastern Europe and other parts of the world in favor of those from Western European countries. The adoption of the new act, under which the quotas were phased out to October, 1968, also removed the subtle but deeply-felt stigma of inferiority that the quota laws imposed on millions of Americans, who implicitly were not fully welcome here.

Of a different yet related order were the developments with respect to reapportionment. When the Constitution was adopted, the population of the country was only 4 percent urban; in 1960, it was 70 percent. State legislatures, however, continued to be controlled by the relatively few people in the rural areas. Attempts at reform failed. As Supreme Court Justice Tom Clark said, "The people have been rebuffed at the hands of the Assembly; they have tried the constitutional convention route, but since the call must originate in the Assembly, it, too, has been fruitless." [13] Malapportionment afflicted other democratic processes besides the state legislatures; for example, the county unit system employed in Georgia's statewide primaries was such that one resident in Echols County had an influence on the nomination of candidates equivalent to that of ninety-nine residents in Fulton County.[14]

Starting with *Baker* v. *Carr* in 1962,[15] the Supreme Court has held that the constitutional conception of political equality means "one person, one vote," or "one voter, one vote." As Justice Douglas stated for the Court in *Gray* v. *Sanders*,[16] "The concept of 'we the people' under the Constitution visualizes no preferred class of voters but equality among those who meet the basic qualifications." In June, 1964, the Supreme Court held that the legislatures of fifteen states, including New York, had been apportioned in violation of the equal protection clause of the Fourteenth Amendment. Litigation challenging the constitutionality of state legislative apportionment was actively pursued in almost every state, and the Court has affirmed and reaffirmed the principle that voters may not be classified on the basis of where they live; that equal representation means "equal representation for equal numbers of people, without regard to race, sex, economic status, or place of residence within a State. . . . Legislators represent people, not trees or acres. Legislators are elected by voters, not farms or cities or economic interests." [17]

---

[13] Justice Clark, concurring, in *Baker* v. *Carr*, 369 U.S. 186 (1962).
[14] *Gray* v. *Sanders*, 372 U.S. 368 (1963).
[15] See note 13, above.
[16] See note 14, above.
[17] Chief Justice Warren for the Court in *Reynolds* v. *Sims*, 377 U.S. 533 (1964).

Answering critics who charged that the Supreme Court had entered the dangerous realm of politics Chief Justice Earl Warren, writing for the Court, said:

Our answer is this: a denial of constitutionally protected rights demands judicial protection; our oath and our office require no less of us. . . . To the extent that a citizen's right to vote is debased, he is that much less a citizen. The fact that an individual lives here or there is not a legitimate reason for overweighting or diluting the efficacy of his vote. . . . A citizen, a qualified voter, is no more nor less so because he lives in the city or on the farm. This is the clear and strong command of our Constitution's Equal Protection Clause. This is an essential part of the concept of a government of laws and not men.[18]

Courts are not as full equipped as they might be to deal effectively with the vast multiplicity and complexity of questions that malapportionment has produced; but in default of action by the legislative branch of government, it did become the duty of the Supreme Court to call on the American people to consider the gross departures from unquestioned principles. On the whole the states have tended to accept what the Court has done.[19] It is not likely that states will persevere in misguided attempts to perpetuate apportionment schemes that tend to silence or to subdue any part of the electorate.

The Ninety-third Congress, convening in January, 1973, was the most representative in American history, for it had more

[18] *Ibid.* The reapportionment principles have been held to apply to local government. See *Avery* v. *Midland County,* 390 U.S. 474 (1968); and to the election of trustees of a junior college district, see *Hadley* v. *Junior College District,* 397 U.S. 50 (1970). See Annot. 18 L. Ed. 2d 1537 (1967).

[19] See Robert B. McKay, "Court, Congress, and Reapportionment," *Michigan Law Review,* 63 (1964), 255–78; Robert B. McKay, "Reapportionment: Success Story of the Warren Court," *Michigan Law Review,* 67 (1968), 223–36; Robert G. Dixon, Jr., *Democratic Representation: Reapportionment in Law and Politics* (New York, 1968); Alexander M. Bickel, *The Supreme Court and the Idea of Progress* (New York, 1970), pp. 151–181.

House members from districts with equal population than any previous Congress. In 385 of the 435 districts, the population varies less than 1 percent; in 41 districts, the deviation is from 1 to 5 percent; and in only 3 is it between 5 and 10 percent. In 1963, just ten years before, in 236 districts the deviation was 10 percent or greater. The average at that time was 17 percent. Before reapportionment the population of the districts ranged from 872,000 to 288,000. The most optimistic observer could not have foreseen when the Supreme Court announced its decision in *Baker* v. *Carr* that the nation would so quickly and almost eagerly adjust to the order to implement the basic democratic ideal of equal representation.

In all these diverse ways, the 1960s saw the largest widening and deepening of the democratic process. Rough places have been made plain as perhaps never before in American history. This is not to say nothing more remains to be done to give full meaning to the concept of "We the people of the United States," or that every American now fully enjoys the rule of law. But while attacks on rights won or refusal to broaden rights must be opposed, it is important to appreciate the fact that some very notable gains have been made, some frontiers have been successfully passed, and some great and fruitful precedents have been established.

But the progress made in extending the application of the rule of law in the 1960s paradoxically was mitigated by outbursts of great unrest and violence which often shocked the nation. President Kennedy was assassinated in 1963, and five years later Dr. Martin Luther King, Jr., and Senator Robert F. Kennedy met a similar fate. Both peaceful and violent mass demonstrations centered upon the war in Vietnam and racial tension and strife, and all too often the general public, alarmed and made fearful by the incessant protest, failed to distinguish between the two.

In 1964 racial disorders broke out in many northern cities, and three young civil rights workers (Michael Schwerner, Andrew Goodman, and James E. Chaney) were murdered in Mississippi. In 1965 a race riot erupted in the Watts section of Los Angeles; in 1966 there were race riots in Chicago,

Cleveland, and other northern cities; in 1968 Chicago police and National Guardsmen fought with demonstrators at the Democratic National Convention. In May, 1970, National Guardsmen killed four students at Kent (Ohio) State University, after officers used tear gas to disperse a demonstration by about one thousand students who were protesting the widening of the war in Indochina. Then students across the country demonstrated their bitterness against both the Kent State killings and the continuation and extension of the war; colleges and universities closed for a few days or for the remainder of the school year. An anti-war demonstration by about 100,000 persons, mostly from campuses, was conducted peacefully near the White House. A few days later in May, at Jackson, Mississippi, a black college student and a black high school student were killed in police gunfire.

These events are cited as characteristic of a decade that was full of turmoil and large-scale disquiet. Everywhere Americans were apprehensive of what the next day might bring, in the black ghettos North and South, on the college campuses and even in the nation's capital. Individual crimes of violence seemed to increase at an alarming rate, perhaps in some way made more threatening by a growth in mass violence. The Watts riots of 1965, the Detroit riots of 1967, the Chicago riot of 1968, the murder of Medgar Evers in 1963, the murder of Malcolm X in 1965, the assassination of President Kennedy, Senator Kennedy, and Dr. King—these and other macabre events threw their dark shadows over the lives of Americans.

Especially among some young people on campuses there developed a mystique of violence that was identified with the New Left, a new creed that dismissed free discussion as old-fashioned gentility and glorified violence as the generator of all that is true and noble. Some college and high school students were such absolutists that they saw no need for discussion. In their misguided view, society's evils were so great that only a total restructuring of society could redress the grievances. Therefore it was legitimate to destroy the opposition by violence. When apprehended by the police or campus officers, they claimed a moral right of amnesty, which they often were accorded. On the other side, they were met by men and officials who, in exercising their vast power, spoke and acted for "law and order" but behaved in an absolutely contrary manner. All too frequently police overlooked the difference between loud demonstration and physical force, and clearly showed that they also accepted a mystique of violence—provided they were the ones who had a monopoly on its use. It sometimes looked as if free discussion and due process, cardinal elements of the Bill of Rights, might get crushed between such irreconcilable opposing forces.

A number of notable presidential commission reports dealt with the issues and problems. The President's Commission on Campus Unrest (the so-called Scranton Commission) distributed responsibility in its late 1970 report among the universities, the students, and the government for provoking campus disorders. The report condemned fanatical student leaders who believed in and practiced terrorism; it blamed weak university administrators, brutal police officers, and demagogic politicians. Urging the president to assert the moral leadership of his office to help bring about a mood of rationality and reconciliation, the report, however, made it clear that the underlying cause of campus unrest had to be faced. It identified three main areas of student concern: the war in Indochina, racial inequalities and injustices, and the values and administration of the universities themselves.[20]

In April, 1968, the National Advisory Commission on Civil Disorders (the so-called Kerner Commission) issued its final report, which stated that "our nation is moving toward two societies, one black, one white—separate and unequal." When the Commission looked at the "basic causes" of our distemper and disorders, it found "the most fundamental" to be "the racial attitude and behavior of white Americans toward black Americans." The report called attention to a climate that tended to approve and encourage violence, a climate formed by white terrorism, by open defiance of law by officials who resisted racial desegregation, and by some protest groups who, going beyond non-violence and the constitutionally protected

[20] Report of the President's Commission on Campus Unrest, *Campus Unrest* (Washington, D.C., Government Printing Office, 1970).

rights of assembly and petition, resorted to violence to attack laws and policies with which they disagreed.[21]

Still another presidential commission addressed itself to the problems of violence and unrest. In 1969, the National Commission on the Causes and Prevention of Violence (headed by Dr. Milton S. Eisenhower) released a report on the violent demonstrations in Chicago at the time of the Democratic National Convention, the so-called Walker Report, which focused a good deal of attention on police mistreatment of demonstrators.[22] In the following year, the Commission issued its final report.[23] The Commission found three basic causes of violence in the United States: First, the sense of frustration felt by millions of Americans who saw a high level of affluence but, because their expectations of participating in such affluence were constantly disappointed, felt goaded toward various kinds of lawless behavior. Second, law enforcement processes, which never had been adequately perfected, had broken down and were patently inadequate to cope with the tide of rising crimes. Third, the belief in the immorality of the Vietnam war and the exposure of white racism converged with other factors to shake the legitimacy of political and legal institutions and respect for law. The Eisenhower Commission envisioned two sweeping objectives for the future of the nation: "to make violence both unnecessary and unrewarding."

While it would be futile to attempt to summarize the Scranton, Kerner, and Walker reports, which come to a total of several thousand pages, it is possible to assert that they are all pervaded by a single spirit—the conviction that crime and violence cannot be cured by any magic formula, such as "law and order," or by any simple device, such as stronger anticrime laws or firmer enforcement of laws. Resort to such actions means only a confrontation between frustration and

[21] National Advisory Commission on Civil Disorders, *Report* (hereafter referred to as *Kerner Report*) (New York, 1968).

[22] National Commission on the Causes and Prevention of Violence, *Rights in Conflict* (New York, 1968).

[23] National Commission on the Causes and Prevention of Violence, *To Establish Justice, to Insure Domestic Tranquility; Final Report* (New York, 1970).

frustration, between anger and anger. This can only add in-justice to injustice, and make a fetish of both criminality and its punishment. All of the commission reports look beyond the immediate scene and its pressures toward broad social reforms which would contribute to the enhancement of human dignity, the enlargement of equality of rights and opportunities, and the strengthening of civil liberties and civil rights.

It was at Greensboro, North Carolina, on January 31, 1960, that the decade's notable civil liberties record began. Anthony Lewis reported on what happened:

> On January 31, 1960, a Negro college freshman in Greensboro, North Carolina, Joseph McNeill, tried to get something to eat at the bus terminal in downtown Greens-boro. Like other Negroes at lunch counters throughout the South and through much of the border area, he was turned down: We do not serve Negroes. But the humilia-tion that so many others had experienced for so long this time set off a spark.
>
> That night, in his dormitory, McNeill asked his room-mate, Ezell Blair, Jr., "What can we do?" Then he an-swered his own question: "Let's have a boycott. We should go in and ask to be served and sit there until they do."
>
> The next day McNeill, Blair, and two of their class-mates, David Richmond and Franklin McCain, sat down at the lunch counter in Woolworth's. When they were not served, they continued to sit there. When they finally left after several hours, they had still not had a cup of coffee, but they did not feel let down.[24]

They returned to Woolworth's the next day, and the national press began to take note. By the fourth day the four students had been joined by others from the area, and more students sat at other lunch counters. And so was born a movement that was to have profound effects on the American people.

These sit-in demonstrators were not outside agitators; they

[24] Anthony Lewis, *Portrait of a Decade* (New York, 1964), p. 94.

were not carpetbaggers; they were not Americans taking advantage of Supreme Court decisions; and they had no ideology. They were simply young American Negroes who had, almost impulsively, decided, at long last, to vindicate their inalienable right to equal human dignity. These young Negro students soon found a leader and a voice in Dr. Martin Luther King, Jr., who came over from Montgomery, Alabama, to Greensboro, and organizations like the NAACP, CORE, and the ACLU lent their support. The sit-in movement gained considerable respectability when John F. Kennedy, in a campaign speech on September 6, 1960, told the American people that the president should use the force of his office "to help bring about equal access to public facilities—from churches to lunch counters—and to support the right of every American to stand up for his rights—even if that means sitting down for them." [25]

No one knows how many demonstrations took place in the early 1960s. According to the Department of Justice, during only a three-month period in 1963, there were 841 demonstrations in 196 cities in 35 states and the District of Columbia.[26] Tens of thousands of Negroes were involved, and thousands were arrested. Local courts imposed jail sentences and fines, and the courts of last resort in the South upheld the convictions. At the end of 1961 the first of such cases reached the Supreme Court. It raised a key question that had to be answered in this and subsequent cases: were the sit-ins legal or should the demonstrators be branded as criminals? It looked as if the country was facing a constitutional crisis.

By this time, some seven years since the decision in the school desegregation cases,[27] it was no longer possible for a state to charge anyone with violation of a statute that compelled or enforced racial segregation. In the early sit-in cases, therefore, the states relied on laws that made "disturbing the peace" a criminal offense. But the application of these statutes

[25] Quoted in Louis E. Lomax, *The Negro Revolt* (New York, 1962), p. 114.

[26] *New York Times*, August 11, 1963, sec. 4, p. 1E

[27] *Brown* v. *Board of Education*, 347 U.S. 483 (1954); 349 U.S. 294 (1955).

to *non-violent* demonstrations raised some serious questions: What "peace" and whose "peace" was being "disturbed"? In the first cases to come before the Supreme Court, it appeared that no one connected with the business establishments had asked the students to leave the lunch counters or the stores; for Negroes were welcome as customers in all departments except where foods or drinks were sold to be consumed on the premises. The shops did not, therefore, wish to identify themselves closely with racial segregation beyond the point required by local law, custom, or pressure.

Many of the shops were part of national chains, and the parent companies tried to avoid the possibility of large-scale customer boycotts in the North, as well as pressures for some of their northern stockholders who were sympathetic to the demonstrations. In the early cases it also appeared that the store managers did not file complaints against the sit-in demonstrators; they merely telephoned the police. In some cases, the police were notified by third parties, evidence that the shops were not eager to antagonize the Negro community. All these developments, important in themselves, had great legal significance, for they showed that *in fact* the demonstrations, conducted peacefully, had caused no "disturbance of the peace." People may have been disturbed in their minds and emotions, but the "peace" of the community had not been shattered.

Fortunately, just as the sit-in demonstrations were getting underway, the Supreme Court, in March, 1960, decided a case which, although at the time it seemed hardly worth much consideration or even mention, proved to be a most serviceable precedent in cases involving thousand of sit-in defendants. The case was *Thompson* v. *Louisville*.[28] It involved only a fine of ten dollars on each of two convictions, but it was an acorn from which there grew a mighty oak.

Sam Thompson was forty-six years old and lived alone in a suburb of Louisville, Kentucky. He was a Negro, but this fact appears nowhere in the record, and his race was not claimed to be of any legal significance in the case. For over thirty years he had worked for the same family as a handy-

[28] *Thompson* v. *Louisville*, 362 U.S. 199 (1960).

man. One Saturday evening Thompson went into a cafe that sold food and beer. After he had been there about half an hour, two Louisville policemen came in on a routine check. They saw Thompson shuffling his feet on the floor. Without being asked by the cafe's manager to do anything, one of the officers walked up to Thompson and asked him what he was doing there. Thompson said that he was waiting for a bus (in fact there was a bus due before long, half a block away, and Thompson had on him a bus schedule). The officer told Thompson that he was under arrest and took him outside. On these flimsy facts a loitering charge was filed against Thompson. After going outside, the officer testified in court, Thompson became "very argumentative"; "he argued with us back and forth and so then we placed a disorderly conduct charge on him." This was all the testimony there was on the charge of disorderly conduct; no one testified that anyone connected with the cafe or any customer had complained about anything Thompson had done.

The Supreme Court unanimously reversed the conviction for loitering and disorderly conduct, and concluded that it was "a violation of due process to convict and punish a man without evidence of his guilt." And thus the *Thompson* case set a logical pattern for the sit-in cases of the early 1960s. For in each instance only a private business was involved, the owner himself failed to complain to the police, there was no force or violence but only peaceful acts, the facts in connection with the arrests showed active zeal on part of the police, and there was no proof that the owner had asked the defendant to leave. The Supreme Court accordingly set aside unanimously the convictions of the sit-in demonstrators.[29]

While basic civil rights issues were not resolved by this approach, the reversal of the convictions by a unanimous Court was widely interpreted as an implied legitimization of the sit-in tactic. In 1963 alone, lunch counters were desegregated in over three hundred cities; and in almost as many cities, hotels and theaters were also desegregated.[30] During a thirty-day period in the summer of 1963, at least fifty cities and

[29] *Garner* v. *Louisiana*, 368 U.S. 157 (1961).
[30] Lewis, *Portrait of a Decade*, p. 103.

towns in the South made some changes in racial segregation practices.[31] The *New York Times* on August 11, 1963, reported that Negroes were especially pleased with the changes effected in Birmingham: "Lunch counters and other facilities in many downtown department and variety stores have been desegregated. Negroes have been promoted to other than menial positions and still others have been hired. City officials have reopened public parks on a desegregated basis."

Despite these constructive effects of the sit-in demonstrations, voluntary desegregation of places of public accommodation or amusement was the exception rather than the rule. Police action against demonstrators continued. Accordingly, the second series of sit-in cases reached the Supreme Court and was decided in 1963. In the *Peterson*[32] case the manager of a variety store in Greenville, South Carolina, called the police, turned out the lights, and declared the lunch counter closed. He asked the ten Negro boys and girls to leave the lunch counter because, he said, integrated service was contrary to local custom and a city ordinance. Though the store manager called the police, he did not ask that the demonstrators be arrested. The demonstrators were charged with trespass and found guilty. The Supreme Court reversed the convictions on the ground that the management had acted in obedience to the city's racial segregation ordinance, which was unconstitutional.

In June, 1964, the Supreme Court decided the third set of sit-in cases, some of which involved the most sticky constitutional issues encountered in such cases, issues that had survived the struggle over lunch counter service. By this time it had become clear to Southern officials that prosecutions of sit-in demonstrators would fail if the record showed that there was, at the time of the arrests, any state or local law that prohibited integrated service; moreover, such prosecutions would not succeed if the demonstrators were charged with breach of the peace or disorderly conduct while the evidence showed that the defendants had acted peacefully

[31] Tuskegee Institute, *Race Relations in the South—1963* (Tuskegee, Ala., 1964), p. 29.

[32] *Peterson* v. *Greenville*, 373 U.S. 244 (1963).

and quietly. *Brown* v. *Topeka* and *Thompson* v. *Louisville* had become insurmountable obstacles. Thus, the only line of attack that remained was the charge of criminal trespass. But to succeed with this tactic, the prosecution would need to show that the shop owners had, as a matter of *private* policy, refused to serve the Negroes, that they called the police in order to have them implement *their own* wishes and policy, and that they had asked the police to arrest and remove from the premises the Negro defendants.

In addition to these factual requirements, in order for a prosecution to be successful a statute was necessary to cover such cases. But not every state was prepared for this contingency. Negroes were not trespassers but invitees when they entered the variety stores or the drugstores. They were welcome as customers in all departments except the "white" lunch counters. But the common-law conception of trespass anticipated only an unlawful *entry*, not an unlawful refusal to *leave* only one part of the premises.

These requirements were tested in *Bouie* v. *Columbia*,[33] where two Negro college students entered a drugstore in Columbia, South Carolina, and took seats in a booth and waited to be served. No one came over to serve them; then an employee put up a chain with a "no trespassing" sign attached. The students remained in their places while white customers were served. The store manager called the police. When they arrived, the manager asked the students to leave because, he said, he would not serve them. When they continued to remain in their places, the police chief asked them to leave. When they refused, they were arrested and convicted of criminal trespass. Although the South Carolina trespass statute prohibited only entry after notice from the owner prohibiting such entry, the state supreme court construed the statute to cover also the act of remaining after receiving notice to leave. The United States Supreme Court reversed the conviction on the ground that the state court had retroactively rewritten the criminal statute, and so the statute, as judicially construed, had become "void for vagueness." [34]

[33] *Bouie* v. *Columbia*, 378 U.S. 347 (1964).
[34] For other and related cases, see Milton R. Konvitz, *Expanding Liberties* (New York, 1966), pp. 319 ff.

It was in *Bell* v. *Maryland*,[35] decided by the Supreme Court on the same day it decided the *Bouie* case, that the Court gave fullest consideration to the trespass issue. The case involved twelve Negro students who went into a restaurant in Baltimore, Maryland. In the lobby they were told by the hostess that the restaurant was not yet integrated; but the students went in and took seats at tables. The manager came over and told them that it was the company's policy not to serve Negroes. He called the police and made out warrants for their arrest. They were found guilty of trespass by unlawfully entering the restaurant after having been duly notified by the owner's agent not to do so. In the Supreme Court, a majority of the justices bypassed the trespass issue and reversed the convictions on the ground that after the convictions Baltimore had enacted an ordinance and the state legislature a statute that prohibited racial segregation in places of public accommodation. Since these enactments came into effect before "final" disposition of the case by the Supreme Court, the majority held that the enactments were relevant. In his opinion for the Court, Justice William Brennan said that the city and the state by their enactments had substituted "a right for a crime."

In concurring opinions Justices Goldberg and Douglas and Chief Justice Warren faced the trespass issue. These justices argued that the trespass convictions, by legitimating the proprietor's attempt to impose his racial policy of segregation, frustrated one of the purposes of the Fourteenth Amendment —insuring the right to enjoy equal accommodations and privileges in places of public accommodation; so the state's failure to protect the right of the Negro students to service at the lunch counters constituted "state action" within the meaning of the Fourteenth Amendment. The state, by using its police, its prosecutors, and its courts to support the lunch counter owner's racial segregation policy, acted as authoritatively as in any case "where the state in one way or another puts its full force behind a policy."

Justices Black, Harlan, and White, in their dissents, also confronted the trespass issue. Justice Black, in an opinion in which the other dissenters joined, argued that the Four-

[35] *Bell* v. *Maryland*, 378 U.S. 226 (1964).

teenth Amendment does not forbid a state to prosecute for crimes committed against a person's private property, however prejudiced the property owner may be. The state, by punishing for the trespass, does not adopt the property owner's bigotry or prejudice.

In his concurring opinion, however, Justice Douglas sufficiently met this complex and difficult point by arguing that what was involved in the Maryland case was not a man's home or his yard. It was, admittedly, private property, but it was property that was serving the public. The Court did not have before it a case of someone opening or closing the door of his home—a place not dedicated to public use. He pointed out that in the 1962 and 1963 terms of the Court, there were twenty sit-in cases, but only two of them involved noncorporate ownership. The other eighteen cases involved corporations, one with 650 restaurants, one with 272 stores, one with 1,307 stores, one with 2,130 stores, and one with 567 stores.

Had a majority of the Court sided with Justice Black, the Court's decision affirming the convictions would have been interpreted as a signal for the southern states to enact adequate trespass laws, through which racial segregation would have been enforced with all the harshness of the "black codes" following the Civil War, and Jim Crow would have been triumphant. And this would have been accomplished under the banner of private property, the right of privacy and free enterprise, terms that conjure up the image of the small, intimate neighborhood shop rather than the 2,130 F. W. Woolworth Company department or variety stores.

The sit-in demonstrations and the southern states' resort to criminal trespass prosecutions for the enforcement of racial segregation showed the desperate need for a strong federal civil rights law. This need was met, in a macabre twist of fate, by the country's emotional reaction to President Kennedy's assassination on November 22, 1963. Less than a week later, on November 27, in his first speech to a joint session of Congress, President Johnson urged Congress to enact a civil rights law, "so that we can move forward to eliminate from this nation every trace of discrimination and oppression that is based upon race or color." On February 10, 1964, the House responded affirmatively by a vote of 290 to 130. On June 16, 1964, the Senate, by a 73 to 27 vote, passed a revised bill. On July 2, 1964, the new law went into effect—almost a hundred years after the Civil War.

What became the Civil Rights Act of 1964 was the end product of a lengthy legislative process. It had started out, on June 20, 1963, as HR 7152, introduced by Congressman Emanuel Celler. At that time the House Judiciary Committee had before it 172 civil rights bills, and the Senate Judiciary Committee 20 bills. Six congressional subcommittees sat for 81 days, heard 269 witnesses and printed 5,791 pages of hearings on HR 7152 and related bills. The House and Senate debates on the bill filled about 3,400 pages of the *Congressional Record,* reporting the millions of words spoken on the floor of the Congress during 809 hours of debate.[36] The legislative mill, like God's, "grinds slow, but sure."

The Civil Rights Act of 1964 is one of the most significant enactments of social legislation in history. By prohibiting discrimination or refusal of service, on account of race, in hotels, motels, restaurants, gasoline stations, and places of amusement, the statute removed the greatest obstacle to the recognition of human dignity. So effective has been the law that one hardly ever hears of a case involving a denial of equal treatment in places of public accommodation or amusement. The debate over "trespass" to "private property" quickly lost its foundation and became a fact of American history and not of American life.

The 1964 law also required that Negroes have equal access to, and equal treatment in, publicly owned or operated facilities, such as parks and swimming pools. It empowered the attorney general to bring suits for the enforcement of school desegregation. The new law was also in effect a fair employment practices act: Title VII banned discrimination by employers or unions.

Title I of the act sought to extend the mantle of legal protection to equal voting rights, a fundamental right of personal expression. It prohibited voting registrars from using different

[36] Marjorie Hunter, *New York Times,* June 20, 1964, p. 10.

standards for white and Negro voting applicants. It required that literacy tests be in writing, thereby reducing the power of prejudiced registrars, and it made a sixth-grade education proof of literacy.

But not all the problems of voting rights were solved by Title I, and soon after passage of the Civil Rights Act leaders of the civil rights movement focused their central concern on the remaining loopholes. In March, 1965, some twenty-five thousand Negroes and whites, led by Dr. King, marched fifty-four miles from Selma to Montgomery, Alabama, to petition Alabama's Governor George C. Wallace for redress of grievances. The petition stated: "We call upon you to establish democracy in Alabama, by taking the steps necessary to assure the registration of every citizen of voting age and of sound mind, by repealing the poll tax in state elections, by opening the registration books at times which are convenient to working people. . . ." [37] But when the marchers reached the Capitol grounds, they were stopped by state policemen. When a delegation sought to see the governor and present the petition to him, word came that his office had closed for the day. Governor Wallace may not have been impressed, but millions of Americans—and millions of others throughout the world—were impressed with the pathos of the words in the petition: "We have come not only five days and fifty miles, but we have come from three centuries of suffering and hardship." Millions watched the march on television and were stirred by Dr. King's Montgomery address: "We are on the move now. Like an idea whose time has come, not even the marching of mighty armies can halt us. We are moving to the land of freedom. . . . Let us march on ballot boxes until all over Alabama God's children will be able to walk the earth in decency and honor."

Less than five months later, on August 6, 1965, President Johnson signed the Voting Rights Act of 1965. Under an "automatic trigger" formula marking the line between discriminatory and non-discriminatory treatment, literacy tests and other disenfranchising devices were immediately suspended in Alabama, Mississippi, Louisiana, Georgia, South

[37] *New York Times,* March 26, 1965, p. 22.

Carolina, and Virginia, and in forty counties in North Carolina. The act gave the attorney general authority to send federal examiners to any county where he believed an examiner was needed to prevent discrimination. Examiners had the right to appoint poll watchers and report incidents of discrimination to the federal district court. The act directed the attorney general to file suits in Texas, Alabama, Mississippi, and Virginia to challenge the constitutionality of poll taxes as prerequisites to voting in non-federal elections. And states were prohibited from making the right to vote dependent on a reading or writing knowledge of the English language; moreover, the law provided that any person with a sixth-grade education in a school conducted in a language other than English may not be denied the right to vote. And annexed to these primary rights was the later Voting Rights Act Amendments of 1970, which virtually abolished residence requirements for voting for president and vice president of the United States.

Some measure of the success of the Voting Rights Act of 1965 may be found in the fact that before the 1968 presidential election, some 800,000 new Negro voters were added to the voting rolls in the South, and by 1970 the figure was nearly one million. In 1971 there were 1,861 elected black officials in the nation, while in 1967 there were only 475. Nearly three-fifths of these officials were elected in the eleven Southern states. In Mississippi in 1964 only 7 percent of the blacks were registered, but in 1970 68 percent were registered. In the 1972 election, thirteen blacks were elected to the House of Representatives, including one from Georgia and one from Texas—the first black members of Congress elected from the South since Reconstruction. In Arkansas 81 percent of black eligible voters were registered, compared with 61 percent of whites.

On June 13, 1967, President Johnson named Thurgood Marshall, former NAACP general counsel, an associate justice of the Supreme Court. The appointment of Marshall, great-grandson of a slave and son of a Pullman car steward, was widely seen as symbolic of the national commitment to racial equality and justice.

But less than a year later, in a cataclysmic tragedy, on April 4, 1968, the whole nation was stunned by the murder of Martin Luther King, Jr. The facts pointed to a white man as the murderer. Army troops ringed the nation's capitol as Negroes rioted, and the National Guard was sent to Chicago, Detroit, Boston, and other cities. Fires, fighting, and looting broke out in many cities. The president called for a joint session of Congress, proclaimed a national day of mourning, and issued a proclamation to deal with violence in the Washington metropolitan area. Schools and colleges cancelled classes. At home and abroad there was great fear over the stability of the country and its government.

By the end of the first week a large measure of calm was restored, and six days after the murder of Dr. King Congress passed and sent to President Johnson the Civil Rights Act of 1968. While proponents of the bill said that it would have passed in any case, there were those who claimed that the assassination of Dr. King influenced the outcome. In any case, the new law made a substantial contribution to the cause of civil rights by prohibiting racial discrimination in housing. The law barred discrimination in the sale or rental of federally owned housing and multi-unit housing where the mortgage was insured or underwritten by the Federal Housing Authority or the Veterans Administration; and it disallowed discrimination in multi-unit housing, excluding, however, owner-occupied dwellings of four or fewer units. The law also barred, after January 1, 1970, discrimination in the sale or rental of single-family houses by real estate brokers, and forbade owners selling their homes without brokers to use discriminatory signs or other such advertisements. (It was estimated that some 80 percent of housing sale transactions were handled through brokers.)

Other provisions of the act provided severe federal penalties for intimidating or injuring civil rights workers or Negroes engaged in federally protected activities, including voting, registering to vote, housing, jury duty and the use of public facilities.

On December 14, 1964, the Supreme Court unanimously upheld the constitutionality of the public accommodations section of the Civil Rights Act of 1964.[38] All nine justices agreed that the section (Title II) was valid under the commerce clause of the Constitution. While the decision was no surprise, it came as a great relief, for it firmly and finally settled the question of the role of the federal government in the protection and enhancement of civil rights.

This role was strengthened further five years later when, on October 29, 1969, the Supreme Court unanimously ruled that school districts must desegregate "at once" and operate desegregated schools "now and hereafter."[39] This decision replaced the principle that desegregation must proceed "with all deliberate speed," formulated by the Court some fifteen years before in the first school desegration case.[40] The Court now made it clear that it meant to follow a much more rigid standard of compliance. The decision was especially significant because it was the first major decision handed down by the Supreme Court under Chief Justice Warren Burger, and also because it was widely interpreted as a rejection of the Nixon Administration's position that school districts should be permitted to delay desegregation and that there should be no haste in the pursuit of the goals set by the Court in *Brown* v. *Board of Education of Topeka.* The Court's meaning was made quite clear when the opinion said that "allowing 'all deliberate speed' for desegregation is no longer constitutionally permissible."

The civil rights sit-ins were of the greatest importance in themselves for what they accomplished for the American Negro in terms of dignity and self-assurance, and also for the civil rights movement. But before long their influence became apparent in other contexts. In the fall of 1964 thousands of young people, university students and young men and women living near the campus, became involved in sit-ins at the University of California's Berkeley campus, which spawned from that time on throughout the country a mixture of campus

[38] *Heart of Atlanta Motel* v. *United States,* 379 U.S. 241 (1964).

[39] *Alexander* v. *Holmes County Board of Education,* 396 U.S. 19 (1969).

[40] See note 27, above.

demonstrations, sit-ins, violence, and riots. What the civil rights movement stimulated was an awareness among young people that they could be socially and politically active, that their actions could produce certain changes in policy, and that to seek redress of grievances the sit-in might be a useful tactic.

The civil rights sit-ins, however, were peaceful. They were guided by the non-violent philosophy of Gandhi and Dr. King. And the civil rights sit-ins were staged at lunch counters and other public accommodations where, as the Supreme Court decisions and the later state and federal civil rights statutes implied, the demonstrators had a right to be and to be served. The campus situation was more complicated. Some campus sit-ins became campus disorders, which stopped classes from being held and the university administration from carrying on its functions; yet others were peaceably conducted and did not interfere with university operations. Some student demonstrations hewed to the line of peaceful protest, but others, guided by radical and revolutionary programs, followed the path of violence.

Moreover, certain legal and constitutional distinctions had to be drawn. It was by no means clear that the students ever had a right to take over and sit in the office of a university official or the entire administration building to the exclusion of persons who clearly had a right and a duty to be in their offices. The Negro students did not occupy seats at lunch counters in such a way that white customers would be shut out. To them the sit-in was a way of reaching a reconciliation; to thousands of students involved in the campus demonstrations, sit-ins were a way of establishing a confrontation. The Negro sit-ins, as Dr. King made it clear, were a form of speech. The Selma marchers' petition to Governor Wallace said: "We must appeal to the seat of government with the only peaceful and non-violent resources at our command: our physical presence and the moral power of our souls. Thus we present our bodies with this petition as a living testimony to the fact that we are deliberately denied the right to vote. . . ." [41]

[41] *New York Times*, March 26, 1965, p. 22.

At a time when highly dramatic means of conveying ideas, even civil disobedience, were labeled symbolic speech, many student demonstrators regarded their actions as a form of speech, as a way of piercing the nation's conscience and informing people about such issues as the war, racism, and poverty. On the other hand, some student demonstrators, through the use of physical force, sought not speech, not deliberation, not negotiation, but radicalization of the campus, even when it meant denying speech to others. When force was met by opposing and stronger force on the part of overreactive police, matters often became aggravated. As a consequence, the composite picture of the campus demonstrations is as much a blur as an articulation.

The Berkeley demonstrations lasted for about three tumultuous months. They started under the leadership of Mario Savio, who was the main force behind the Free Speech Movement. When the university suspended eight students who had demonstrated against a rule forbidding solicitation of political funds on a small strip of land on the campus, Savio led about one thousand students and non-students into Sproul Hall, the main administration building. Carrying food, blankets, guitars, and books, they locked the doors. The chancellor of the university asked them to leave, but only a few departed; the rest barricaded the stairs and occupied the second, third, and fourth floors. When the university officials felt that they could not persuade the demonstrators to vacate Sproul Hall, they called the police. It took the police, on December 3, 1964, twelve hours to arrest 796 students. Most of those arrested got off with suspended sentences, or the charges against them were dropped. But Savio and several dozen others were found guilty of resisting arrest and other offenses, and several served brief jail terms. Before long the Free Speech Movement seemed to have become the Filthy Speech Movement, in which students and non-students carried obscene signs and shouted obscenities. Tension remained high and in November, 1966, there was another clash between demonstrating students and police at Berkeley. Four students and six non-students, including Savio, were arrested.

In February, 1967, in a demonstration on the University of

Wisconsin's Madison campus, about two hundred students threatened to keep the chancellor in his office unless the university put up bail money for eighteen anti-war demonstrators who had been arrested by the Madison police. The chancellor put up the money. In the following October a more violent demonstration was held to oppose the war in Vietnam. The students crowded into a three-story building where representatives of the Dow Chemical Company, which manufactured napalm, were recruiting for their company. The representatives left, but the students continued to occupy the building. When they refused to leave, the university called the police. The students responded by throwing rocks and bricks. In the ensuing melee three policemen and sixty-five students were injured.

In April, 1968, Columbia University students seized and held five buildings for about a week. These seizures followed by several days the seizure of Hamilton Hall by black students. The main point of the dispute between students and administration was opposition by students and by members of the Negro community to proposed construction of a gymnasium in Morningside Park, located between Columbia and Harlem. A contributing cause of friction was Columbia's affiliation with the federally sponsored Institute for Defense Analyses, an affiliation perceived by many as university support for warmaking. About one thousand policemen were needed to remove the students from the buildings. The students broke in, opened files, and littered the president's offices in Low Memorial Library. They refused to leave the buildings when ordered to do so by the university and the police, and had to be dragged out. As they appeared, some sang *We Shall Overcome* or *The Battle Hymn of the Republic*, and some shouted obscenities.

There was no question that the students' disruption halted the educational process, but the behavior of New York City's police deserves similar condemnation. Brutality was charged against low-ranking police, who, in disregard of the orders of their superiors to limit the use of force, vented the emotional feelings of society at large against youth and their different life styles. The police indiscriminately beat and arrested people, including some who were mere onlookers and uninvolved in the protest. Some students were injured and 250 were arrested.

In the space assigned to this chapter, it is impossible to do more than let these all-too-brief summaries stand as representative of the events that shook American colleges and universities—and American society—beginning with the Berkeley episodes in 1964. It was not until the academic year 1969–70 that relative calm was restored. During the years of turmoil there were also crises on the campuses of Howard, Stanford, Northwestern, Cornell, Massachusetts Institute of Technology, San Francisco State College, City College of New York, Harvard, New York University, and the University of Chicago.[42] Student radicals rallied under various banners: Students for a Democratic Society (SDS), groups inspired by Maoism, Leninism, Stalinism, Trotskyism, and other leftist ideologies. Extremist members of SDS formed the "Weathermen" and carried out acts of vandalism in several cities. Black students, inspired by the cry for "black power," also seized buildings and resorted to other forms of militant action.

These convulsive events posed a definite challenge to the generally accepted methods of free and open debate. This problem was expressed in a letter that on April 3, 1969, the ACLU addressed to leaders of the academic community, reflecting both historic commitment to fundamental constitutional liberties and grave concern over resort to force and violence. The statement said, in part:

We believe in the right and are committed to the protection of all peaceful, non-obstructive forms of protest,

[42] The literature on campus disorders is voluminous. Perhaps the best collection of documents and statements may be found in the two volumes edited by Immanuel Wallerstein and Paul Starr, *The University Crisis Reader* (New York, 1971). Several books on the Berkeley events are: Michael V. Miller and Susan Gilmore, eds., *Revolution at Berkeley* (New York, 1965); Seymour Lipset and Sheldon S. Wolin, eds. *The Berkeley Student Revolt* (New York, 1965); Christopher G. Catope and Paul G. Zolbrod, *Beyond Berkeley* (New York, 1966). For documents on the New Left, see Paul Jacobs and Saul Landau, *The New Radicals* (New York, 1966). (All of the books cited in this note are available in paperback editions.)

including mass demonstrations, picketing, rallies, and other dramatic forms. However, we are deeply disturbed about some methods that some student activists have used in the attempt to achieve their ends; methods which violate and subvert the basic principles of freedom of expression and academic freedom. Protest that deprives others of the opportunity to speak or be heard, or that requires physical take-over of buildings to disrupt the educational process, or the incarceration of administrators and others, are anti-civil-libertarian and incompatible with the nature and high purpose of an educational institution.

In disagreeing with these methods the ACLU took special pains to point out that student protests on the whole "have in great degree been motivated by extraordinary selflessness, idealism, and altruism." The statement noted student concern with society's materialism, "the plodding pace toward de-segregation and equal rights," the immoral basis of the Vietnam war, the university's service to the military, and the need for greater student participation in the governance of educational institutions which so affect their lives.

But these strong feelings, along with lack of direct access to mass communications media and the "stubborn and often recalcitrant resistance to desirable change," could not excuse these types of specific action the ACLU condemned:

In December of 1968, students at New York University's Loeb Student Center stopped an address by Nguien Huu Chi, the South Vietnamese permanent observer at the UN, by draping a Nazi flag across him, hurling an egg, and pouring a pitcher of water over him. They then invaded another room, seized the notes of James Reston, executive editor of the New York *Times,* and tore them to bits. He left without delivering his address.

In January, 1969, at a symposium at Northwestern University on confronting change, student activists shouted down all but the most radical speakers.

In February [1969] at Harvard University, students disrupted a course whose focus they resented.

In March [1969] Professor John H. Bunzel, of San

Francisco State College, whose views are unpalatable to some student activists, was drowned out in a flood of shouts and questions in his classroom.

At a conference on "World Problems and American Change," on March 22, 1969, Arthur J. Goldberg, former Supreme Court justice and United States ambassador to the United Nations, was shouted down by about thirty youngsters who dumped the head of a pig on the speaker's table.

The statement of the ACLU reminded the activists among students and faculty that

> violence and the threat of violence may be used in "bad" causes as well as in "good" causes. They were employed by the Nazis in Germany and by Hungarian fascists to shut down universities or oust particular faculty members or students. They were used in the attempt to block the admission of James Meredith to the University of Mississippi and to block integration widely across the South. And there are those who today would use these methods to destroy our universities, not to reform them.

As noted earlier in this chapter, student demonstrations were both peaceful and violent. Whatever their style, the question repeatedly was asked, what lay behind the sudden and dramatic outbursts of protest? There were those who claimed that the campus disorders were justified because peaceful forms of protest had failed, because democratic processes had been unresponsive to the legitimate grievances of minority groups and even of the masses of students, because many students had been denied equality of opportunity, because the universities had become too closely linked with the defense machinery of the government, and because students had no voice in the governing of institutions which had such a pervasive impact on their lives.

Whatever the reasons, the fact is that in the 1960s important progress was made in meeting these complaints. State and federal courts, acting in cases sparked by student protest and recalcitrant university attitudes, handed down hundreds of decisions that affirmed the rights of students. The courts affirmed that students had the rights of due process and equal protection of the law in all matters involving campus discipline; that they did not surrender their liberties under the First Amendment when they came to their campus—they had the constitutional right to invite and hear speakers who represented unpopular or radical causes; that they had free access to the courts for the vindication of their rights as people and as citizens, and their rights as students. Students had the constitutional right to hold mass meetings if they could attract to them the masses of students. They had the right to act as the Negro sit-in demonstrators had acted at the lunch counters: to assert and exercise their rights without violence or the threat of violence, and without impairing the equal rights of others.

But the trouble was that these decisions were not nearly as interesting or satisfying as the existentialist "happening" of the moment, the direct confrontation between the student and the "establishment." And so thousands of students allowed themselves to be led by a few hundred dedicated militant activists who insisted on instant satisfaction of their demands and whose interests lay not in the reform of the universities but in the radicalization of university students and in the radical reform of American society.

But radicalization through sacrifice of basic democratic procedures? The heart of the ACLU statement is that while students, like all other Americans, have the right to become radicalized and to transform their society and its institutions, they have no right to attempt to achieve these or other ends by means other than those guaranteed by the First and Fourteenth Amendments, by speech, publications, peaceful assembly, free association, peaceful petition for the redress of grievances, the legislative process, the judicial process—by full use of all the democratic processes and the institutions these processes have created.[43]

No matter how one views the campus events of the decade, there is general consensus that the traumatic experiences

[43] See ACLU pamphlets, "Academic Freedom and Civil Liberties of Students in Colleges and Universities," April, 1970; and "Academic Freedom in the Secondary Schools," September, 1968.

suffered by American colleges and universities in the 1960s did change them. University reforms had been long overdue, and many reforms were initiated. The idea of *in loco parentis* faded, curriculum revision was achieved, student representation in institutional governance was increased, an atmosphere of reduced rigidity and more openness marked the campus scene. Some of these changes were for better and some for worse. But what remains are the spiritual wounds which will probably not heal for many years.

One of the main preoccupations of Americans in the 1960s was crime—crime in the streets, crime in the nation's capital, crime in the cities, crime in the suburbs. At times Americans considered crime a greater problem than the war in Vietnam. One of the most important studies of crime was the report of the President's Commission on Law Enforcement and Administration of Justice, chaired by the then attorney general, Nicholas Katzenbach. The report was published in 1967 under the title *The Challenge of Crime in a Free Society*. It did not, however, receive the attention it deserved, perhaps because it was a document of over three hundred double-column pages written in sedate language, and did not propose an easy solution that could be stated in a banner headline. Anticipating the later Kerner, Scranton, and Walker reports, the Katzenbach report concluded that:

> The most effective way to prevent crime is to assure all citizens full opportunity to participate in the benefits and responsibilities of society. Especially in inner cities, achievement of this goal will require extensive overhauling and stengthening of the social institutions influential in making young people strong members of the community —schools, employment, the family, religious institutions, housing, welfare, and others. Careful planning and evaluations and enormous increases in money and personnel are needed to expand existing programs of promise and to develop additional approaches.[44]

[44] President's Commission on Law Enforcement and Administration of Justice, *The Challenge of Crime in a Free Society* (Washington, D.C., Government Printing Office, 1967), p. 293.

While no one doubted that there had been an increase in crime in recent years, there was general agreement among experts that statistics more often reflect statistical techniques than criminality itself. Notwithstanding this difficulty, Congress and public officials generally had no doubt that public anxiety about crime—the fear of mugging, the fear of forcible entry into one's home or office—had been greatly increased.

Since most crimes are committed by the young, and since the young today make up a larger percentage of the population than ever before, the fear and distrust of the young exacerbated the normal generation gap. This fear and distrust were aggravated by the campus unrest and disorders, dropouts from high school and college, hippies and yippies, mass demonstrations in which youth dominated the scene, mass rock festivals, and the revolution in sex mores and morals.

Crime accentuated not only the generation gap but also the wide chasm between the races. Since crime rates are much higher in large cities than elsewhere, and since within cities crime rates are higher in Negro slum areas than elsewhere,[45] most white Americans simply saw an intimate connection between criminality and the Negro race. They paid no attention to the fact that the most frequent victims of crimes of violence are themselves persons who live in the city slums. The Task Force Report on Crime, prepared for Vice President Humphrey in 1968, pointed out that 84 percent of assault victims and 70 percent of murder victims in Washington, D.C., were black.[46] Nor did the public pay attention to the fact that historically the slums have always been the main breeding places of criminality, no matter what racial group lived there.

Blame for the rising crime rate was also placed on the Supreme Court for a series of decisions that set up stronger constitutional guidelines for the police to follow when they seek information or evidence from a suspect. In 1964 the Court generated a controversy when it reversed the conviction of Danny Escobedo for the murder of his brother-in-law. The Supreme Court held in a 5–4 decision that Escobedo's volun-

[45] *Kerner Report*, p. 266.

[46] "Order and Justice," Task Force Report to Vice President Humphrey. James Q. Wilson, Chairman. September 16, 1968.

tary confession was inadmissible because it was made after he had requested the assistance of counsel and was refused that assistance by the police, and because he had not been advised that he had the constitutional right to remain silent.[47]

The attacks on the Court increased in extent and intensity two years later when it handed down its decision in *Miranda*,[48] which went beyond *Escobedo*. In its 5–4 *Miranda* decision the Supreme Court formulated the following guidelines: (1) a suspect must be informed of the right to remain silent; (2) a suspect must be told that anything he or she has said can be used against him or her; (3) a suspect must be told of the right to the assistance of counsel; (4) defense counsel must be provided if the suspect asks for counsel but cannot afford to engage one; (5) the prosecution must prove that the suspect knowingly waived his or her rights if the confession was made without counsel being present; (6) prolonged interrogation will be construed as lack of such knowingly made waiver of rights; and (7) if the suspect indicates in any manner that he or she wants to remain silent, even after starting to talk, questioning must end.

The majority opinion, written by Chief Justice Warren, referred to the long history of documented police brutality during the period of in-custody interrogation, and said that while such brutality is the exception, unless a proper limitation is placed upon custodial interrogation there can be no assurance that such practices will be eradicated in the foreseeable future. It was toward such eradication that *Escobedo* and *Miranda* were striving. Said the Court:

> We have concluded that without proper safeguards the process of in-custody interrogation of persons suspected or accused of crime contains inherently compelling pressures which work to undermine the individual's will to resist and to compel him to speak where he would not otherwise do so freely. In order to combat these pressures and to permit a full opportunity to exercise the privilege against self-incrimination, the accused must be ade-

[47] *Escobedo* v. *Illinois*, 378 U.S. 478 (1964).
[48] *Miranda* v. *Arizona*, 384 U.S. 436 (1966).

quately and effectively apprised of his rights and the
exercise of those rights must be fully honored.

The Court made clear that the decision was not intended
to hamper the traditional function of police officers in investigating crime, or to interfere with general on-the-scene
questioning as to facts surrounding a crime when the persons
questioned are not under restraint. Yet police and other law-
enforcement officials throughout the country protested that the
Court was "pampering" criminals and disregarding the right
of the people to live securely and peacefully. High public
officials, including members of Congress, spoke out intem-
perately against the Warren Court and its decisions.

Instead of taking great pride in the civilized standards
formulated in *Miranda*, critics have used the decision and the
Warren Court generally as a scapegoat for failure of government to face the real issues in crime as stated in many voluminous, documented reports, starting with the Wickersham Report
of 1931 and culminating with the Presidential Commission
reports of the 1960s. All of the reports warned against the
temptation to think that crime can be solved by official repression. Yet the tendency has been to disregard the positive social
measures recommended by the reports and to concentrate
emotion, money, and other resources on conventional "law
and order" methods and procedures.

An example of what has happened is the Omnibus Crime
Control and Safe Streets Act of 1968. The temper of Congress,
as its various committees considered the bill, may be gauged
from the fact that the version approved by the Senate Judiciary
Committee curtailed the Supreme Court's jurisdiction in state
confession cases, and restricted federal habeas corpus jurisdiction regarding applicants for the writ who are in state custody.
These provisions fortunately were eliminated on the floor of the
Senate. As enacted, the bill vests power in the trial court to
determine if the confession was "voluntarily given." The act
formulates tests the court is to use, but there is the decisive
provision that the "presence or absence of any of the above-
mentioned factors to be taken into consideration by the judge
need not be conclusive on the issue of voluntariness of the

confession." In signing the bill, President Johnson referred to this provision as "vague and ambiguous," and said that the federal practice will in the future "conform to the Constitution." After passage of the act, Attorney General Ramsey Clark instructed federal prosecutors to adhere to *Miranda,* notwithstanding the 1968 act, but when Attorney General Mitchell assumed office he leaned heavily the other way.[49]

A previous section of this chapter referred to the Civil Rights Act of 1968. A part of that statute is an Anti-Riot Act.[50] Sections 2101–2102 provide that it shall be a federal crime to travel from one state to another or to use interstate communications with intent to incite riot. The statute defines a riot as an act of violence by one or more persons constituting an assemblage of three or more persons, if the act constitutes a clear and present danger of damage or injury to person or property. It also makes it a crime to threaten the commission of an act of violence by one who is part of such an assemblage, provided there exists the ability immediately to execute such a threat. The term "incite a riot" is defined to include urging or instigating persons to riot, but excludes the mere oral or written advocacy of ideas or expression of belief "not involving advocacy of any act or acts of violence or assertion of the rightness of, or the right to commit, any such act or acts."

It was under this new statute that the Chicago Seven case came up.[51] On February 18, 1970, after five days of deliberation, a federal jury found the defendants—after a turbulent trial that lasted twenty-one weeks—not guilty of conspiring to incite riots during the 1968 Democratic National Convention in Chicago, but convicted five of crossing state lines with intent to incite riots. Two defendants were acquitted of both counts against them. The guilty verdicts were returned against David

[49] See Robert A. Burt, "Miranda and Title II: A Morganatic Marriage," *Supreme Court Review,* 81 (1969).

[50] The anti-riot section was passed as a rider to the Civil Rights Act under pressure from Senator Strom Thurmond of South Carolina and other southern Senators.

[51] Originally there were eight defendants. But the case of Bobby G. Seale, Black Panther leader, was severed after a series of courtroom outbursts that ended with his being bound and gagged. Later the government dropped the case against him.

Dellinger and Rennie Davis, leaders of the National Mobilization Committee to End the War in Vietnam, and Abbie Hoffman, Jerry Rubin, and Tom Hayden, all prominently identified with the New Left and the anti-war movement. Judge Julius J. Hoffman, who presided at the trial, imposed sentences of five years and $5,000 fines on each of the five convicted men, and $60,000 in court costs on the group.

While the jury deliberated the verdict, Judge Hoffman imposed jail sentences on the defendants for contempt of court. These sentences ranged up to nearly two-and-a-half years. He also imposed a sentence of four years and thirteen days in jail on William M. Kunstler, chief defense attorney, for fanning "the flames of disorder" during the trial, and nearly two years in jail for Leonard I. Weinglass, another defense attorney.

While the case was pending before Judge Hoffman, proceedings were instituted to get a judicial declaration that the anti-riot statute was unconstitutional, but both a federal district court judge and a federal court of appeals judge [52] held that the questions as to the act's constitutionality were not substantial enough to warrant impaneling a statutory three-judge court to pass on the challenge.

The ACLU and many Americans considered the Chicago case one of the most important political trials in American history. In a brief supporting the defendants' motion to dismiss the indictment, the ACLU showed that the purpose of the statute was to discourage the "outside agitator" from crossing state lines in order to "stir up trouble" and "cause riots." Behind this charge was the recognition that the southern legislators who sponsored the act had in mind black militants like Stokely Carmichael and H. Rap Brown as well as "Communist agitators." The ACLU pointed out that the statute was aimed at crossing state lines with intent to incite a riot rather than actual participation in riots by "outside agitators." But, the ACLU brief contended, there is a constitutional right, under the First Amendment, to be an "outside agitator." Americans have the right to travel. They have a right, under the Constitution, to be concerned with conditions in the state of

[52] *National Mobilization Committee v. Foran*, 297 F. Supp. 1 (1968); 411 F. 2d 934 (1969).

Illinois, for example, though they may be residents of the state of Maine or Maryland. In crystal-clear words, the brief stated:

> The activities of the freedom riders in the South furnish a good example of the importance of this institution [the "outside agitator"]. So do the voter registration drives, in which many young people from all parts of the nation have participated. Likewise representatives of national organizations such as the NAACP can show local people, often poor and frightened, what can be done about the injustices they suffer. . . . Most importantly, outside agitation represents communication between people from different parts of our federal union, interacting to solve problems, which though seemingly local, may be national in scope. If we are truly to be a nation, freedom of expression can know no boundaries. . . .

The ACLU also contended that the statute is unconstitutional on its face because vague and overbroad, in violation of the First Amendment and the Fifth Amendment; the emphasis in the statute is not on participation in or instigating a riot but on crossing a state line with a certain "intent." The stress is on the "evil intent," thus making the defendant's state of mind when crossing a state line the critical question. But a person's state of mind is precisely what the First Amendment protects.

Throughout the country, indeed throughout the world, attention was focused on the Chicago Seven case because it provided an occasion for a constitutional test of the 1968 act. But even more because of the conduct of the trial itself, evidenced by the bizarre antics of some of the defendants, the unrestrained and undignified outbursts of defendants' lawyers, and the often demeaning and combative actions of the trial judge —his scornful sarcasm, his biting, prejudicial rebukes. The trial became a public spectacle and an open disgrace to the administration of criminal law in the United States. No matter what may be the ultimate fate of the 1968 statute, the trial of the Chicago Seven was a disservice to the ideal of the rule of law.

It was perhaps with some of these considerations in mind that the Supreme Court, in a March 31, 1970, decision otherwise unrelated to the Chicago Seven case, said in an opinion by Justice Black:

> It would degrade our country and our judicial system to permit our courts to be bullied, insulted, and humiliated, and their orderly progress thwarted and obstructed by defendants brought before them charged with crimes. As guardians of the public welfare, our state and federal judicial systems strive to administer equal justice to the rich and the poor, the good and the bad, the native and foreign born of every race, nationality and religion. . . .
> But, if our courts are to remain what the Founders intended, the citadels of justice, their proceedings cannot and must not be infected with the sort of scurrilous, abusive language and conduct paraded before the Illinois trial judge in this case.

Our heritage, said the Court, cannot endure if the vital issues in individual cases cannot be resolved in the courts, for if their resolution cannot be reached there, "it will be reached elsewhere and by other means, and there will be grave danger that liberty, equality, and the order essential to both will be lost." [53]

On November 21, 1972, almost three years after the trial, the United States Court of Appeals for the Seventh Circuit reversed the five convictions in the Chicago Seven case. The court held that the "antagonistic" courtroom demeanor of Judge Hoffman and of the prosecutors would require reversal if other errors did not. The court, however, by a 2–1 vote upheld the constitutionality of the anti-riot statute, which has come to be known as the "Rap Brown Act." Judge Wilbur Pell in his dissent argued that the statute infringed First Amendment freedoms and was unconstitutional also because of vagueness. Following the decision the government announced that it would not appeal the reversal of the five convictions.

In 1973 the contempt convictions were reversed, with instructions from the Court of Appeals that the charges be

[53] *Illinois* v. *Allen,* 397 U.S. 337 (1970).

brought before a judge other than Hoffman. At the new trial, the original 160 charges were reduced to 52 specifications, and the defendants were convicted on 13 of them, all misdemeanors. An appeal to the United States Court of Appeals for the Seventh Circuit is pending.

The 1960s opened with a body-blow to literary censorship. There was poetic justice in the way this was accomplished, for the new freedom to read was ushered in with the publication of D. H. Lawrence's *Lady Chatterley's Lover,* which had aroused the ire of book-burners for years.

The ground for this development had been prepared in the 1957 decision of the Supreme Court in *Roth* v. *United States.* In that decision the Court held that though obscenity is not within the area of constitutionally protected speech or press, it is vital that the standards for judging obscenity shall "safeguard the protection of freedom of speech and press for material which does not treat sex in a manner appealing to prurient interest." Accordingly, the Court rejected the traditional (so-called Hicklin) test as unconstitutionally restrictive insofar as it permitted judgment on the basis of the effect of isolated passages on the most susceptible reader. The new test laid down by the Court called for judging a book or other publication as a whole, and only its effect on the average or normal person could be considered. The Court further held that sex and obscenity are by no means synonymous. Obscene material, said the Court, "is material which deals with sex in a manner appealing to prurient interest." The portrayal of sex "in art, literature, and scientific works," the Court added, "is not itself sufficient reason to deny material the constitutional protection of freedom of speech and press."

Roth and several other cases decided in the late 1950s, however, involved no important book against which the new standards could be tested. It was fitting that the first significant test should be presented by D. H. Lawrence's famous novel. No major author of the twentieth century had suffered more from puritanical and sadistic literary censorship than had Lawrence. On March 25, 1960, the U.S. Court of Appeals for the District of Columbia unanimously upheld the decision of a federal district court which had issued an injunction restraining Postmaster General Arthur E. Summerfield from barring copies of the book, published by Grove Press, from the mails.[54] The postmaster general, on the advice of the Department of Justice, did not appeal the decision to the Supreme Court. A few months after the postmaster general's decision, Penguin published the book in England—some 200,000 copies. Attacked as obscene, the book won an acquittal from a jury sitting at Old Bailey. The effects of these decisions have been immeasurable.

In 1961 Grove Press published Henry Miller's *Tropic of Cancer,* a favorite target of "anti-smut" crusaders. The Post Office Department banned the book but, on the advice of the Department of Justice, withdrew the ban after a few days. The Customs Bureau confiscated a copy of the book brought in by a traveler, but in August, 1961, acting on the advice of the Department of Justice, the Bureau lifted its prohibition on this book as well as on two other books by Miller. Thus, with relatively little fuss, all federal restraints on *Tropic of Cancer* collapsed.

Several months later Grove published a paperback edition of the book at ninety-five cents, and by early 1962 some 2,500,000 copies were in print. Since the federal authorities would take no action against the book, local communities moved in to fill the prosecution vacuum; by mid-June the publisher was involved in over sixty cases. The result, as could have been expected, was hopeless confusion. In 1962 the Supreme Judicial Court of Massachusetts, in a 4–3 decision, held that the book was not obscene and was entitled to protection under the First Amendment. In 1963 the Supreme Court of California unanimously reached the same conclusion. But a week later the New York Court of Appeals, the state's highest court, decided by a 4–3 vote that the book was obscene under that state's obscenity statute.[55] In June, 1964, the United

[54] *Grove Press* v. *Christenberry,* 276 F. 2d 433 (1960). See for the Roth case and generally on this topic Konvitz, *Expanding Liberties,* chap. 5.

[55] See Konvitz, *Expanding Liberties,* pp. 214–216.

States Supreme Court ended the confusion by reversing in a 5–4 decision a Florida ban on the book.[56]

The last of the trilogy of books, the treatment of which symbolized traditional censorship, was *Fanny Hill, or Memoirs of a Woman of Pleasure,* by John Cleland. First published in London in 1748–49, the book had moved in the literary underground for over two centuries. In 1963 G. P. Putnam's Sons published it and at once faced trouble from the Corporation Counsel of the City of New York. In July, 1964, the New York Court of Appeals, by a 4–3 vote, set aside a lower court's injunction against Putnam. The majority referred to the decision of the Supreme Court in favor of *Tropic of Cancer* only a fortnight before. The eighteenth-century novel, said the Court of Appeals, "does not warrant suppression"; and it is unlikely that the book will have "any adverse effect on the sophisticated values of our century." [57]

These legal victories on behalf of *Lady Chatterley's Lover, Tropic of Cancer,* and *Fanny Hill* are regarded as great gains for both literature and freedom. But their free publication and sale generated the production of and brought into the open marketplace a great mass of "underground" pornography, publications which could make no claim to literary merit. Newsstands displayed openly books and periodicals with lurid covers that appealed exclusively to a wide variety of sex interests. Shops that made a specialty of such wares developed in San Francisco, New York, and other cities.

The freer attitude toward sex and literature carried over into motion pictures. A series of Supreme Court decisions went far to loosen the hold of censorship on the showing of movies. In 1959 the Court set aside the ban by the State of New York on a film based on *Lady Chatterley's Lover.*[58] In 1965, in *Freedman* v. *Maryland,*[59] the Court, in a unanimous decision, held that, to meet the constitutional test, a system of movie censorship must contain certain defined procedural safeguards,

---

[56] *Grove Press* v. *Gerstein,* 372 U.S. 577 (1964).
[57] *Larkin* v. *G. P. Putnam's Sons,* 252 N.Y.S. 2d 71 (1964).
[58] *Kingsley International Pictures* v. *Regents,* 360 U.S. 684 (1959).
[59] *Freedom* v. *Maryland,* 380 U.S. 51 (1965).

as follows: (1) the censoring agency, rather than the exhibitor, must have the burden of instituting a judicial proceeding; (2) any restraint prior to the judicial proceeding can be only for a brief period to preserve the status quo; and (3) there must be assurance of judicial review. The broad grounds of this and other decisions made prior restraint or subsequent punishment almost impossible. While at one time there were some ninety local censorship boards, by 1970 official censorship was found primarily in Maryland and in the city of Chicago.

In the 1920s, as a response to public indignation over sensational films and the unconventional lives of movie stars, the Motion Picture Association of America, Inc., formulated its own Production Code, in order to head off stringent legal censorship. The Code placed taboos on certain subjects and severely restricted treatment of others. In 1956 the Code was relaxed in certain respects, and in 1968 a system of so-called voluntary ratings or classification was substituted for prohibitions. As revised in 1970, the system called for the following ratings: "GP" for films suitable for general attendance, though with some parental discretion advised; "R" for restricted films, to which persons under seventeen would not be admitted unless accompanied by parent or guardian; and "X," for films not open to persons under eighteen at all.

Every machine, as Justice Oliver Wendell Holmes once remarked, has its frictions, and there was no reason to assume that a movie-classification system, operated by the movie industry itself as a form of self-regulation, would be free of mistakes or would not lead to abuses.

After some time, dissatisfaction was expressed with the ratings. One parental and moralist complaint was that movies rated "GP" should have been given an "R" or even an "X" classification—parents said that their children were exposed to sadistic violence, flagrant sex, dirty words, and other unsavory features, with a kind of public seal of approval. Another complaint was that some theaters had begun to specialize in movies rated "X," so that some movies were made especially for these theaters and their clientele. The "X" rating came, therefore, not as a by-product, but as the pattern to which the movie was fitted. Creative people within the film industry—writers, producers and directors—backed by civil libertarians also criticized the Code as an inhibition on personal expression.

The changes wrought by the Supreme Court in removing the shackles of literary and film censorship did not go unchallenged. Indeed, the 1960s was marked by considerable public concern, and even indignation, over what appeared to many to be a gross debasement of public taste and morals. Much of the indignation was directed at the Warren Court for allegedly opening the floodgates to "dirty" books, pictures, and movies.

That the Supreme Court itself was aware of the explosive nature of the issues can be inferred from the fact that on the same day that it decided in favor of *Fanny Hill,* it upheld the conviction of Ralph Ginzburg for sending through the mails four issues of *Eros* magazine and two other sexually-oriented publications, and the conviction of Edward Mishkin for procuring and publishing fifty books with assorted titles that empasized deviant sexual practices.[60] On the one hand, said the Court, a book cannot be proscribed "unless it is found to be *utterly* without redeeming social value." This is so even though the book has prurient appeal and is "patently offensive." But the Court held up another side of the coin: a court may consider the way a book is advertised. If the advertising shows that the book is commercially exploited for the sake of its prurient appeal, to the exclusion of other values, then it can be banned. The Supreme Court found that Ginzburg's advertisements were a deliberate representation of the publications as "erotically arousing."

Since there were fourteen opinions in the three cases decided on the same day, one can see how complex were the questions and the judicial attempts to answer them.

In 1968 the Court, by a 6–3 vote, made another concession to censorship. A New York statute prohibited the sale of obscene materials to minors under seventeen years of age. The operator of a small stationery store-luncheonette was convicted of selling some "girlie" magazines to a sixteen-year-old boy, publications which admittedly would not have been obscene

[60] *Ginzburg* v. *U.S.*, 383 U.S. 463 (1966). *Mishkin* v. *N.Y.*, 383 U.S. 572 (1966).

for adults. The Supreme Court upheld the conviction, holding that the statute did not invade the constitutional liberties of minors.[61]

In the many opinions written by the Supreme Court Justices in the 1960 censorship cases, some differences among them kept recurring. The more important ones were these:

1. Justices Black and Douglas were against any form of censorship. They took the position that the First Amendment leaves no power to suppress, control, or punish the publication or distribution of any publication, writings, or pictures on the ground that they are "obscene."

2. Justice Stewart thought that the First Amendment still left power to control or punish the distribution or publication of "hard-core pornography." He admitted, however, that he probably could not define the term, but added: "But I know it when I see it. . . ."[62]

3. Justice Harlan contended that in federal cases, there must be a federal standard, under the First Amendment; but for state cases, the Court should allow the states and the state courts greater latitude in determining what may be banned as obscene.

4. Chief Justice Warren and Justice Tom Clark contended that in all cases, federal or state, the "community standards" by which obscenity may be tested should be those of the various states in which the federal or state cases arose rather than a single national standard. The role of the Supreme Court would then be to review the record to see whether there was "sufficient evidence" to sustain the finding of the federal or state trial court. In Justice Warren's words: "This is the only reasonable way I can see to obviate the need of this Court's sitting as the Super Censor of all obscenity purveyed throughout the nation."[63]

5. All the members of the Court, except Justices Black, Douglas, and Stewart, as noted above, held that a state may not interfere with the publication or distribution of literary

61 *Ginsberg* v. *N.Y.*, 390 U.S. 629 (1968).

62 *Jacobellis* v. *Ohio*, 378 U.S. 184 (1964).

63 Chief Justice Warren's dissenting opinion in *Jacobellis* v. *Ohio* (see note 62, above).

material that may be described as "obscene" unless these three elements coalesce:

a. the dominant theme of the material taken as a whole appeals to prurient interest in sex;

b. the material is patently offensive because it affronts contemporary community standards relating to the description or representation of sexual matters; and

c. the material is *utterly* without redeeming social value.[64]

Justice White, however, would not view the social value of the publication as an independent factor in the judgment of obscenity.[65]

6. Except for Justices Black and Douglas, all the members of the Court agreed that the First Amendment leaves some room for restricting obscenity for minors.

Notwithstanding all these considerations, the Supreme Court in the 1960s did sit as a supreme board of censors, and it was not uncommon to hear snide remarks about the "Nine Old Men" viewing dirty movies or poring over dirty books and pictures. This did not improve the image of the Court. There were many open attacks on the Court and its function and rulings in obscenity cases. So infuriated were certain segments of the public and government leaders that congressional and state legislative hearings were held on how to control obscenity—and, in all seriousness, how to control the Supreme Court.

In response to these pressures, Congress established in 1967 a Commission on Obscenity and Pornography. The statute setting up the Commission stated that Congress found the traffic in obscenity and pornography to be "a matter of national concern." The federal government was said to have "responsibility to investigate the gravity of this situation and to determine whether such materials are harmful to the public, and particularly to minors, and whether more effective methods should be devised to control the transmission of such materials." To achieve this end, the advisory Commission's

[64] *A Book Named "John Cleland's Memoirs of a Woman of Pleasure"* v. *Attorney General,* 383 U.S. 413 (1966).

[65] Justice White's dissenting opinion in *Jacobellis* v. *Ohio* (see note 62, above).

purpose was to make a thorough study "which shall include a study of the causal relationship of such materials to antisocial behavior, to recommend advisable, appropriate, effective, and constitutional means to deal effectively with such traffic in obscenity and pornography." In January, 1968, President Johnson appointed the eighteen members of the Commission, with William B. Lockhart, dean of the University of Minnesota Law School, as chairman. In September, 1970, after close to two years of careful and exhaustive study, the Commission submitted its report, with six members dissenting.[66] As soon as its contents became known, the report itself became a storm center of controversy.

And no wonder. For the report recommended the repeal of all laws that impose sanctions on the use of obscene materials by adults. It also recommended repeal of the new laws that charted out an area of restrictions with respect to exposure of minors to obscene materials. The Commission, however, recommended that availability of certain pictorial materials may be prohibited to minors, and, moreover, that legislation may bar display of such pictorial matter for sale in a manner which permits children to see materials which cannot be sold to them.

To the credit of the Commission majority, its recommendations met head-on the central argument in this emotionally charged area: did the viewing of obscene materials really produce such social evils that infringement of First Amendment guarantees was warranted? The Commission concluded that it did not, saying that it "does not believe that a sufficient social justification exists for the retention or enactment of broad legislation prohibiting the consensual distribution of sexual materials to adults."

As soon as these recommendations became known, and even before the public had a chance to see the report and judge it on its merits, the Senate, by vote of 60–5, in October, 1970, passed a resolution which repudiated the majority report on two grounds: that the findings and recommendations were not supported by the evidence, and that the Commission had not complied with the mandate of Congress. And President Nixon

[66] The report was published by the U.S. Government Printing Office in 1970 and by Bantam Books in the same year.

joined the chorus of objectors in a sharply worded statement on October 24, 1970:

> I have evaluated that report and categorically reject its morally bankrupt conclusions and major recommendations.
>
> So long as I am in the White House, there will be no relaxation of the effort to control and eliminate smut from our national life. . . .
>
> American morality is not to be trifled with. The Commission on Obscenity and Pornography has performed a disservice and I totally reject its report.[67]

The Commission report was treated scornfully not only because of its recommendations but also because it had supported experiments to determine, if possible, the effects of obscene materials on adults. For years the core question for civil libertarians in the battle over obscenity was whether the freedom to read and see should be restricted in the absence of proof that obscenity produced anti-social consequences. Many Americans disagreed that this was an open issue. They supported a dissenting Commission member's rhetorical question: "Why was it necessary to conduct dozens of experiments and interviews at taxpayer expense to demonstrate the obvious —that human beings are aroused by erotic materials?" [68] But this kind of remark contributed only to the confusion and obfuscation, for the emphasis in the search for empirical data was on *anti-social* effects of exposure to obscene materials. What the Commission report stated was this: "Analyses of the United States crime rates do not support the thesis of a causal connection between the availability of erotica and sex crimes among either juveniles or adults. Because of limitations in both the data and inferences which can validly be drawn from them, the data cannot, however, be said absolutely to disprove such a connection.[69] From the attacks on the report by President Nixon, some senators, and some dissenting members

[67] *New York Times*, October 25, 1970, p. 71.

[68] Charles H. Keating, Jr., "The Report that Shook the Nation," *Reader's Digest*, January, 1971, p. 38.

[69] *Commission on Obscenity and Pornography, Report* (New York, 1970), p. 286.

of the Commission, one would hardly suspect that the report was written in such cautious terms. They closed their eyes to the careful wording of the Commission's conclusion:

> Research to date thus provides no substantial basis for the belief that erotic materials constitute a primary or significant cause of the development of character deficits or that they operate as a significant determinative factor in causing crime and delinquency.

This conclusion is stated with due and perhaps excessive caution, since it is obviously not possible, and never would be possible, to state that never on any occasion, under any circumstances, did any erotic material ever contribute in any way to the likelihood of any indiviual committing a sex crime. Indeed, no such statement could be made about any kind of non-erotic material. On the basis of the available data, however, it is not possible to conclude that erotic material is a significant cause of sex crime.[70]

It is true that the Commission did consider studies of the effects of erotica on sexual arousal, emotions, and attitudes, quite apart from the relation of erotica to delinquency and crime, and perhaps the Commission would have been wise to have avoided getting into this thicket. But within the context of the total report, the consideration of these studies made a positive contribution toward a broader understanding of the more specific data on the relation of erotica to crime,[71] and they certainly were germane to the task that Congress set before the Commission.

From the point of view of constitutional law, the Commission report should have strong relevance, for it bears on the question whether obscene publications create a clear and present danger to an important interest that the state has a right to protect. While the Supreme Court has expressly held that obscenity is not within the guarantee of the First Amendment, and while only Justices Black and Douglas dissented from this position, the *fact* is that obscenity is constitutionally protected. In the 1960s the Court gave obscenity ample "breath-

70 *Ibid.*, pp. 286–287.
71 *Ibid.*, pp. 197 ff.

ing space"; the Court acted *as if* obscenity is in fact protected by the First Amendment.[72] In the light, then, of this consideration, the question of the clear and present danger ascribable to obscenity as a cause assumes prime importance.

The pressures for federal legislation to deal with obscenity were intense in the 1960s, as may be measured by the fact that some two hundred bills were introduced. In 1967 Congress passed an act dealing with unwanted "pandering advertisements" of erotic materials sent through the mails. The act made it possible for an addressee to request the Post Office to instruct the advertiser to strike from the list the complaining individual's name. The addressee himself decides what is obscene and unwanted. By the end of 1969, over 300,000 persons had obtained orders striking their names from such lists. The ACLU objected that the law now made each citizen in the country a censor, even covering such materials of social value as birth control bulletins, sex manuals from respected medical sources, and even general ACLU publications which the addressee could claim were erotica! In 1970, in the *Rowan* case, the Supreme Court unanimously upheld the act as constitutional. It interpreted the act as giving no censorship power to the Post Office; its only power—and duty—was to fulfill the wishes of the addressee to have his or her name stricken from the mailing list. The decision of the addressee was not to be questioned.

Another law, enacted in 1970, goes one step beyond the 1967 law. It allows a person to direct the Post Office to stop any mailer from sending "sex-oriented" advertisements even if the individual has not received any. The Post Office is required to maintain a list of all persons making such requests, and for a fee, must make available a copy of the list to any mail-order business firm. The fee charged by the Post Office is by no means a nominal one. Two key cases challenging the 1970 law were heard by three-judge federal courts in New York and California. The New York decision upheld the constitutionality of the 1970 law, but mandated certain technical changes in mailings of such advertisements that mitigated the law's harm. The Post Office adopted these changes in its regulations. The

[72] See Konvitz, *Expanding Liberties,* p. 239.

California case resulted in a temporary restraining order against the Post Office. Neither case has been appealed to the Supreme Court. If a case does reach the Supreme Court, in all likelihood the Court will see the 1970 law as an extension of the 1967 act: enhancing the citizen's freedom of choice without enlarging the power of the Post Office.

As the outbursts against the Commission report, the congressional legislation, and other events indicate, the American people were not likely to let empirical and other objective studies and constitutional debate settle the emotional, psychological, moral, and religious feelings that the obscenity issue generates. Open prostitution, increased venereal disease, openly avowed homosexuality and lesbianism, group sexuality, some radical expressions of women's liberation, the easy availability of contraceptives, the large number of legal abortions, the near-nudity in women's dress, the new permissiveness among high school and college students in sexual relations—all these and other developments will continue to be seen as *direct effects* of erotica, and therefore consequences of the Warren Court decisions, and of ACLU positions and work over the past half-century. Yet any such simplistic answer falsifies our view of reality. In our complex society today, it is doubtful if it is any longer possible to single out one factor as alone the villain in the drama.[73] Besides, there always remains Thoreau's reminder that we are double-edged blades, for every time we sharpen the virtuous or evil side of the moral razor, the return stroke strops the opposite side.[74]

The vicious attacks on the "Warren Court" (the term was used pejoratively), which became a staple item in the arsenal of right-wing and conservative rhetoric, were heightened as a result of several decisions in the decade upholding the principle of separation of church and state. The swirl of controversy began on June 25, 1962, when the American people

[73] See Konvitz, *Expanding Liberties*, p. 172.

[74] In a series of cases decided by the Supreme Court in 1973, the position that had been advocated by Justices Warren, Clark, and Harlan, as summarized on pages 260–61, was adopted by a 5–4 vote, with Justice White agreeing with the four Nixon appointees.

learned that the Supreme Court had ruled by a 6–1 vote that the official prayer used in many schools in New York State was unconstitutional. Justice Stewart was the lone dissenter.[75]

In his opinion for the Court, Justice Black held that recital of the prayer was in fact a religious activity, and therefore an unconstitutional violation of the "no establishment of religion" clause of the First Amendment. The fact that non-observing pupils might be excused did not save the constitutionality of the practice, since the prayer was found to be an "establishment" of religion in the constitutional sense.

The prayer that had been approved by the Board of Regents of the State of New York was as follows: "Almighty God, we acknowledge our dependence upon Thee, and we beg Thy blessings upon us, our parents, our teachers, and our country." The school boards argued that since the prayer was "non-denominational," it was not an "establishment" of any one religion, and therefore constitutional. But the Court saw through this sophistry. The prayer expressed certain religious beliefs, and these beliefs when expressed in the prayer in the public schools constituted a state "establishment" of them.

That a great deal depended on the outcome of the case was manifested by the fact that twenty states had filed friends of the court briefs urging the constitutionality of the prayer. The ACLU and leading Jewish organizations led the forces opposing the prayer. As soon as the Court's decision was announced, the floodgates of vituperation opened. Congressman George Andrews of Alabama said, "They put the Negroes in the schools and they've driven God out." Cardinal Spellman spoke for many churchmen and church groups when he said: "I am shocked and frightened that the Supreme Court has declared unconstitutional a simple and voluntary declaration of belief in God by public school children. The decision strikes at the very heart of the Godly tradition in which America's children have for so long been raised." [76] The National Association of Evangelicals called for a constitutional

[75] *Engel* v. *Vitale*, 370 U.S. 421 (1962). Justices Frankfurter and White did not participate.

[76] *New York Times*, June 26, 1962, p. 17.

amendment to allow prayers in the schools, and at once the Senate had before it many versions of such an amendment. However, strong opposition was mounted. In November, 1962, all efforts to override the decision and to open the public schools to religious exercises were condemned in a forceful statement submitted to the Senate Judiciary Committee by 132 deans and professors of law and political science.

In the following year the Supreme Court again invited abuse and attacks when it ruled that use of the Lord's Prayer or the devotional reading of the Bible in public schools was unconstitutional.[77] The decision was 8–1, with Justice Stewart again the lone dissenter. In his opinion for the Court, Justice Clark stressed the constitutional principle of neutrality in church-state matters:

> The place of religion in our society is an exalted one, achieved through a long tradition of reliance on the home, the church, and the inviolable citadel of the individual heart and mind. We have come to recognize through bitter experience that it is not within the power of government to invade that citadel, whether its purpose or effect be to aid or oppose, to advance or retard. In the relationship between man and religion, the State is firmly committed to a position of neutrality.

While Roman Catholic churchmen reacted with alarm, the National Council of Churches and Jewish groups hailed the decision.[78] As between Roman Catholics and Protestants, this meant a reversal of traditional roles; historically the public school had been the captive of the Protestants, and Catholics had always objected to the infiltration of Protestant Christianity into the public schools.

But after the passage of some months, Catholic church groups also seemed to temper their opposition to the Court's 1962–63 decisions. By the spring of 1964, 147 resolutions had been introduced in the House of Representatives calling for a

[77] *Abington School District* v. *Schempp and Murray* v. *Curlett*, 374 U.S. 203 (1963).

[78] *New York Times*, June 18, 1963, p. 1. See also Konvitz, *Expanding Liberties*, pp. 44–45.

constitutional amendment to overrule these decisions. The House Judiciary Committee held hearings for seven weeks but could not agree, and laid the matter aside. Educators, legal scholars, and scores of organizations testified for and against the proposal. Leading Protestant groups appeared to oppose the resolutions. However, the Roman Catholic Church took no position, and after the hearings the legal department of the National Catholic Welfare Conference and the Catholic Press Association came out publicly against tampering with the First Amendment.[79]

Before the Supreme Court decisions, thirty-seven states and the District of Columbia permitted religious exercises in their public schools; twelve of these expressly allowed and thirteen of them required Bible reading. It was estimated that a majority of the nation's schools conducted Bible reading. The Court's rulings did not end the practices everywhere. Immediately after the 1963 decisions, the state superintendent of education in South Carolina stated that religious exercises would continue in his state's public schools, and open or covert defiance was by no means uncommon. It was ironic and tragic that schools which claim to inculcate American ideals and values, including respect for the Constitution and the rule of law, should resort to practices that could only teach children to have a cynical regard for fundamental laws and principles.

This cynical flouting of the Supreme Court's rulings also went on unabated over the years in the Congress. The 1964 stalemate over a constitutional amendment to permit prayers in the public schools did not end the matter. The battle was rejoined in August, 1971. When Congress adjourned for its summer recess, there were 191 signatures on a petition to take the amendment away from the House Judiciary Committee where it had been bottled up and send it to the House floor. Only 28 more signatures were needed to accomplish this. The necessary signatures were obtained and on November 8 the House voted down the amendment after intense debate. But the vote was 240 for the constitutional amendment and 162 against—only 28 votes short of the required two-thirds majority. A national effort featuring the leaders of more than

[79] Konvitz, *Expanding Liberties*, p. 45.

thirty-eight leading religious denominations and organizations which spoke out against the proposed amendment was necessary to kill the proposal. Presumably the pro-prayer forces will continue the battle, so this item, too, will remain unfinished business on the agenda not only of Congress, but also of the American people.

Although the question of religious exercises in the public schools was settled as a constitutional matter, legislators and courts faced a new church-state challenge, the question of aid for parochial schools. Since 1947, when the Supreme Court upheld as constitutional the use of public funds to reimburse parents for the transportation of their children by bus to and from parochial schools,[80] primarily Catholics tried to find ways to extend the principle of this decision to other aspects of parochial schools. In the 1960s they acutely felt the need for such financial aid. At the end of the decade there were over eleven thousand Catholic educational institutions, with well over four million students. Costs were rising, and parents found it difficult to pay tuition fees. As a result, there were some two thousand fewer schools than there had been in 1965, with about 1,200,000 fewer students.

There were fewer religious teachers for the schools, which were forced to employ many lay teachers who had to be paid salaries that were far in excess of those paid to teachers who belonged to religious orders. Building and maintenance costs were constantly rising. In some places, Catholic spokesmen warned that unless government aid was given, all parochial schools would have to close. Non-Catholics became concerned as they had never been before, for in some states as many as one-fifth of all elementary and secondary school pupils attended parochial schools. Nationally, the figure was one-tenth. In some cities the figure was staggeringly high; in Philadelphia, for example, one-third of the schoolchildren attended parochial schools.

Pressures grew to erase the strict constitutional line drawn against government help to religious schools, a strong barrier to government-funded programs of aid to education. The breakthrough came with the theory which argued that the government benefit was going to the child rather than the school.

[80] *Everson v. Board of Education,* 330 U.S. 1 (1947).

On this basis, for example, the state could pay the cost of textbooks used in non-religious courses in parochial schools. This was done in New York by a statute that went into effect in 1966. In that state, close to one million pupils, or about one-fifth of all schoolchildren, attended parochial schools. The statute required local school boards to purchase tetxbooks and lend them without charge to all schoolchildren, without regard to whether they attended public or parochial schools. Only secular books, not religious books, could be loaned; no funds or books were given directly to the parochial schools.

In 1968 the Supreme Court upheld the act as constitutional under the religion clauses of the First Amendment.[81] Justices Black, Douglas, and Fortas dissented. The Court's opinion by Justice White said that since attendance at an accredited parochial or private school satisfies the state's interest in the education of its children, the state has a proper interest in the manner in which those schools performed their secular educational function. "The law," said the Court, "merely makes available to all children the benefits of a general program to lend schoolbooks free of charge." The general public acceptance of the parochial school, said the Court, showed that they were performing, "in addition to their religious function, the task of secular education."

This decision in the *Allen* case was naturally taken as a green light for state legislation that would extend further financial aid. But such steps to broaden the Court's ruling were of no avail. In 1971 the Supreme Court struck down a Rhode Island law under which 250 parochial school teachers were paid up to 15 percent of their salaries for teaching secular subjects, and also a Pennsylvania act which earmarked $20 million a year for parochial school teachers of secular subjects.[82] Though the statutes, said Chief Justice Warren Burger,

[81] *Board of Education* v. *Allen*, 392 U.S. 236 (1968).

[82] *Lemon* v. *Kurtzman, Earley* v. *DiCenso, Robinson* v. *DiCenso*, 91 S. Ct. (1971). In *Tilton* v. *Richardson*, 91 S. Ct. 2091 (1971), decided the same day, the Court upheld as constitutional the Higher Education Facilities Act of 1963, under which construction grants were made to church-related colleges and universities. The vote was 5–4. Two days after these decisions, the Court affirmed the decision of a three-judge federal district court which invalidated a Connecticut statute similar to the Pennsylvania law (*Sanders* v. *Johnson*, 91 S. Ct. 2292 [1971]).

intended to promote secular state obejctives, both involved excessive entanglement of state with church, and therefore violated the religion clauses of the First Amendment. (These decisions were especially notable for the fact that they spoke for eight justices of the Court, including the two Nixon appointees, Chief Justice Burger and Justice Blackmun. In the 1968 and 1972 presidential campaigns, Nixon went on record as favoring "parochaid.")

The decisions in the school prayer and "parochaid" cases by no means terminated the agitation in which they had their origin. The plight of the parochial school has continued, and with rising costs the economic pressures on these schools are likely to become aggravated. Legislatures have been and will be pressured to resort to all sorts of devices to circumvent, if possible, the Supreme Court decisions. Thus in September, 1971, Pennsylvania passed a bill providing $75 for each elementary school pupil and $150 for each high school child attending parochial schools. Again the theory was "child benefit." But in April, 1972, a three-judge federal court held the act unconstitutional, for the *effect* of the grants was to support religion. So, too, in April, 1972, another such court held that Ohio's parent-reimbursement plan was unconstitutional. In October, 1972, the Supreme Court, by an 8–1 vote, affirmed the decision in the Ohio case without an opinion, thus closing off to legislatures the plan of making direct tuition grants to parents.

Other state ventures were similarly rebuked. In May, 1972, Governor Nelson Rockefeller signed a New York law which provided tuition assistance payments and income tax credits to families with incomes of over $5,000 who paid tuition for their children to attend a non-public school. The tax credit idea received the endorsement of both President Nixon and Senator George McGovern when they campaigned in 1972. In October, 1972, a three-judge federal court held unconstitutional the part of the New York law that provided for tuition grants to parents of non-public school pupils. It also reaffirmed a previously imposed ban on state payments to non-public schools for maintenance and repairs. But the court called for further review of income tax benefits. However, the question of the constitutionality of New York's method of providing "paroch-aid" was settled by the Supreme Court in June, 1973. After upholding the lower court's ruling on tuition grants and payments for maintenance and repairs, the Supreme Court held that the tax benefits also infringed the separation principle. Like the tuition grants, tax benefits "represent a charge made upon the state for the purpose of religious education," the Court said.

The 1960s also saw a constitutional challenge to the Sunday closing laws which prohibit commercial business from being transacted. These laws could easily be traced back to the colonial "Lord's day" laws, and their religious origin could hardly be denied. Almost the only ones who suffered from the laws were Jews, Seventh Day Adventists ,and Seventh Day Baptists, who observed their Sabbath on Saturday. However, the rise of suburban shopping centers and discount houses, which wanted to take advantage of the desire of many people to spend part of Sunday shopping, touched off a drive to abolish the Sunday closing laws. Lined up against these interests were city merchants, some labor unions, and church groups, especially those associated with the Lord's Day Alliance.

In time four cases worked their way up to the Supreme Court. These involved attacks on the Pennsylvania and Maryland statutes by a highway discount house, and opposition to the Pennsylvania and Massachusetts laws by Jewish merchants who kept their places of business closed on Saturdays for religious reasons. In 1961 the Court upheld the constitutionality of the laws,[83] but it took eight opinions and about fifty thousand words to explain the decisions. On the basic issue of constitutionality, only Justice Douglas dissented. As to whether the laws, by failing to exempt merchants who observed Saturday as their day of religious rest, violated the free exercise of religion clause of the First Amendment, Justices Douglas, Brennan, and Stewart dissented.

[83] *McGowan* v. *Maryland,* 366 U.S. 420 (1961); *Gallagher* v. *Crown Kosher Super Market,* 366 U.S. 617 (1961); *Two Guys from Harrison* v. *McGinley,* 366 U.S. 582 (1961); *Braunfeld* v. *Brown,* 366 U.S. 599 (1961).

The Court held that, even though it was clear that originally the Sunday laws were intended to aid the Christian religion, "as presently written and administered, most of them . . . are of a secular rather than a religious character." Their secular purpose is to provide a single, uniform day of rest. Therefore, these laws do not violate the establishment clause. As to the claims of those who observed Saturday as their day of rest and were thus compelled to observe two days of rest, while the Court recognized the economic burden the laws imposed on them, it rejected the claim that this unintended and indirect effect violated the free exercise clause.

While these decisions seem to have put a quietus on the constitutional issues, they actually accelerated two developments that had been started long before the Court acted in 1961: (1) a widespread disregard or liberalization of the Sunday closing laws as more stores, in and outside of cities, stay open on Sunday, often catering specially to the Sunday trade; and (2) some—though far from sufficient—liberalization of laws as they affect merchants whose day of rest is Saturday. And in cases under Sunday closing laws which did not involve places of business, the Supreme Court has upheld the claims of seventh-day observers under the free exercise clause.[84]

As the economic plight of urban areas grew in the 1960s, marked by the desperate need of cities for more and more money, the problem of tax-exemption of churches for property used for religious purposes took on special significance. The Supreme Court evaded this sticky issue during the decade, but finally in 1970, by a 7–1 vote, it upheld the constitutionality of such exemption authorized by state law.[85] In an opinion by Chief Justice Burger, the Court held that since the exemptions were granted to all houses of religious worship, and such houses of worship were included within a broad class of property owned by non-profit organizations—hospitals, libraries, professional and historical organizations—it was apparent that the legislative purpose was not aimed at establishing, sponsoring, or supporting religion. The Court also held that the exemptions created only a minimal and remote

[84] *Sherbert* v. *Verner*, 374 U.S. 398 (1963).
[85] *Walz* v. *Tax Commission*, 397 U.S. 664 (1970).

involvement between church and state, and that this was far less than would be the case if the state did tax church property. Only Justice Douglas dissented from the decision, citing the figure of $141 billion as the total assets of churches, and stating that their annual income is at least $22 billion. It has been estimated that the total value of the real estate owned by churches comes to $80 billion, and that if this property were not exempt, it would yield $2.2 billion per year in taxes.

But the American people are not alarmed by such allegations. There may be some murmurings here and there, but the contrast between the temper of the times and that of the years of Henry VIII as he openly confiscated, appropriated, and distributed the large property holdings and other assets of the churches is, indeed, very sharp. Americans probably accept the view expressed by Justice Brennan in his concurring opinion in the tax-exemption case:

> Government grants exemption to religious organizations because they uniquely contribute to the pluralism of American society by their religious activities. Government may properly include religious institutions among the variety of private, nonprofit groups that receive tax exemptions, for each group contributes to the diversity of association, viewpoint, and enterprise essential to a vigorous, pluralistic society. . . . [The tax exemptions] merely facilitate the existence of a broad range of private, nonprofit organizations, among them religious groups, by leaving each free to come into existence, then to flourish or wither, without being burdened by real property taxes.

The war in Vietnam provoked some serious questions as to the "neutrality" of the religion clauses as applied to institutional religion and to unattached conscience. Comment on the cases that revolved around this distinction must first start with the highly important case of *Torcaso* v. *Watkins*,[86] decided by the Supreme Court in 1961. The case made no great noise, but the Court's decision became, in unforeseen ways, the cornerstone of rulings in later cases involving conscientious objection to war.

[86] *Torcaso* v. *Watkins*, 367 U.S. 488 (1961).

The Maryland constitution, as construed by the state's highest court, required a declaration of a belief in God as a qualification for public office. Torcaso, appointed as a notary public by the governor, was refused a commission to serve when he stated that he would not declare a belief in God. The United States Supreme Court unanimously upheld Torcaso's constitutional right to his commission. The state's requirement of a declaration of a belief in God, said Justice Black, invaded Torcaso's freedom of religion. Neither the federal nor any state government can pass laws or impose requirements "which aid all religions as against non-believers, and neither can aid those religions based on a belief in the existence of God as against those religions founded on different beliefs." At this point Justice Black said in a footnote: "Among religions in this country which do not teach what would generally be considered a belief in the existence of God are Buddhism, Taoism, Ethical Culture, Secular Humanism, and others."

Four years later the Supreme Court applied the spirit of the *Torcaso* case to conscientious objectors. The draft law exempted from combatant training and service in the armed forces persons who, by reason of their "religious training and belief," were conscientiously opposed to participation in war in any form. The act defined the term "religious training and belief" as "an individual's belief in a relation to a Supreme Being involving duties superior to those arising from any human relation, but [not including] essentially political, sociological, or philosophical views or a merely personal moral code." In the 1965 *Seeger* case,[87] the Supreme Court unanimously held that Congress, when it used the expression "Supreme Being" rather than the designation "God," was clarifying the meaning of "religious training and belief" "so as to embrace all religions. . . . " Then the Court, in the opinion by Justice Clark, went on to say: "We believe that under this construction, the test of belief 'in a relation to a Supreme Being' is whether a given belief that is sincere and meaningful occupies a place in the life of its possessor parallel to that filled by the orthodox belief in God. . . . Where such beliefs have parallel positions in the lives of their respective

[87] *U.S.* v. *Seeger*, 380 U.S. 163 (1965).

holders we cannot say that one is 'in a relation to a Supreme Being' and that the other is not."

In order to save the constitutionality of the congressional provision respecting conscientious objectors, the Court gave to the act's essential phrases—"religious training and belief" and "in a relation to a Supreme Being"—the breadth and sweep of meaning it gave to the word "religion" in the First Amendment in the *Torcaso* case. In sum, a "religion" that does not teach a belief in the existence of God is still a "religion" in the constitutional sense. Within the phrase "religious training and belief," said the Court, would come "all sincere religious beliefs which are based upon a power or being, or upon a faith, to which all else is subordinate or upon which all else is ultimately dependent. The test might be stated in these words: A sincere and meaningful belief which occupies in the life of its possessor a place parallel to that filled by God of those admittedly qualifying for the exemption comes within the statutory definition."

A majority of the Court in 1970 took a further step in *Welsh v. United States*.[88] Welsh's application for exemption as a conscientious objector had been rejected by the Selective Service System, and he was subsequently convicted of refusing to submit to induction. The Supreme Court, by a 5–3 vote, reversed the judgment of conviction. Noting that Welsh claimed he believed killing was morally wrong, but that his views were not "religious" in any traditional sense, the Court held that in order for conscientious objection to qualify as "religious," it is necessary that the registrant's opposition to war stem from his moral or religious beliefs about what is right and wrong, and that these beliefs be held with the strength of traditional religious convictions.

If an individual deeply and sincerely holds beliefs which are purely ethical or moral in source and content, but which impose a duty of conscience to refrain from war at any time, these beliefs function as a religion in the person's life, and thus the individual is as entitled to a "religious" conscientious

---

[88] *Welsh* v. U.S., 398 U.S. 333 (1970). Chief Justice Burger and Justices White and Stewart dissented. Justice Blackmun did not participate.

objector status just as is someone who derives opposition to war from traditional religious convictions. Justice Black, in an opinion in which Justices Douglas, Brennan, and Marshall joined, said that the relevant provision of the statute "exempts from military service all those whose consciences, spurred by deeply held moral, ethical, or religious beliefs, would give them no rest or peace if they allowed themselves to become a part of an instrument of war." [89]

No one concerned with the progress of civil liberties can question the great contribution made by the *Seeger* and *Welsh* cases toward the enhancement of conscience under the religion clauses of the First Amendment. While technically the Supreme Court in these cases professed to engage only in interpreting the will of Congress, the formulation took the form it did only because of the Court's understanding of the spirit and the demands of the First Amendment.

Yet perhaps the most important contribution to religious liberty was made, not by the Supreme Court, but by the American people when, in November, 1960, they elected the first Roman Catholic president of the United States. Perhaps no single event in American history so clearly and definitively demonstrated the American idea of religious liberty as did the election of John F. Kennedy as president. Yet one may wonder if the American people could have given this dramatic confirmation of their adherence to religious liberty had they not been prepared for this act by the work of the Supreme Court, by the teaching function it has performed as it has struggled to give intellectual, political, and moral meaning to the forty-five words that comprise the First Amendment.

As he turned his civil rights papers over to the Lyndon Baines Johnson Library in Austin, Texas, President Johnson

[89] See Milton R. Konvitz, *Religious Liberty and Conscience* (New York, 1968), in which it is argued that the First Amendment should be interpreted in a way that would make religion and conscience approximate one another. See also *U.S.* v. *Sisson*, 297 F. Supp. 902 (1969), opinion by Judge Wyzanski); app. dism. 399 U.S. 267 (1970). In *Gillette* v. *U.S.*, and *Negre* v. *Larsen*, 91 S. Ct. 828 (1971), the Court, by 8–1 vote, held that the draft act exempts those who are conscientiously opposed to participation in all wars but not those who object only to participation in a particular war.

said: "I'm kind of ashamed that I had six years and couldn't do more." This honest and pathetic confession could in a way stand as the judgment on the American people and their government of the 1960s.

Through all the shattering noise and violence, through the murders and assassinations, through the riots and the burnings, there will be noted by the historians some great achievements of the human spirit: the peaceful, dignified marches and demonstrations led by Martin Luther King, Jr., for which he rightly won the admiration of the world and the Nobel Peace Prize; the enactment of the Civil Rights Acts of 1964 and 1968 and the Voting Rights Act of 1965; the repeal of immigration laws that were based on the shameful, discriminatory national origins quota system; the commitment to deal with poverty and health as grave national problems; the reapportionment of state legislatures and congressional districts, to end our rotten boroughs and to give fuller meaning to representative democracy; the federal commitment to give substantial federal aid to schools, colleges and universities; the emergence of the ideal of the right to know, freedom of information, the right of the public to know what its officers and servants do or are up to; and a virtual end to governmental censorship of literature and the arts.

It will be remembered that it was in this decade that America's disadvantaged and overlooked minorities—the blacks, the American Indians, the Puerto Ricans, the Chicanos—made their appearance on the public stage and made their bid for equal rights, equal privileges, equal dignity. They got out of the melting pot, and by their actions and words made it clear that they had no intention of allowing themselves to be melted down and out; the "ethnicity" always implicit in the idea of American pluralism began to make itself heard and known.

These are no mean achievements. And they are more than institutional gains; they represent some deep changes in attitudes.

And yet, despite—and maybe in part because of—these gains and victories, we are left with the feeling of shame that we had ten years and didn't do more. We made some wonderful starts. We formulated grand designs, as in our war on poverty, but failed to take the giant steps that were required. Time and again one had occasion to recall Heywood Broun's observation: "I have known people to stop and buy an apple on the corner and then walk away as if they had solved the whole unemployment problem."

Then, too, it should be said that every solution has a nasty way of generating its own problems. It is only the utopian who thinks that there are total, ultimate answers to deeply rooted, complex social and moral questions. For the problem is not only to set up new guidelines for future action, but also to find ways to remove *now* the effect of past inequalities and injustices; and the latter is by far the more difficult problem. Unlike Moses, we have no way of leading to the Promised Land only those who had never known the effects of slavery. Our generations overlap, and no one now wants to reconcile himself to the limitations and disadvantages imposed on him by past laws, customs, and moral standards and attitudes that were rooted in inequality, discrimination, and economic, political and social subordination. He wants not only the promise of a better life for his children, but a better life for himself here and now. And who can blame him?

At the end of the decade we were, therefore, on the threshold of the new but standing on the old. Like President Johnson, we felt both joy and grief, both hope and despair, both pride and shame. There was the bottle with what we had poured into it, but Oh! the pity of it that we had not poured more.

PAST, PRESENT, AND FUTURE

ALAN REITMAN

The cataclysmic events which have marked America's development over five decades of wars, economic depression, and social upheaval make piecing together the major themes in that span of civil liberties history a formidable assignment. Indeed, the selection of a set of unified themes that would describe the course of civil liberties in a half-century of wide social transformation seems an impossible task. However, in the spirit of challenge—the yeast of civil liberties endeavor—perhaps the reader will join me on a journey to probe the main elements of the fifty-year struggle for liberty, cast in the setting of what Edmund Spenser called "the ever whirling wheels of change."

The events reported and evaluated in the five essays require analysis under these major headings:

The impact on rights of a drastically altered society constantly confronted by tremendous strains and pressures, and the key question of how civil liberties are employed to attain personal freedom.

The roadblocks placed in the path of liberty which impede the individual's exercise of freedom.

The role of major institutions, courts, media, education, and religion in protecting—or weakening—the values of liberty.

Whether the past can illuminate the present and future course of civil liberties, and a look at the 1970's.

Given the record of the past and the present, what is *now* needed to defend the spirit and letter of the Bill of Rights—a pragmatic examination of the tools and techniques being utilized and a discussion of what more needs to be done in an era of new hazards.

The use of power has always been viewed with deep suspicion by those who regard personal liberty as the natural state of man. This mistrust turns to opposition when power is improperly exercised by government. From the inception of the United States, citizens always have railed against the heavy hand of government when it interfered with fundamental rights, articulated frequently as denials of civil liberties.

Long before World War I, strong protests were voiced against government's abuse of its authority, in such milestone episodes as the Alien and Sedition Acts, the monumental conflict over slavery (marked by suspension of the writ of habeas corpus and punitive loyalty oaths during the Civil War), the struggle of workers to organize labor unions, and the Comstock law and highly restrictive federal censorship policies. This danger was enlarged with the extension of federal governmental power during World War I. That war opened the door to what has been the dominant development over five decades: the growth and extension of centralized power, espe- by the executive branch of government.[1]

This expansion, which so greatly influenced the civil liberties scene, stemmed from the existence of huge problems which defied local solution: two major world wars; an economic depression which brought the nation to the brink of collapse; and the propelling of the United States into the self-assigned position of world leader in far-flung competition with

[1] It was not until the late sixties and the seventies that serious efforts were initiated to decentralize governmental power, not only at the federal level, but within lower governmental units as well; such decentralization remains largely unattained.

a different and feared economic and social system, an international rivalry which produced two other costly and lengthy military conflicts. Under the battering pressures of such historical forces, the original ideal of limited government, so closely connected to the ideal of personal liberty, was bound to be diluted.

Each of the five decades offers clear illustrations of how the magnification of government power interfered with the rights of people: the frenzied Palmer raids and mass deportations of aliens in the twenties; the use of congressional investigation as a political weapon in the thirties; the dragnet loyalty-security probes in the forties and fifties; and the usurpation of power in the sixties in order to wage undeclared war in Vietnam.

The dimensions of libertarian concern with governmental power become more sharply focused as the size of government bureaucracy swells. According to the Statistical Abstract of the United States, in 1920 the federal employment roster covered 1,034,418 civilian and military employees in twenty-eight departments, boards, and commissions. Fifty years later the work force was 5,803,276 persons in sixty-six departments and other units, an increase of more than 450 percent.[2] This rise, given heavy impetus by the New Deal's centralization of power, inevitably led to a burgeoning of administrative machinery that not only affected the rights of these workers (for example, Hatch Act prohibitions against political activity) but also spawned administrative and quasi-judicial action in which the rights of the ordinary citizen were frequently trampled. From the NRA days of the New Deal to the officialdom of World War II, the post-war loyalty-security investigatory apparatus and the recent governmental structures designed to dispense aid to the poor and other disadvantaged persons, thousands and thousands of citizens were subject to investigation, harassment, and punishment which curbed their freedom.

If size is a criterion for evaluating how government tampered with rights, its handmaiden was the discriminatory way

---

[2] The problem of size was accentuated by the rise in the number of state and local government employees. In 1929, the first year reported by the Statistical Abstract, the total was 2,532,000; in 1970 the figure was 7,055,000, an increase of more than 150 percent.

in which inflated government utilized its power in enforcing the law. The FBI vigorously pursued violators of "regular" criminal statutes, but frequently refused to investigate violations of federal civil rights laws when such cases touched on politically sensitive civil rights issues. Federal budgets amply financed the degrading investigations of the House Un-American Activities Committee, but limited funds to agencies responsible for administering civil rights laws.

Legislators were adept at obfuscation and delay in blocking the required denial of grants to undeserving school systems which refused to comply with Supreme Court rulings on school segregation. The Law Enforcement Assistance Administration used funds primarily to purchase tanks and other police hardware instead of developing programs instructing police in the law's responsibility to uphold constitutional rights. Even the battle over presidential impounding of some, but not all, congressionally authorized funds reflects the problem. All these examples, and myriad others, are signposts of how both raw and sophisticated power was shamelessly used in selective, discriminatory application of the law.

Over the five decades, as new crises produced demands for more governmental involvement in the lives of people, the typical civil liberties alarm, "too much government power results in denial of liberty," was frequently and correctly sounded. But that was only half of the story. The other side of the coin was that large, centralized government could produce positive gains for liberty. Power could be employed not only to curb rights, but to protect and extend them, as witness the Wagner Act's government-mandated guarantee of labor's right to organize, which embraced the rights of free speech and assembly; the slow but definite strides towards racial equality which culminated in major legislative breakthroughs; and the precedent-making programs providing legal counsel to the poor.

This presented a problem for civil libertarians: whether their instinctive distrust and fear of government power could remain a constant principle in defense of liberty, or, depending upon the issue of the moment, could be taken out of mothballs, like changes in clothing, and then locked away again for another season. For those who regarded government as the chief culprit in denying fundamental rights this was an unsettling situation. And, as if this was not enough to rattle those committed to keeping the citizen free of government intrusion into private affairs, there was the problem of reconciling the growing notion that affirmative government action is necessary to make enjoyment of rights a reality with the fact that government can take away as well as give rights. Birth control programs aimed at improving life in the ghettos may run counter to the free choice of some blacks who see an increased black electorate as a way of building political power.

This perplexing question, which runs throughout the changes wrought in American society, is not resolved by turning for guidance to the record of the separate branches of government or particular political administrations. At different times in the past fifty years the different branches found themselves characterized both as defender and usurper of the citizen's liberty. In the fifties the legislative branch practiced McCarthyism and approved the executive department's pervasive apparatus for judging an employee's loyalty-security status; a decade later Congress became the focal point for attacking the executive's overreach of power in pressing on with the Vietnam war.

The judicial branch, hardly a torchbearer for liberalizing constitutional doctrine in the forties and early fifties, except in the racial equality area, leaped forward in the late fifties and sixties with pace-making decisions in the criminal justice, political rights, and racial fields; yet in the seventies, as society retreated to a more conservative line, the courts cut back on individual rights. In the thirties and sixties the executive branch answered pleas for help to insure rights and enlarge their scope. Yet this is the same branch which now is denounced for assembling over the years a huge array of powers which have been used to deprive people of their rights.

The labeling of particular administrations as "liberal" or "conservative" is a superficial and inadequate method for deciding how the mix of government and power affected individual liberties. In the Republican era of the twenties, the Harding-Coolidge team showed some understanding of the need for amnesty for World War I draft resisters, but practiced a tough anti-strike line that limited the freedom of labor.

The New Deal used government power in the labor-management arena to win rights for workers and their unions, an essential advance; but this same administration was ambivalent to the Dies Committee, gave the FBI the first go-ahead to wiretap, and did not oppose the Smith Act's prohibition of mere advocacy of revolutionary doctrine.

In a later decade, Harry Truman stingingly rebuked Congress for creating the Subversive Activities Control Board, but still initiated a sweeping loyalty program enveloping millions of government employees. Dwight Eisenhower, albeit reluctantly, sent federal troops into Little Rock to uphold the rule of law in the Supreme Court's unanimous decision on school segregation, but weakened that same rule of law by refusing to meet head-on the peril of McCarthyism. And Lyndon Johnson touched off the legistative machine that produced the most significant civil rights legislation since the Civil War but also accelerated an undeclared war which exacted from thousands and thousands of Americans a vast toll of lost freedom.

In a similar vein, the high office held by officials invested with authority, especially those heading the agency charged with concern for justice, offers no clue to resolving the conflict over the duality of government's power. For an attorney general like Harlan Fiske Stone, who put an end to investigation of personal political beliefs and ssociations; a Ramsey Clark, who drew the curtain down on wiretapping; a Frank Murphy, who established the affirmative Civil Rights Division in the Justice Department, there was also a Herbert Brownell, who used raw, unverified FBI data to stoke the cold war fires with charges of treason; a John Mitchell, who arrogantly argued that the president's authority to place taps on citizens' telephones rested on an unchallengeable claim of national security which overrode the law-making power of Congress.

Confusing and jagged as the lines were between power used both to deny and to provide personal liberties over the half-century, a sense of purpose and achievement does emerge. The struggle to maintain a proper balance between the two, often forgotten in the heat of a particular social controversy, assured the keenest efforts in behalf of liberty. And, of course, operationally a demarcation was made between attacking governmental power used to violate rights and supporting governmental power employed to enforce rights—while in the latter case keeping a weather eye out for misuse of authority.

This pragmatic approach applies especially to the decade of the sixties, a period of economic and social experimentation in which the power of government was enlisted on the side of the poor. For the first time, disadvantaged segments of society were assured rights which would begin to make them equal before the law with others of a higher economic or social position.

After all these explorations of government power and their impact on rights, this obvious truth remains: that the enjoyment of civil liberties in a democratic society depends entirely on how people perceive rights and their function, on how hard they demand and struggle for rights, and on whoever possesses power and the machinery to use it.

But even this conclusion does not sufficiently explain the effect of a perpetually shifting society upon rights (and vice versa). Deeper probing reveals the cardinal questions which have been the integral links in the civil liberties story of the five decades: do civil liberties merely accord specific rights to people, or do they provide the machinery for engineering social change? Can these two approaches be harmonized? Must they collide? Or are the means and the ends both equal parts of the struggle, justified by the fact that however used they are what maintains freedom and democracy?

One textbook response is that civil liberties guarantee all persons equally the exercise of certain fundamental rights, those codified into constitutional pronouncements of freedom of speech, press, religion, assembly, due process, and equal treatment before the law, and representing also the sense or "spirit" of liberty which undergirds these guarantees. The philosophical bases for this position stem from the early Greeks and the humanitarian concepts of the Judaic-Christian heritage, a view of people as possessing dignity and worth, personally free but still part of a larger brotherhood entitled to enjoy these rights.

Advocates of this abstract, principled definition of civil liberties also assert an utilitarian value for the Bill of Rights. They believe that not only society's stability but its ability to resolve social problems stems from the full exercise and protection of rights possessed by all. For example, the amalgam of expression in the "marketplace of thought" leads to new, acceptable solutions to social ills, and strict adherence to due process and equality of treatment under the law drains off frustration and bitterness which alienate citizens from their government and make them prey to provokers of violence and social turmoil.

But this view of civilized, rational man is challenged by the sharp realities of life over the ages, the fact that conflict and struggle between competing political, economic, and social philosophies are the core of human history and shape the relationship between people more often than respect for "natural rights."

So, as nations battled in the five decades over these philosophies and their interpretations of personal freedom in a changing world, part of that argument was whether civil liberties are freedoms to be enjoyed by all because they are indigenous to man's human state, or are primarily instruments to be utilized in struggles to reform society, a mechanism for social change. This latter view, naturally connected to society's failure to meet human needs, was stressed throughout the half-century. It came to public attention most forcefully in the last decade, when the wide economic and social gaps between the poor and non-poor, the white and non-white, were etched on the American conscience.

Society's failure to bridge the chasm between the advantaged and disadvantaged generated myriad cases arguing for constitutional guarantees on which all could agree. But it also bred the argument that the chasm required more drastic civil liberties action, including support of preferential treatment and special economic assistance. This group or class approach, which claimed that economic and social inequalities are evils which government must correct under the rubric of a government-enforced right of equality, was sharply disputed by libertarians who perceive civil liberties as rooted only in the concept of individual rights and personal merit.

To pose the issue in such sharply defined terms does not mean that these trains of separate civil liberties attitudes always ran on separate tracks. Or that the discord was wrapped in asbestos, safe from the bubbling cauldron of social conflict. In each decade, the effort to maintain civil liberties, no matter from which part of the spectrum its defenders came, were part and parcel of the struggles which divided the changing society, and both affected and were affected by great clashes—the public anxiety over the Russian Revolution, the economic collapse of the Depression era, World War II and the postwar pressures on liberty, the cold war's toll of freedom, and the subsequent "revolutions of rising expectations."

Indeed, because these struggles swirled around deeply felt political, economic, and social convictions about the nature of American society and government, civil liberties often became the focus of attention, if not the favorite whipping boy, of contesting—and often polarized—forces in society. Even though its voice is somewhat muted now (perhaps only temporarily), the ultra-right assailed libertarian defense of free speech for Communists or other political dissidents of the left as a camouflage hiding more radical endeavors to destroy the existing system. Similarly, the far left criticized libertarian defense of a pro-Nazi's or pro-Fascist's speech or assembly rights as "muddled thinking" that hindered the movement toward uprooting the "decaying social order."

Sometimes this debate over the means and the ends, the philosophical contest between principle and pragmatism, split the civil liberties camp. When Fred Beal, a Communist Party leader convicted of murdering a sheriff during the Gastonia, North Carolina, textile strike of the late twenties, jumped bail and fled to the Soviet Union, libertarians who had backed bail as a simple due process right felt betrayed. Others, declaring themselves equally committed to the civil liberties creed, explained the bail jumping as a necessary step against "capitalist class vengeance" as represented in the "infamous Gastonia verdict." [3] In World War II, when Japanese-Americans were

---

[3] This statement comes from an October 31, 1930, letter from William Z. Foster, chairman of the Communist Party of the United States, submitting his resignation as a member of the advisory National Committee of the American Civil Liberties Union and as an ACLU member. Foster was sharply critical of the ACLU's attack on the bail jumping. He said

herded into detention camps, some libertarians initially defended the evacuation as a necessary step to protect national security in war-time, while others indignantly charged the government with wholesale violations of due process and with racial discrimination.

The clash between the means and the ends often faded when history easily joined the two philosophies in a mutual endeavor. In the twenties the ACLU gave strong assistance to the United Mine Workers Union when it risked the brutal beatings of company-controlled police to hold meetings in the coal mining region of West Virginia's Logan County. Similar aid was given in the thirties when the budding CIO won through the courts the right of free speech and free assembly for its organizers. The resulting victory for recognition of industrial unions led to economic gains for workers which illustrated the relationship between abstract rights and specific social objectives. The analogy can be drawn with later struggles by other groups: Blacks, Puerto Ricans, Mexican-Americans, teachers, students, and the poor have won recognition if not adequate acceptance of their programs by their constant demand for or exercise of free speech, due process, and equal treatment. And the pattern is being repeated now by women, homosexuals, prisoners, and the young.

However, the lines became blurred, as did the consequences for civil liberties and society, when dramatic political change switched the abstract absolutists and the social instrumentalists from the same track onto different paths. As discussed by Jerald S. Auerbach in his essay, the classic example is the "loyalty oath" controversy of the thirties within the ACLU, which revolved around an organizational resolution adopted in the aftermath of the Soviet Union's pact with Nazi Germany. The resolution barred from service or employment on the governing councils or staffs of the ACLU any supporters of totalitarianism, defined as members of Communist or Fascist parties or the Ku Klux Klan.

that he was forced to the conclusion that by its actions in the Gastonia case, the Union is "no longer seriously engaged in the fight for civil liberties . . . and that the workers have nothing to expect from [the ACLU] in the way of assistance in their desperate struggle against capitalism."

With the hindsight of the McCarthy era and today's revelations of pressures exerted by the government on citizens' political beliefs and associations, the thirties episode seems an infringement of First Amendment principles. On the ground of absolute principle, it was; although defenders of the policy pointed to the need at a time of convulsive political change for preserving organizational integrity by including in leadership positions only those committed to non-totalitarian standards. But regardless of the conflict over principle, the episode takes on a less than absolute proportion when evaluated not only as a simple matter of right or wrong or as a reflection of the political loyalties of that period, but against the need for preserving an organization so that it could go on defending the civil liberties of all, including those advocating totalitarianism.

No one knows exactly what would have happened if the resolution never had passed, or if, as a consequence, Elizabeth Gurley Flynn had not been expelled from the board of directors of the ACLU. The Union's position before the country as an impartial defender of the Bill of Rights might have remained unchanged and its work continued undisrupted. But, given the mood of national revulsion against the German-Russian pact as an abdication of principle, and the havoc created by Soviet supporters' takeover of organizations through anti-democratic methods, it is at least a fair assumption that the ACLU might not have withstood the battering attacks which an absolute stand would have provoked, or that it might have had its civil liberties directions altered. And what was essentially a small, private organization might have sunk into oblivion.

The choice was based not on the desire to court majoritarian approval or right-wing support but on the need to prevent impairment of the Union's function, and consequent loss for civil liberties, a serious reduction of credibility before courts and legislatures when the ACLU defended the civil liberties of all persons and groups, even those inimically regarded because of their noxious political views. In retrospect, might not the decision in the oath controversy have produced more gain than loss for civil liberties?

This interpretation is further elaborated by Osmond K.

Fraenkel, a general counsel of the Union, a distinguished constitutional expert, and a firm opponent of the ACLU "loyalty
oath." In a statement to me on May 4, 1973, Mr. Fraenkel said:

As one of those who opposed the 1940 resolution and voted
against the expulsion of Elizabeth Gurley Flynn, whose
informal counsel I was at the hearing, I think the large
amount of space given by Jerald S. Auerbach to this episode
is disproportionate. It is true, of course, that there was a
strong public relations concern about the role of the Union.
I think this was prompted less by anti-Communism as
such than by fear that if we got into the war the Communists would be opposing it, as the Socialists did in
World War I, no one at that time expecting Germany to
invade Russia.

I believe the 1940 resolution was proposed so as to
make it possible for the Union to support Communists in
such an eventuality should their freedom of speech be
restricted.

It is certainly misleading to convey the impression that
adoption of the resolution subverted the protection of the
Bill of Rights for all persons. That was certainly not true
of the ACLU in any respect whatever. It should be noted
that in 1939 the ACLU sent me to Washington to testify,
on free speech-association grounds, against what later became the Smith Act; [4] and in 1942 the ACLU supported
the appeal of the Trotskyites when they were convicted
under the Smith Act.

In the decades following, the Union remained steadfast
to its only purpose of defending the Bill of Rights for all,
including Communists and other advocates of political
unorthodoxy, even while asserting its separation from those
doctrines. This occurred in cases defending the right of
Communists to teach and to hold government jobs; and in
resisting numerous Smith Act prosecutions, the federal
loyalty program, and the outrageous depredations of the
McCarthy and House Un-American Activities Committees.

---

[4] The federal statute which prohibits conspiring to advocate, or to
teach doctrine advocating, the violent overthrow of the government.

Civil liberties incidents, including clashes between purists and instrumentalists, obviously make their impression on the political struggles which mark the changes of a particular era, and often seem totally to envelop the conflict. Even today the tension between those committed to a more traditional position and those motivated by the desire for necessary social reform ignite the sparks of new civil liberties debates. But to claim, as some do, that these incidents can largely affect, if not determine, the outcome of the political struggle is to assign them too great an importance.

While the thirties episode within the ACLU stood as a symbol of anti-Communist feeling that infected many private liberal organizations, the controversy was not the prime cause of the anti-radical sentiment which flooded the country, then and subsequently. This sentiment was fed by forces much larger and more powerful than the internal ACLU dispute. Domestic and foreign political conflagrations, war itself, and fundamental philosophical differences over economic and social systems were the real causes of the nation's attitudes in the decades from the forties on, including its treatment of civil liberties. And considering the ebb and flow of both history and civil liberties (witness today's rapprochement with the Soviet Union) what was regarded in the twenties as a "crucial" situation falls today into a less decisive category, especially as new and complex problems emerge to demand the energy and attention of libertarians.

The libertarian creed inevitably recognizes strain between order and freedom as the natural state of affairs in the relationship of government to the individual. The former seeks stability so that it can carry out its governing function and preserve its existence; the latter chafes against restraints which curb diverse expressions of personal liberty and impede the development of human potential. In times of national crisis, real or presumed, these two forces dramatically clash; then government unleashes its tremendous power to achieve its objectives, and the individual is hard pressed to prevent the submerging of rights.

From the twenties to the seventies the United States experi-

enced almost perpetual crises, the result of worldwide upheaval: the rise and fall of Fascism, the vast expansion of
Communism, the revolutionary impact of nuclear weapons on
military and foreign policy, even the ups and downs of détente
with the Soviet Union. We were engaged in military hostilities
for almost fifteen years, and the cold war existed for nearly
twenty.

Throughout the five decades, all these events created an en-
circling climate of restriction which became the major enemy
of freedom. But the conflict between government and the individual was most sharply exemplified by war itself and the
repression of liberty that accompanied it.

World War I produced unprecedented violations of individual rights, sedition laws that punished political comment, censorship of communications, jailing of conscientious objectors
and police raids on Socialist and anti-war organizations. Indeed, so jarring were these occurrences that in 1920 [5] they led
a determined, dedicated group of lawyers, religious leaders,
social workers, and social reformers to establish the ACLU
and make defense of liberty an organized affair.

And the adverse effects on liberty of that war lingered on. As
Paul L. Murphy relates, government continued to crack down
on the politically unorthodox, an expression of fear about the
assumed menace of the Russian Revolution which both fed
and paralleled public feeling. Labor's organizing efforts were
taken as evidence of an alien philosophy, particularly when
Communists and Socialists identified their cause with workers'
rights. And censorship of publications was accepted.

A better overall record, due in part to a developing consciousness in the previous decades about civil liberties, was
posted in the World War II period. However, that perilous
time still was replete with incidents of infringed personal
rights.

The mass evacuation of Japanese-Americans from the West
Coast, although explained as a security measure, reinforced
national attitudes of racial discrimination, as did the inferior
treatment accorded blacks in the armed forces. A censorship

[5] Actually, the seeds were planted in 1917, when the National Civil
Liberties Bureau was formed to combat war-time violations of rights.

system over certain kinds of communication prevailed. Economic controls were imposed that often neglected due process. And criminal penalties were sought against those who merely advocated philosophies regarded as "un-American," advocacy unconnected to specific acts of violence or personal harm.

Other military conflicts, even though less sweeping than World Wars I and II, made deep incursions into civil liberties. The Korean War fed the flames of McCarthyism, a fire which burned into a fear-ridden America the acceptance of violations of civil liberties because their exercise jeopardized the "higher public need," national security. And while freedom of speech, assembly, and association flourished to a much larger extent in the Vietnam war than in other periods of military conflict,[6] the government not only spied on, harassed and jailed thousands of Americans for daring, on political and conscience grounds, to express opposition, but sent thousands more to their death in an undeclared war regarded as unconstitutional by major segments of the population.

The war-time repression of rights in the five decades created one strange paradox. This was a unique dialectic of war, that repression itself can draw public notice to how certain groups, both in and outside the armed forces, are denied liberty and thus strengthen the drive to advance rights. Because of their harsh treatment in World War I, the problems of conscientious objectors were raised to public consciousness; in World War II and the Korean War, the plight of blacks was highlighted; and the war in Vietnam, seen through a moral prism affecting mainly the young and poor, increased interest in the problems

[6] There are many reasons why the Vietnam war did not produce the large-scale denials of liberty that usually occur in war. The nation was not on a complete war-time footing, thus avoiding the imposition of controls over people's everyday lives. Unlike World War II, the Vietnam war was not fully supported by the citizenry. Strong opposition took the form of active protests, joined by the predominantly middle-class parents whose sons were threatened by the draft. The sixties also were invigorated by the moral conviction of the civil rights crusade, which legitimized protest against the Vietnam war. Also, the nation had just recovered from the McCarthyism of the fifties, whose abuses of civil liberties were an educative force in the next decade for understanding why the Bill of Rights must be defended.

of groups hitherto regarded as not covered by the Bill of Rights.

But basically, the effect of the half-century's tension between war and liberty was highly destructive. Odd as it may seem in a society so committed in principle to libertarian standards, when constitutional freedoms were particularly endangered there was little reluctance to override these freedoms. The call to patriotism which war engendered was a powerful emotional cry which turned people away from reason. Yet, precisely at those times, one would think that the best in the American tradition would have asserted itself. It is in crisis seasons when public officials seize on threats to the state to limit freedom, when fear of dissent and willingness to conform prevails, that the faith should be kept. The failure to maintain that faith in war-time situations spoke to the question of whether Americans actually understood and believed in their rights. It also raised the question which libertarians debated but did not agree on: whether, since war creates such heavy pressures on liberty, the surest protection for the Bill of Rights is the elimination of war.

It would be a mistake to dwell entirely on war as the only creator of roadblocks which impede the course of liberty. Over the half-century an arching pattern of government depredation appears, with the most dominant element being the fear of an alien philosophy whose economic and political system challenged our own. Undoubtedly perceived and felt by the populace as a realistic danger, this fear was heightened and often manipulated for political gain by the executive and legislative branches, with the result that personal rights were seriously impaired.

The greatest damage flowed from the all-embracing anti-Communist loyalty-national security fetish, the most common reaction to fear of foreign enemies. This consuming passion began with the local "red scares" of the twenties; the Dies (House Committee on Un-American Activities) Committee investigations followed, and were aped by that committee's successors; then came sweeping executive department loyalty program and the McCarthy era's *Sturm und Drang* investigations. Even by the sixties, when the country had regained some

sense of balance, too many Americans still labeled anti-war
and civil rights protests as "disloyalty to the system," and
cheered severe government measures to thwart and punish
such protests. So ingrained and commonplace were these governmental pressures on civil liberties that it wasn't until the
seventies, as the international political scene took on a different hue, that charges of disloyalty began to fade from public
consciousness. However, the institutionalization of these abuses
is still to be fully uncovered and rooted out, as evidenced by
the Nixon administration's outrageous employment of bugging, wiretapping, breaking and entering, and political surveillance—all under the magic umbrella of preserving national
security.

If government was the main villain in the play of pressures
which blocked the exercise of liberty, then the citizenry also
deserved top billing in the cast of characters. Of course governmental power and how it was used was the dominant factor
in shaping public attitudes toward civil liberties. But, unless
we accept the notion of a totally supine citizenry, totally uninvolved or unconcerned about the state of liberty,[7] to assert
that officialdom alone was responsible for violations absolves
the public of its share of responsibility. The fact is that the
public joined the government in a friendly partnership to in-
fringe rights.

The American society is composed of diverse sections, all
with different ideas as to what economic and political philosophy should prevail. But, despite the support given to the social
pioneering of liberals in the halcyon days of the New Deal,
the abortive promise of the New Frontier, and the creative
contributions of the Great Society, preservation of the status
quo has been society's paramount theme. This psychological
fact of life was the connecting thread over the five decades in
the blanket of fear about change that frequently and effectively obstructed the utilization of liberties or their extension.

[7] Many persons do accept this idea, believing that understanding of
civil liberties is still a province reserved for intellectuals or the more
highly educated. However, the events of the sixties and seventies which
popularized the issue of rights for many people may be changing public
knowledge about and receptivity toward civil liberties. The problem of
popular understanding of civil liberties is discussed below, pp. 337–40.

More significantly, what this attitude strikingly demonstrated
was how often the public's fear of the unknown was a flight
from reality and a retreat into fancy.[8]

There was widespread public support for the mass deportation of aliens in the twenties, a reaction to the dread of the
Russian Revolution's influence and spread. Yet, despite Trot-
sky's cry for a worldwide uprising of the masses, there was
little basis for such apprehension in this country. The wave of
criminal syndicalist prosecutions of the IWW in the early
years of the decade was rooted in fear of new ideas about the
nature of economic and social systems, not in hard evidence
of planned revolution.[9]

Similarly, the governmental investigating power, beginning
with the Lusk Committee inquiries in New York State in the
twenties, and continuing through the Fish and Dies committees and their satellite committees down to the apex of the
McCarthy-type investigations of the fifties, was invoked with
public backing, primarily to block the infiltration of Communist ideology rather than as a response to actual armed insurrection or overt acts of sabotage.

Even in less earth-shattering realms, the populace's fear of
the new took its toll of liberty. Geologist John Scopes, who
simply wanted to acquaint his Tennessee high school students
with the theory of evolution, left his job because the frightened local citizenry did not want their fundamentalist understanding of existence challenged.[10] Fifteen years later the
Jehovah's Witnesses ran into difficulties with local authorities,
who regarded that faith's religious belief in refusal to salute

[8] This evaluation does not belie the fact that during the half-century
real dangers confronted the country. Strong measures were necessary to
deal with certain international and domestic problems. But the existence
of such dangers did not require the kind of response from government
and the public which assailed individual rights.

[9] The bombings by anarchists and IWW disciples, while threatening,
and regarded by people as aiming at destruction of the government,
were isolated examples rather than a grand design.

[10] Although Scopes resigned his teaching post and was fined in the
famous "monkey trial" that ensued, the worldwide publicity given the
Clarence Darrow–William Jennings Bryan confrontation enlarged public
understanding of academic freedom and free speech.

the flag as a threat to established conformist standards, which, in the officials' benighted notion of security, tied the community together.

Reflected in the public's attitude toward change was deepseated hostility and prejudice toward particular groups of Americans. Because of these attitudes, rooted in fear, those who demanded their rights were perceived as seeking to destroy the power of groups whose rights were already recognized, rather than as seeking a share of that power. Yet these anxieties, too, had little substance in reality.

Labor unions undoubtedly have made industry unhappy with their insistence on a fair share of the economic pie, but their recognition has not sounded the death-knell of American capitalism. Indeed, the stability brought to the industrial arena by unions, when accepted and dealt with, has strengthened the economic system. The entrenched power of law, status, and custom was applied in all sections of the country by masses of citizens opposed to the elimination of racial segregation. While evidences of racism abound and are hard to root out, and delay, circumvention, and other forms of opposition still mark the civil rights scene, large cracks in the wall of discrimination have occurred without the total destruction of society that some predicted. A beginning has been made in the sharing of power upon which social peace depends.

In drawing together the mosaic of the citizenry's failure to respect rights, which both fed into and were fed by government's own disregard of individual liberties, a natural question that springs to mind is why people acted in such a fearful manner. Granted that the stakes of power and privilege were high and that the demands for rights came from sources outside the mainstream, the majoratarian public's overreaction to emerging concepts and movements is puzzling when measured against freedom's rich background of constitutional guarantees and historical tradition. Why, in the face of change, was commitment to civil liberties values so woefully weak?

There is one answer which has special meaning for the seventies, when life's pressures seem inexorable. There has always been in the American strain a reliance on and desire for simplistic solutions to social problems, particularly when disliked changes are necessary to deal with them. Rather than face the truth we look for the easy way out, for scapegoats, hoping to avoid the deep and often disturbing thought necessary to accept change. Time and again over the five decades, this evasion of reality has rent the fragile fabric of liberty.[11]

When fear of Marxist ideology first struck, rather than examining domestic social evils and correcting them so as to minimize the appeal of the new ideology we instead cracked down on those who expressed dissent from the existing order.

When minorities demanded equal protection of the law, rather than applying constitutional guarantees fairly we instead allowed the criminal justice system to parcel out different brands of justice for the rich and poor, for the white and non-white.

When crime became an issue of major concern, rather than relieving the economic causes which, despite current counter-theories, are still the major source of crime, or recognizing the need to humanize prisons, we instead fashioned tougher "law and order" methods which only compounded the disillusionment and tension, thus leading to further crime.

When students rebelled against, among other things, archaic rules and institutions which had little meaning in their lives, rather than studying carefully the merits of their complaints and the frustration represented by their protests we instead sought repressive legislation and applauded overreactive police assaults on *all* forms of campus protest.

When the Presidential Commission on Obscenity and Pornography recognized the reality of changing sex mores and recommended legislation sensibly distinguishing between free-

[11] Actually, the *reality* of denied rights also violated libertarian standards. It was the frustration, born of institutions' failure to meet needs, that produced the violence of the sixties which in many ways reduced observance of civil liberties. The reality of the disadvantaged was far from that of the majority of Americans whose post–World War II affluence helped them to hide from the hard truth of social inequality. Indeed, even when existentialist behavior assumed its most drastic form, violence, this was in large part a reaction to the neglect of people's needs by those in power. And while violence did impair the exercise of civil liberties, the reality is that it also dramatically focused attention on the unmet needs, thus forcing the public to accept some social reforms.

ing adults to read and see materials of their choice and pursuing non-legislative positive approaches to sexuality, rather
than accepting this important distinction we instead excori-
ated the Commission, sought safety in more criminal prosecutions, and vented our wrath on the "libertine" Supreme Court.

When the Supreme Court clarified the demarcation between
church and state, rather than approving the decision as a
strengthening of religious freedom we instead heaped condemnation on the Court and sought to handcuff its authority, for-
getting that an independent judiciary is a key bastion of freedom.

Why was commitment to civil liberties values so poor, especially in times of intense public controversy? Was our pen-
chant for simplistic solutions an example of a mechanistic culture in which problems can be solved by applying some handy
tool, or a kind of "instant gratification" syndrome caused by
the conditioning of mass advertising? Was it a lack of political
awareness and sophistication, contrasted with such nations as
England and France, where active political participation more
fully acquaints people with the substance of power and, therefore, its dangers? Was it the huge rise of government employment at all levels which built within millions of government
workers and their families the feeling that protest against inroads on liberty would threaten their job security? Was it the
failure of educational institutions to instill within young people a real understanding of the worth and necessity of civil
liberties?

To stress the neglect of libertarian values and the distortions
of reality by the status quo public which curtailed rights is
not to ignore the tremendous progress achieved over the five
decades in certain key areas. Enormous advances have been
made by labor unions in their struggle to organize, secured by
their rights of free speech and free association. Comparative
peace now reigns on the industrial front, a scene marked by
violence and repeated use of federal troops and state militia
in the first two decades. Mob fury, which erupted frequently
in the early decades, is now exceedingly rare, and lynchings
have disappeared.

The evolving concept of racial equality, incorporated in laws

and court rulings even if not sufficiently an everyday practice
in the lives of people, is a major triumph over the fixed order.
Other definite gains include the recognition of indigents' legal
rights, additional due process reforms in the criminal justice
system, the broadening frontiers of free speech, and the clearer
definitions of church-state separation—all pioneered by the
the Supreme Court in the fifties and sixties.

But every success came only after hard tussles with forces
which held stubbornly to their frightened perception of an
enlarging scope of liberty. Each forward step was won only
by long, sometimes excruciating effort that taxed the spirit and
conviction of those who battled for liberty. Civil rights legislation came only after beatings, lynchings, and other painful
indignities of the body and soul. Free speech and free association rights for workers came only after shootings, harassment,
and economic pressures exerted by industry. Today's greater
latitude for the expression of unorthodox ideas by political dissenters came only after the sufferings of earlier non-conform-
ists who served prison sentences after government prosecution
or were pilloried by congressional investigating committees.

In tracing the roadblocks placed in the path of liberty over
five decades, a familiar pattern emerges. It is true that there
were always new kinds of movements and groups (and some
that remained the same) which jousted with government and
the majoritarian status quo public. And the techniques of repression took on different, complicated forms, as witness the
rise of electronic eavesdropping and computerized record-
keeping, which have so stealthily invaded privacy. But there
is a repetition in civil liberties conflict which makes it clear
that the struggle to preserve liberty is always constant and
that fundamentally nothing really changes. A sense of *déjà
vu* hovers over the historical record.

In the twenties William J. Burns, head of the "radical division" within the Bureau of Investigation, played on the fear of
infiltration to win congressional appropriations for his undercover political police apparatus; in the decades following,
J. Edgar Hoover sounded the same clarion annually to obtain
always-increasing budgets for the FBI. The local confrontations of the thirties, pitching mine workers battling for union

recognition against the local constabulary egged on by coal operators, parallels Cesar Chavez's battles in the 1960s and still today to organize farm workers against the bitter resistance of farm growers and their sympathetic local police.

The federal government's seizure in 1918 of books and records of the National Civil Liberties Bureau, precursor of the ACLU, was matched by government raids against Communist dissenters at the Bridgman, Michigan, convention of the twenties; harassment of the German-American Bund and other pro-Nazi groups in the thirties; and again by the photographing and auto-license recording of anti-war demonstrators in the sixties, not to mention the "plumbers'" invasion of Daniel Ellsberg's psychiatrist's offices. States' investigations of so-called subversive activities in the early decades were a forerunner of later-day McCarthyism, and World War I's federal anti-sedition laws certainly resemble the Smith, Mundt-Nixon, and McCarran acts of subsequent years.

The call to conscience and dissent was heard in decade after decade. Writer Upton Sinclair's jailing in 1923 for reading the Bill of Rights at a San Pedro, California, street meeting, a challenge to the police's unconstitutional disruption of striking workers' assemblies, was cut from the same cloth as Benjamin Spock's and William Coffin's defiance of laws penalizing counseling of anti–Vietnam war resistance.

Such religious leaders as Norman Thomas and John Haynes Holmes, by their moral indignation, rallied public support to oppose World War I attacks on civil liberties, as did the writings and speeches of the Berrigan brothers in the Vietnam war decades later.[12] The analogy drawn between amnesty and respect for the right of individual dissent from government's military action was argued at the time of Woodrow Wilson's rejection of amnesty, as it is today in the face of Richard Nixon's adamant stand.

This précis of revolving-door pressures on civil liberty could be seen as proof that people and government never learn and that the drive to reduce individual liberty will never be halted. However, a totally pessimistic appraisal is wrong. There have

---

[12] The Berrigans also engaged in various forms of civil disobedience. These violations of law were different from writings and speeches.

been victories over repression. Resistance to violations of liberty has grown over the years. The business of civil liberties defense, no matter how heavy the assault, is now on a full-time, organized basis and is winning new adherents. There is a strong and spreading corps of experienced civil liberties attorneys and a rising consciousness within the bar. A body of legal decisions exists, especially at the Supreme Court level, which provides a foundation on which to construct further challenges. These legal successes, or even the failures, stimulate and shape campaigns toward attaining new frontiers of personal rights.

Nevertheless, the protection of liberty against government and citizen sway remains an uphill fight. The maxim of the American Civil Liberties Union, "history creates our clients," still rings true. Societal pressures of a particular period [13] undoubtedly will produce fresh "enemies" seen as threats to the status quo and will harden attacks on a new social movement's or organization's civil liberties. Vigilant and militant defense of these civil liberties may even reintroduce the shallow thinking of super-patriots who reject the Voltairian concept ("I disapprove of what you say, but I will defend to the death your right to say it"), and confuse defense of a group's liberty with sympathy for the cause or philosophy espoused by the group—a simplistic "guilt by association" label which has dogged many libertarian efforts to protect the Bill of Rights.

But, just as the edge of such old saws has been dulled in recent years by greater public recognition of civil liberties conflict, the roadblocks in the path of liberty could be eased. The obstacles might be cleared by dint of the progress achieved through law and public opinion, aided by the press. But, more importantly, achievements will be made by those who

[13] These pressures are often seen as a reaction to shifts in values, but over the decades these changes were more often one of form than of real substance. The flappers of the twenties were kin to the hippie culture of the sixties and the communes of the seventies. The hip flask and marathon drinking bouts of the earlier period offered the same release as do drugs today. The connecting links were rebellion against the existing mode of life, especially among the young. This led to new forms of personal behavior in both decades which were categorized as discarding of old values.

have the will to struggle for their own rights, and who by their endeavors lead government and the public to recognize the unreality of imagined dangers, the need for change, and the importance of civil liberties in constructing a truly free and open society.

The evolving pattern of civil liberties over five decades was molded not only by the citizenry at large, by particular national administrations, and by the march of historical events. Large institutions of power which held key positions in society were both affected by these forces and played their own special role in influencing how much or how little liberty was exercised. This was certainly true of the courts, the mass media, education, and religion in the 1920–70 period.[14]

As the enumerated constitutional guarantees of the Bill of Rights are the individual's basic protection against denial of rights, the Supreme Court record offers the best guideposts for evaluating the judicial institution's contribution in the five-decade story. Since the authors of the previous chapters describe specific court decisions and their significance in more detail, only an overall comment is necessary at this juncture.

Historians, lawyers, and other students of government hotly disagree on particular stands of the Supreme Court and their importance. But all would agree that the Court's decisions were the largest and most positive factor in advancing civil liberties, by writing into the "law of the land" many elementary tenets of the libertarian creed.[15]

This trend began in the 1920s when, led by the dissents of

[14] The current scene is marked by sharp breaks with traditional values and a questioning of the importance of some institutions in people's lives. However one judges the strength of institutions today, over the half-century they definitely influenced the civil liberties scene.

[15] Indeed, over the fifty years the Court's attitude to the Bill of Rights shifted remarkably to a uniform national policy invalidating various sorts of state and local restrictions on individual freedom. The lines of permissible action have been greatly extended and the power to protect rights strengthened, reflecting the welfare state's general protection of citizens. In turn, national consciousness about the rule of law has included strong belief in the role of the Court, as shown by the failure of such disparate measures as FDR's court-packing plan and congressional legislation to limit the Court's jurisdiction.

Justices Louis Brandeis and Oliver Wendell Holmes, the Court adopted the idea that state and local action which limited application of the Bill of Rights was superseded by the federal Constitution's guarantees made applicable to the states by the Fourteenth Amendment's equal protection and due process clauses. With this precedent-shattering concept as the wedge, the high court more and more accepted as its function the safeguarding of human rights, a sharp break from its previous championing of property rights.

Freedom of assembly and association for radical—defined then as Communist—groups enlarged the scope of First Amendment protections in the thirties. Similar concern for unfettered debate was illustrated by the Court's defense of the right of the press to function free of government pressure, carved out in cases invalidating licensing and special tax requirements which served as a suffocating prior restraint. In the same decade, key decisions upholding the constitutionality of the Wagner Act's principle of collective bargaining and the voiding of municipal ordinances designed to block labor organizers' free speech and assembly rights gave further evidence of the Supreme Court's ability to influence the social direction of the nation by equalizing the power of labor and management.

The discriminatory nature of the double-standard criminal justice system was opened to public inspection by decisions in the Scottsboro case reversing the rape convictions of black defendants whose rights to a fair trial had been denied. These laid the groundwork for later pioneering decisions in housing, education, and public accommodations cases which more directly confronted the issue of racial discrimination and cracked open the segregated patterns of American life.

So sweeping was the Supreme Court's interpretation of the Fourteenth Amendment's equal protection clause that it attached this section to a vital area not directly related to racial discrimination. This had widespread ramifications. The battery of decisions reapportioning political districts broke the tight control held by small rural areas over many state legislatures and paved the way for the more populous urban-suburban sectors to obtain a fairer share of political power at the state and congressional levels.

As America emerged into the *realpolitik* of the post–World War II period, the motion picture industry, which since the twenties had been viewed as merely flashing entertainment on the silver screen, was finally recognized by the Court as a medium deserving First Amendment protection because films contain information, opinion, and ideas—a recognition which aided the fight against state and local film censorship.

The shibboleths of Comstockery, which deprived the public of authors' full portrayals of life's realities, including the taboo subject of human sexuality, began to fade as the high court offered definitions of obscenity which, while not matching an absolutist interpretation of protected free expression, were more in keeping with the reality of changing mores.[16]

The biggest leap forward for the protection of individual rights by the Supreme Court came in the late fifties and the sixties under the wise and humane leadership of Chief Justice Earl Warren. To a nation finally sick of McCarthyite excesses, the high court, while not always meeting constitutional challenges head-on, found ways of voiding the convictions of witnesses cited for contempt when they refused to answer questions of congressional committees whose investigations touched inviolate areas of free speech and free association.

This sensitivity to the human condition and to the importance of shielding dissent from the massive power of government was shown also in the many decisions validating sit-ins and other forms of peaceful civil rights protest, and in the criminal justice rulings that assured indigents their right of counsel in criminal proceedings and required police to treat suspects and defendants with the fairness commanded by the Constitution.

The fresh respect for strict adherence to constitutional standards which colored this whole period was illustrated by the series of decisions clarifying the separation between church and state. Entering into the highly controversial realm of

[16] Gratifying as these decisions were, the Court's attempts to define obscenity were unsuccessful, not surprising in an area where subjective feelings rather than objective criteria make definition so difficult. The fact that in the seventies the Burger Court refused to accept the idea that an adult, if he/she so wishes, has the right to buy or see anything substantiates the subjective nature of the whole obscenity debate.

religion, the Supreme Court accepted its responsibility by drawing clear lines barring direct or indirect government support to religious institutions, particularly in the field of education.

Over the five decades the Court built a firm framework of constitutional support for an enlarging view of individual freedom. However, by no means was its record entirely positive. While the Court made vast strides in carving out new constitutional frontiers, many of its decisions were less liberating and assented to restrictions which reflected the popular mood of the moment.

The public's failure to understand that the First Amendment protected the most obnoxious speech, so long as it was divorced from dangerous, implementing action, was symbolized in the Court's acceptance of a group libel law and convictions for strong public utterances distasteful to the listening audience. Under war-time exigencies of the forties the Court bowed to military authorities by permitting the evacuation of Japanese-Americans into detention camps. Under like pressures of the Cold War in the following decade the government's loyalty program was held valid, with a passing bow of respect for due process standards.

At the height of McCarthyism the Court also backed the position of both the legislative and executive branches that the threat of Russian aggression warranted congressional exposure of present or former Communist sympathizers and prosecution of Communist leaders simply for conspiring to advocate revolutionary doctrine, without a shred of real evidence that such doctrine would be put into action. And, as Milton R. Konvitz emphasizes, in the turbulent sixties the Supreme Court failed a nation sharply divided on the Vietnam war by refusing even to hear argument on the claim that the waging of war by the president without seeking congressional approval was an unconstitutional act.

The Supreme Court's advances and retreats exemplified a general paradox of civil liberties, that gains and losses are part of the total record and sometimes intersect. The Court's path of progress was not always straight, and was sometimes confusing. In the early fifties, when the free speech and association rights of individuals came under fierce attack, the Court could turn away the pleas of political dissidents, but at the same time favor the pleas of others claiming abridgment of individual rights because of racial discrimination. Undoubtedly, the Court's composition, its leadership, the nature of world events, and the citizenry's acceptance of its decisions [17] helped to shape this influential institution's approach to and impact on civil liberties. But despite the uneven course it traveled over five epochal decades, the Supreme Court charted, for the entire nation, an indelible upward curve of liberty that developed a clearer picture of what individual rights are and why they must always be vigorously defended.

Society's respect for rights and the individual's freedom to use liberty depend upon more than laws and court rulings. They rest also on attitudes formed as a result of information, opinion, and ideas imbibed from the channels of communication, the mass media.

This institution's influence on the half-century's civil liberties tally sheet can best be evaluated by separating the record of the print media—newspapers, books, and magazines—from that of the electronic media—motion pictures, radio, and television. The distinction is drawn because of the different functions they serve, rather than the existing, albeit contested, dissimilarity in constitutional protection between print and film media, and radio-TV—the latter not enjoying full First Amendment press freedoms because the limited spectrum space on the air makes its channels subject to regulation by the Federal Communications Commission.

[17] While the words of Finley Peter Dunne's Mr. Dooley, "th' supreme coort follows th' iliction returns," proved correct at times, there is good evidence that despite popular pressures in many crucial periods the Court firmly adhered to its own view of constitutional issues. In the late fifties and sixties the Court displayed proper independence in the face of widespread public and congressional dismay over church-state, obscenity, criminal justice, and civil rights decisions. Despite proposed constitutional amendments and legislation avowedly aimed at clipping the Court's wings, the Court did not waver. The efforts to undo the Court's decisions failed, and it remained for a new Court which included the appointees of Richard Nixon to change its direction in some of these areas.

Whatever one's position on this troublesome constitutional question, the fact is that despite their economic-advertising base and entertainment features, the print media are primarily geared toward dispensing information and the film and broadcasting media are primarily in the business of providing entertainment.

During the five decades, were newspapers the paragon of enterprising journalism in supplying information and opinion in vital civil liberties areas? Hardly. Like the rest of society, most newspapers were not attuned to the needs and aspirations of disadvantaged groups. They did not adequately report the problems, views, and activities of racial minorities and the poor until the insistent demands of such groups spilled over into behavior that made them "news." It was left to journals of opinion and books to dissect social changes and analyze their meaning for liberty. Nor did newspapers adequately examine the cruel abuses of the criminal justice system or the workings of the educational structure as they affected teacher and student rights—until the victim groups' protests sparked open physical confrontations which became top news stories.

With the exception of a few nationally focused newspapers, civil liberties coverage dwelt on local issues, as it still does. Useful as these exposures of local controversy were, the failure to cover adequately the larger civil liberties scene limited public understanding of how liberties were being denied on a national basis.[18]

Even when abuses of government power which denied individual rights were unveiled, this performance of the press's historic role featured only the surface facts; newspapers did not dig deeply enough into background causes or interpret the forces locked in conflict.[19] Government's refusal to turn over

[18] It is true that when historical pressures made civil liberties a major national news topic, such as the McCarthyite attacks of the fifties, these episodes received increased national coverage. And certain local cases, like the Scopes trial, the Scottsboro case, and General MacArthur's Anacostia Flats attack on the Bonus March of World War I veterans in 1932, were given national attention. But these were dramatic exceptions to the general rule of limited national coverage.

[19] The failure of newspapers to plumb the depths of government's betrayal of individual rights is not a thing of the past. The Washington

information to the press, the vast problem of secrecy inveighed against today in ringing editorials upholding the "public's right to know," was not always as vigorously challenged as it should have been.[20]

But if newspapers were lax in aggressively pursuing these civil liberties–related goals, they nevertheless exercised their freedom to publish, often in a highly sensational manner, prejudicial information about a defendant's background prior to trial.[21] Such publication raised the vexing problem of press responsibility for violating the right of fair trial, an element of the Bill of Rights deserving equal status with freedom of the press.

It would be wrong to call for sanctions against the press for publishing prejudicial information, but it is true that overzealous reporting and editorial irresponsibility have played a large role in whipping up public passion and interfering with the calm and orderly consideration of facts, the heart of the judicial process's search for truth. Whatever praise the press deserves for digging out wrongdoing by public official and private citizen alike should be qualified because of the way such information was presented to the public, including prospective jurors. And the excuse that excesses are the price that must be paid to keep the press free to do its basic reporting job is not sufficient to override its insensitivity to due process —as recognized by the press itself in recent efforts to work out an accommodation with bar associations and judges.

As the inexorable pressures of history shaped the civil liberties situation, the print media were affected by these events

press corps has admitted that hundreds of Washington correspondents neglected their duty in not earlier unearthing the facts of Watergate. If it was not for the *Washington Post's* two reporters, Bob Woodward and Carl Bernstein, the whole affair might never have come to public attention.

[20] Even today, when the press seems so alert to government pressures on its freedom, it is being criticized for not sufficiently using the Freedom of Information Act, which permits groups, including newspapers, to challenge in court a government department's rejection of a request for information.

[21] Radio-TV news reporters and executives must share in this criticism for repeatedly airing such information, especially those employed by the influential medium of television.

and indeed helped to form them. At times in key situations they were strong defenders of civil liberties values, such as in their objections to the frenzied overreaction to the Russian Revolution in the twenties and the Dies Committee and other governmental loyalty inquiries of the thirties. But the tradition of John Peter Zenger and editorial independence was cast off in the xenophobia of the Cold War forties and fifties. Editors and publishers joined the government pack in ferreting out alleged Communists and Communist sympathizers and exposing them to public opprobrium.

The responsibility of the print media in helping to create the McCarthy monster has been amply documented. Hindsight merely adds the observation that the page-one publicity given his wild charges undoubtedly inflamed public feeling and provoked that era's easy acceptance of gross violations of free speech and due process.[22] But it was also the press, a minority at first belatedly joined by others, which published dissenting views and carried the editorial fight to McCarthy. At a time of aggravated national excitement, these efforts at least kept the standards of civil liberties alive in the public mind so they could be reclaimed when a calmer day allowed them again to flourish (a lesson to be learned by civil liberties proponents in the seventies who so utterly despair about current attacks on the Bill of Rights).

If the print media in the middle decades did not always display the courage one might expect from an institution protected by a firm constitutional guarantee, it fulfilled its informing function far better during later civil liberties crises, most particularly those arising from the civil rights revolution and the opposition to the Vietnam war.[23]

---

[22] It is unfortunate that present-day trends toward investigative reporting and personal journalism were not on the newspaper scene in the fifties. This might have resulted in earlier exposure of the evils of McCarthyism. However, the high-pitched tension of the U.S.–Soviet confrontation still would clearly have outweighed any personal deflation of the Wisconsin senator.

[23] The press's consciousness was raised by those two major social developments, but it never fully caught the scope of social change in this decade, especially the *depth* of the counter-culture's feelings. It was left initially to the new, struggling brand of journalism, the "under-

Not because of personal conversion to these causes, but because these movements produced major news, those who controlled the print media at first cautiously opened their pages
to stories and editorial opinion on these great controversies.
Then, caught in the crisis of conscience and the call to personal witness which both these movements created for the
American public, the print media assumed a more affirmative
role and presented a steady flow of news and analyses of these
social conflicts and their consequences. The general atmosphere of expanding personal freedom which civil rights and
anti-war activists symbolized in the sixties even carried over
to the newspaper office. A new and still unsettled relationship
between reporter and editor began to develop, focusing on
reportorial freedom and joint decision-making about the editorial product.

All these changing attitudes produced a fresh tone of editorial independence and awareness of First Amendment values, buttressed in large measure by Spiro Agnew's broadside
attacks on the media and the hard fight over the Pentagon
Papers. Yet serious structural problems remained that imposed
severe limits on the press's informing function.

The rise of suburban newspapers and the creation of new,
community-type magazines was an invigorating step. But this
was offset by the economic realities which caused the number
of daily newspapers to diminish and a number of national
news magazines to cease publication. These developments,
coupled with the cross-ownership of different kinds of media,
posed the ever-present hazard of monopolization of news,
which can stultify public thought and discussion.

The problems of the print media over the five decades in
discharging their responsibility to inform the public did not
overly concern the two other channels of communication,
whose power to influence public thinking was, and still is, so
great.

The motion picture and radio-TV industries, despite some
welcome recent changes, perceived their function to be the

ground" press and campus newspapers, to explain in the face of governmental and educational institutions' pressures the resistance and cyni-
cism of the young to the existing social structure.

presenting of entertainment, not the interpreting of political and social discord. As William Preston, Jr., notes, blandness and fear of controversy were the hallmarks of the product they gave the public in the early decades. So dependent were films and radio-TV upon the mass, common-denominator audience that they chose box office profits over social responsibility.

This abdication of an affirmative duty to explore societal problems was not the only evidence of these media's failure to utilize their special status and power to inform the public about civil liberties values. At times they were directly responsible for vitiating these values, as part of the pack that chewed at the vitals of free speech, free association, and due process. In the cold war forties and fifties, Hollywood's fulsome endorsement of unquestioning super-patriotism, not simply in film content but through employment clearance of "loyal" performers who steered away from unpopular political causes and organizations, was aped by radio-TV moguls. Their Jello-like adherence to constitutional principles strangely overlooked the fact that these guarantees provided the underpinning for the very freedom under which they operated.

Blacklisting was an abject rejection of First Amendment values and exposed the corporate cowardice of the two industries. By bowing to the pressures of the day they effectively destroyed or seriously injured the careers of many people and denied the public the benefit of their creative talent. Blacklisting was also an insult to the intelligence of the American public, by insisting that they judge a film or TV program on the basis of the political attitudes of the writers, actors, and producers responsible for the production, rather than its content and artistic merit. It was basically another example of how raw fear fostered conformity, encouraged escapism, and blocked citizens from exposure to the variety and reality of life, including political and social conflict.

This harsh appraisal of movies and radio-TV is softened by developments in recent years which forced on these media certain departures from their norm. With the more open society forged by the social protest of the sixties, Hollywood's film fare took on a bolder complexion. Taboos on the treatment of sex, violence, divorce and race relations, decreed by the industry's all-powerful code, were lifted. Whether they liked it or not, Americans were exposed to slices of real life that shocked and sometimes horrified them. But credit for the new film wave hardly was due to a suddenly discovered sense of social responsibility on the part of industry leaders. The different Hollywood pictures were more a reaction to new, acceptable modes of social behavior and to the necessity to match the frankness of foreign film imports and the competition of TV. Whatever the reason, and whatever the level of art and creativity—with personal expression free, some productions were good and others bad—films that provoked thought and debate on what is happening in the world were made available to the public.

The march of events also brought about changes in the electronic broadcasting field. In the loyalty-security investigations of the fifties, the all-seeing eye of the TV camera exposed public and private personalities and frequently smashed reputations and careers. But these adverse results were countered by the courageous Edward R. Murrow programs, which laid open the depredations of Senator McCarthy and his cohorts. Murrow's style of personal TV journalism has not been equaled, but his skillful use of television's power to unfold social problems paved the way for later electronic journalists to disclose a host of abuses, such as those brought to light by the rising social awareness of the sixties, and those which continue today.

Yet, despite the magnified growth of TV's power to expose, the extended speech heard as a result of radio open-mike and TV talk-shows, and the increasing public attention given to TV coverage of the news, the overall tendency of the medium was still to feature entertainment and avoid controversy.[24] In this regard, the Federal Communications Commission was rarely the citizen's champion, despite its clear statutory charge

[24] Radio-TV's entertainment function *is* important. The public needs relief from the painful realities of everyday life, which a variety of entertainment provides. The quarrel is with the disproportionate share of time given to these programs and the lack of access by different minorities to their own groups and to the majoritarian public.

to defend the public's interest. Granted its difficult regulatory assignment, walking a tightrope between general overview and control of programing content, the FCC trod lightly on the industry's toes when citizen-consumer demands were made that those granted a license to use the public's airwaves be required to provide better service to the public.

With certain exceptions—as in the forties, when a liberal philosophy prevailed at the Commission, or in the sixties when an occasional maverick like Nicholas Johnson, who really believed that radio-TV can be made to work in the public interest, managed to make his voice heard—the Commission's membership was predominantly industry-oriented. The FCC saw networks and station licensees first as operators of businesses and second as servants of the public. This economic emphasis dominated the entire broadcasting structure and was reflected in FCC decisions. Despite an occasional recognition of the public interest, such as adoption of the Fairness Doctrine, the Commission's protection of the industry's economic status [25] over the years is shown in license awards and renewals, obstacles to discussion of unorthodox issues, and restrictions on innovative communications systems.

There are, however, some heartening signs on the horizon which indicate that libertarians' desire to strengthen the medium's informing role may be at least partially realized. Despite setbacks caused primarily by the lack of adequate long-range financing, educational—or public—television now offers a variety of instruction and cultural programs. The new-style investigative reporting introduced by print journalism, an offshoot of the "muckraking" journalists of the early twentieth century, is being paralleled in radio-TV and offers bright prospects for more intensive presentation of issues. The technological revolution of cable communication, which permits an almost infinite number of wired channels and thus

[25] The officially reported huge profit margin shows that the broadcasting industry quite clearly recognized the economic stakes which dictated network and station decisions on program emphasis and allocation of prime time. According to the FCC's annual reports for the 1966–71 period, television profits totaled $2,795,000,000, and radio profits were $584,000,000. The combined figures represent a 35 percent increase over the five-year period.

breaks the log-jam created by limited spectrum space on the air, could enormously enlarge diversity by opening up vast opportunities for individuals and groups to present their views. And organizations representing different minority interests are learning how to use the governmental process to challenge before the FCC and the courts the right of station operators to keep their licenses when their programing does not conform to the public interest standard set forth in the federal communications law.

Just as the mass media unquestionably were an important force over the half-century in shaping public attitudes toward the content and spirit of civil liberties, another major institution with similar influence was education. It was a veritable battleground of civil liberties strife, not surprising in view of the natural interconnection between liberty and places of formal learning. Wittingly or unwittingly, educational institutions are one of the dominant transmitters of values in society, including the precepts of individual rights. And those frightened souls who blindly struck out against rights as proof of the "excessive personal freedom and permissiveness" in American life saw schools and colleges as carriers of just such a dangerous philosophy which had to be rooted out.

The result was massive and inevitable attacks on education over the decades.[26] The school and college campus had been the arena in which young people, breaking away from home and hearth, could be exposed to different ideas and approaches to life—in politics, economics, religion—and to contact with other kinds of people. So it was natural for those who feared change, especially as world events forced the nation into uncharted and difficult paths, to resent and attack the educational process, the place where new thought and new action occurred.

The drive to extirpate novel and alarming ideologies left its mark on civil liberties. The hunt for subversives, defined as

[26] The fact that one of the American Civil Liberties Union's earliest substantive committees was its Academic Freedom Committee, organized in 1924, suggests the strong assaults mounted against education even in the early part of the half-century.

those who departed from the norm, usually began with books and teachers perceived as the vanguard of the revolution. If one traces the resolutions of American Legion conventions, the Lusk and Rapp-Coudert state legislative investigations of subversives right down to later exposures by the House Un-American Activities Committee, McCarthy, and their local counterparts, the central theme is how "un-American" teachers poisoned and brainwashed the minds of the young. The rash of loyalty oaths in the fifties, explained so fully by John Caughey, was simply a replica of previous periods in which teachers and education were the first targets, and as a result, free expression and association were diminshed.[27]

In the early decades, organized, effective opposition by the educational profession to these maraudings enjoyed limited success. The American Association of University Professors was on the scene, attempting through lengthy, academic-style investigations focused on university violations to blunt the impact of insensitive and often politically inspired legislative and community attacks. But it was often left to individual teachers and their inspired students, backed by the ACLU and ad hoc groups, to openly contest violations of intellectual freedom.

Defense of academic freedom was at first a budding concept, limited to a teacher's right to inquire into truth and express views, not the broader civil liberties values of due process and non-discrimination; and even the narrow definition was not accepted by all sectors of the educational establishment.

Moreover, a definite line was drawn between lower and higher education, with defense of rights applied almost entirely to the former in cases affecting professors, not students, and very occasionally to a campus newspaper defying institutional policy. But at all levels of education the notion of *in*

[27] The pressures exerted were not always based on loyalty and patriotism in the political sense. John Scopes was under fire for his views on evolution; Bertrand Russell's appointment at the City College of New York was cancelled because of his outspoken opinions on sex; and, more recently, long-haired students were harassed because their different appearance was stupidly interpreted as a "clear and present danger" to educational authority.

loco parentis prevailed. Educational institutions were expected by the community to serve as surrogate parents, invoking tight discipline and authority and dispensing learning that would not touch the sensitive nerve of controversial social conflict which might disturb the existing order.

This attitude, with its obvious sacrifice of civil liberties values, was hardly surprising given the very close relationship of public schools and colleges with state legislatures, which, as the community's representatives, parceled out educational funds. Administrators, fearful of budget cuts, were not likely to offend those who held the purse-strings. And since legislatures were predominantly controlled by persons satisfied with the status quo, controversial teachers, departures from standard curriculum, even books challenging existing modes of thought were often the losers in situations in which educational officials pandered to legislators.

Private colleges had a more independent stance, but even their thinking was affected by irate alumni warnings of reduced contributions if a controversial subject was too zealously pursued or a campus personality too strongly defended. Moreover, in the fifties and sixties, as governmental research needs brought huge financial grants to private colleges, the line between public and private institutions faded, and government influence seriously affected, if not compromised, the independence which is the true mark of educational freedom.

It remained for the social unrest of the sixties, powered primarily by the challenge of young people, black and white, to race discrimination, the Vietnam war, and poverty, to produce marked changes in education. Civil liberties principles were tested and broadened in that struggle.

The rioting, violence, and direct disruption of meetings and classrooms on the part of some—but far from all—students soured the general public and political leaders on the student cause and led to repressive measures. But, wrong as such student behavior was, it did, along with the ferment stirred by non-violent student demonstrators, center attention on the need for educational reform.

The whole idea of students as people entitled to exercise rights won acceptance as a result of student rebellion against things as they were. Administrators—some convinced that a more open atmosphere should prevail and that young people should be entrusted with the responsibility for developing campus policies that affect their lives so directly, others bowing to student pressure just to restore peace on campus—did accept changes that brought about a freer climate in colleges and universities, in curriculum, living conditions, and institutional governance.

The drive even extended to secondary schools, where insistence upon such basic rights as non-censorship of newspapers, distribution of political literature, invitations to controversial speakers, no locker searches without a warrant, and fair hearings in disciplinary cases won widening affirmation. Indeed, the emphasis on rights broadened the base of academic freedom in educational institutions. From the original interest in protecting free research and expression by teachers, the notion of academic freedom incorporated due process and equal protection guarantees as well. Utilizing the legal process, students in colleges and secondary schools surprisingly won a number of major court victories. While no nationwide pattern was set, the principle of *in loco parentis* was considerably weakened. And the example set by students provided a lesson for their elders. Professional educational organizations, particularly the large teachers' associations, began to display new vigor in asserting their rights and attacking grievances within their profession.

Although new pressure points developed in the large urban areas beset by racial tension in the schools, civil liberties in the field of education experienced a general upswing. These advances opened wider the doors of freedom for the larger society outside.

Many modern-day religious leaders have despaired over the loss of formal religion's influence in the crush of contemporary pressures. Cataclysmic events which sweep away societal bounds and traditions create alienation and fear that make it difficult for individuals to sustain their religious faith; yet others perceive today's social decay as an invigorating challenge to try to refashion religious institutions. No matter how one evaluates religion's present strength as a force in American life, over the five decades it played a remarkable role on the civil liberties stage.

Major religious leaders lent their names to and were actively involved in the organization of the American Civil Liberties Union in 1920.[28] Over the decades individual clergymen personally intervened in many important cases which dot the civil liberties record: the early defense of dissenters in World War I, the Scopes case, the attack on company-derived injunctions to block labor's organizing efforts, the counterattack against the loyalty-security hysteria, and, of course, the moral crusades against racism and the Vietnam war which so gripped the conscience of America.

But to say that the institution of religion was united in stoutly championing the Bill of Rights would be inaccurate. Indeed, in many instances certain religious groups were responsible for violating the tenets of liberty. Although the lines were not always rigidly drawn, the division was primarily between the Roman Catholic Church and its influential army of lay organizations on the one hand and the Protestant and Jewish faiths on the other, a separation which reflected their differing religious philosophies. The Catholics' tight adherence to authority and discipline led to a distrust of the free mind and spirit, and the liberal Protestant and Jewish view of people emphasized their personal conscience and responsibility.[29]

Three areas exemplify this basic distinction. From the 1920s

[28] Among the founders were a number of clergymen, including William M. Fincke (Presbyterian); John Haynes Holmes (Unitarian); Judah L. Magnes (Reform Judaism); A. J. Muste (Dutch Reformed); John Nevin Sayre (Episcopal); and Bishop Charles D. Williams (Episcopal). Monsignor John Ryan, a liberal Catholic, gave active support in the early years and served on the Union's governing council. The Reverends Ward and Holmes led the Union's board of directors over the first thirty years, Ward as chairman from 1920 to 1940 and Holmes from 1940 to 1950.

[29] The division was not absolute. A substantial part of Protestantism, especially the fundamentalist sects, shared the Roman Catholic belief in tight adherence to authority and discipline, and frequently supported the latter's stand on civil liberties issues. And a liberal Catholic wing, most notably reflected in the weekly magazine *Commonweal*, sought to apply the gospel to matters of conscience and rights.

on, the Roman Catholic Church was in the vanguard of those urging strong loyalty and security measures to protect the nation against "godless Communism." A natural reaction to the triumph of anti-religious Marxist philosophy in the Russian Revolution, the Church feared the spread of Marxism in the United States and committed itself to its domestic extirpation. Loyalty oaths, loyalty investigations, loyalty parades, non-hiring or actual firing of teachers suspected of Communist leanings were all energetically backed by Catholic organizations, capped by the effusive support given Senator McCarthy's maraudings in Washington and his followers at local levels.

On the contrary side, although conservative Protestant leaders joined in the anti-Communist chorus, large numbers of Protestant clergymen discharged their religious fervor in causes espousing social justice, such as protecting the rights of workers in labor-management confrontations and aiding Southern blacks victimized by race discrimination. A number of them, such as Bishop G. Bromley Oxnam of the Methodist Church, who became a target of House Un-American Activities Committee wrath, feared that the panoply of loyalty-security measures were actually (as they were) a device to stifle dissent and to preserve the status quo. This same concern for freedom of political association and freedom of speech was shown by rabbis and by the influential Jewish lay organizations. Before and after Hitler's holocaust, they could easily point to the connection between religious discrimination and the handcuffs placed on First Amendment guarantees.

A second divergence came in an arena of civil liberties struggle which directly challenged the mainstay of the libertarian creed—the rights of individual free expression and intellectual choice. Here the battle to censor books and movies was vigorously waged, not only by Catholic societies such as the Legion of Decency and the Knights of Columbus, but from the pulpit itself. Sunday morning sermons urged parishioners not only to boycott individual films with "evil" content but to punish exhibitors by staying away from the offending movie house for six months or a year. Lists of approved and disapproved books were also handed out for local checking as to their sexual emphasis.

Many of these drives were successful, especially at the corner candy store level, since the owner of a nickel-and-penny business, so susceptible to neighborhood pressures, could ill afford to defy those who supplied an approved label for window display only if the magazines and books within passed muster. Similar prior restraint pressures at a more sophisticated level, but with similar effect, were applied in Hollywood through the industry's code office.

Protestant and Jewish opposition to censorship crusades did not equal the vigor manifested against the loyalty drives to enforce political orthodoxy. These religious leaders understood the connection between freedom of creative expression and a healthy democracy, the antithesis of conformity, and some did criticize the moves to censor. But as certain of the expressions dealt with sex, violence, and the main bugaboo, obscenity, they were less prone to defend materials (and many publicly attacked them) that were felt seriously to undermine morals, especially among the impressionable young.

Whatever disaffection there was on the part of the Protestant and Jewish faiths from anti-censorship campaigns was more than made up for by their patient efforts in a third area, the maintenance of separation of church and state, especially in the crucial sector of education. Here old religious rivalries, going back to Martin Luther's freedom-of-conscience break with Catholicism and to the persecution of Jews over the centuries by religiously dominated governments, came to the fore.

The belief that government should lend its vast power to inculcate religious values in public schools, strengthened in the last two decades by the economic need to shore up the faltering system of parochial education, motivated Catholic insistence on religious observances in public schools and on direct and indirect financial assistance to private education— all in the name of the First Amendment's guarantee of freedom of religion. An equally-determined counter-drive was mounted by major Protestant and Jewish groups to eliminate from public schools such overt religious practices as state-authorized Bible reading, prayers, and religious holiday observances, and to block various legislative devices aimed at obtaining public funds to support religious schools—all in the name of the no-establishment-of-religion clause of the First Amendment. The Protestant-Jewish coalition emerged as victor from the legal battleground, the Supreme Court, whose decisions, overall, favored a clear-cut separation between churches and the state.

The Court's rulings, however, did not end the quarrel. They prompted a new round of struggle, an effort to overturn the prayer and Bible-reading decisions by amending the Constitution. Only repeated counter-campaigns in the sixties and seventies, in which religious forces played a decisive role, defeated various amendment proposals in Congress. Strangely, many Protestant clergy fought to re-introduce religious prayers in the schools, while the Roman Catholic bishops quietly opposed such constitutional amendments.[30]

If the major faiths were not fully united in all these key areas of civil liberties concern, a better, although not complete, record of unity was posted in recent decades in the spheres of race discrimination and the Vietnam war. Beginning with the first stirrings of opposition to racial inequality, the three faiths voiced support of efforts to provide a full measure of human dignity to oppressed minorities; however, practical application of their commitment awaited the conscience-awakening civil rights movement of the sixties, in marches, demonstrations, congressional lobbying, and various economic aid programs.

The nation's obeisance to the Vietnam war as a roadblock to worldwide Communist advance was initially accepted, if not approved, by a majority of clergymen. But as the killings and horror of that war mounted, more individual clergy and finally their official orders joined actively in the street protests and political pressures brought to bear on United States

---

[30] The United States Conference of Bishops in 1973 revised this position, on the ground that a broader constitutional amendment was needed, one that would also include a range of religious practices in the schools. This is not acceptable to prayer-amendment proponents because they fear that such a broad approach is self-defeating.

policy. Indeed, the moral condemnation heaped on the government by religious spokesmen and their orders ultimately helped to hasten the end of the war.

The long course of human history over the centuries records one apparent truth: the past is kin to the present and future. Events of the seventies largely substantiate this aphorism. Once again the weight of societal pressures, built up by a turn to the political right, worked, at least in the pre-Watergate stage,[31] to place civil liberties under great stress. And yet, as in prior periods, there is the paradox that at a time when rights are under severe attack there are also demonstrable gains, mainly the extension of rights to groups of Americans previously seen as second-class citizens not entitled to the liberties and freedoms enjoyed by others.

Lyndon Johnson's Great Society of the sixties was ballyhooed as a harbinger of vast social progress through programs to remove inequities suffered by racial minorities, the poor, and other disadvantaged segments of society. A mood of hope was in the air as new programs took root which had as their base direct assistance to people and enlargement of their rights. An image of concern for rights was projected (although the president's destruction of personal liberties caused by his stubborn continuation of the Vietnam war contradicted this image).

But, as the decade drew to a close—shaken by such shattering incidents as the assassinations of John F. Kennedy, Robert

[31] The startling revelations of Watergate, highlighted by the White House's abrogation of constitutional rights and the rule of law, were a tremendous educational experience for the public. At this writing, in the winter of 1973, it is still too early to determine what the lasting effect will be. But certain positive signs are in the wind. Juries in political dissent cases continue to return not-guilty verdicts; the FBI, under a new director, promises a more even-handed approach in applying its investigative power; radio-TV networks, despite strong presidential criticism, pledge to retain controversial programing; and, in the political sphere a number of police chiefs in major cities who rose to the mayor's seat on a strict law-and-order platform have been defeated for reelection. So, as in the case of the McCarthy-era fifties, it may be that disclosure of abuses of rights will lead to greater respect for libertarian values.

F. Kennedy, and Martin Luther King, Jr.; repeated, high-decible anti-war demonstrations; campus protests which substituted angry physical confrontation for the conventional realm of reasoned debate; rising urban crime rates; and a new civil rights militancy—the majority of citizens turned away from innovative programs that emphasized equality of rights. Instead they opted for calm and no further change, a tough law-and-order stance (in fact a cover for basic prejudice against blacks, other minorities, and the poor, all blamed for creating social unrest), a flight from social responsibility.

The route chosen to achieve this end was the election of Richard M. Nixon, who pledged an administration that would return America to its "basic values," which to both the candidate and the electorate meant not support for constitutional rights but the stand-pat majority's wish to eschew further social experimentation and to cut back on attempted reforms. And the Nixon administration fulfilled its pledge to a great extent by its court appointments, legislative master plan, and maneuvering to dismantle the structure of the Great Society and its institutionalized aid programs. The result was that in many key areas civil liberties was the loser.

Despite the temporary glee occasioned by the Senate's refusal to approve two Nixon appointees who hewed to his conservative line, the Supreme Court has been recast to reflect a generally stiffer attitude toward constitutional rights. Although the Burger Court has not actually overruled any of the libertarian decisions of the Warren Court, it has limited many of them in important aspects.

Incursions have been made into the due process protections previously won for criminal suspects and defendants and into the free speech and association sector, most notably through the 1973 obscenity decisions, which threaten to unleash forces clamoring for new local censorship campaigns. And, perhaps most important, the Court's more conservative stance is being demonstrated by its refusal to accept and rule on cases which might have breathed fresh life into constitutional guarantees. Even the Court's positive decisions curbing capital punishment, voiding anti-abortion laws, and standing firm on church-state separation fail to negate the overall lessening of concern for individual rights in the present Court's decisions.

In the legislative arena, the dire warnings sounded about the 1968 omnibus crime law proved correct. That panacea for "crime in the streets" did little to make citizens more secure, but did much to reduce the protections of the Fourth and Fifth Amendments. The crime law greatly weakened the privilege against self-incrimination by reducing immunity coverage before legislative bodies and grand juries; abuses by grand juries were especially severe, as they coerced witnesses into giving testimony used in government surveillance of peaceful political activity. This same law legitimized illegal searches and seizures by a system of court-approved wiretapping which reversed a thirty-four-year-old federal law prohibiting tapping. The result was that between 1968 and 1971, 1,118,912 conversations involving 77,227 persons were recorded by governmental agencies.

By attacking busing programs, an immediate method of desegregating schools, a majority of members of Congress expressed the public's repudiation of racial integration when brought too close to home. For the first time in two decades the federal government gave up on affirmatively pressing for broadening of rights to blacks and other racial minorities; instead, through the Nixon administration, it led the fight against a central measure to achieve the integration mandated by the Fourteenth Amendment's equal protection clause. Even though anti-busing bills and amendments were turned back, civil rights forces suffered a serious setback. The administration's actions shored up the evasive moves and resistance of those committed to preserving discrimination and segregation by signaling the nation to slow down its efforts to achieve real equality.

If supporters of the president, a diminishing lot in the post-Watergate days of late 1973, pointed to the enlarged budget and increased powers given the Equal Employment Opportunity Commission as evidence of civil rights progress, the record is replete with counter-examples that more than offset the EEOC gain: the active opposition to the legislatively authorized extension of the voting rights law (affecting southern states seeking to circumvent the power of blacks at the ballot box); the Department of Justice's ignoring of complaints by southern blacks that the voting rights statutes were not being enforced; the failure to present to federal grand juries the killing by Mississippi police of the Jackson State students or the slaying of the Orangeburg, South Carolina, students by state troopers; and the disclosure of how the Administration's vaunted "minority capitalism" program was pockmarked by awards to political favorites.

Similarly, the Nixon administration showed its attitude toward social welfare programs by gutting the OEO's legal services program, which had provided an effective right of counsel to poor people, and by abandoning its original family assistance program, which had included substantial right of privacy protections. In the absence of a strong administration push, Congress turned a deaf ear to myriad bills legislating penal reform and the end of the death pealty in federal cases (although in the latter instance the Supreme Court's anti–capital punishment decision removed the sense of urgency about the federal bill). Repeated calls for investigation of the Department of Justice's infringements of justice were never answered.

The Administration's adherence to a social philosophy that was bound to affect individual rights adversely was shown by its callous disregard of those particularly sensitive First Amendment areas of free press, free speech, and free association: the Pentagon Papers ruckus, in which the White House used its power and authority to try to muzzle the press's disclosures; the cloak of "national security" thrown over government agencies to block media efforts to obtain information about government operations; and the parallel use of the "executive privilege" claim, which hampered Congress in obtaining facts that would enable it to discharge its legislative function.

The Nixon-via-Agnew campaign against alleged prejudicial news reporting, followed by the White House crackdown on radio-TV networks for commentary and programs critical of Vietnam military operations, coupled with the government's warning to the media "you do invite the government in" unless better balance is achieved in the print and electronic media— all these, augmented by the Watergate disclosures of the tapping of reporters' phones and the inclusion of journalists on the political enemies lists, symbolized a desire to control the media for administration purposes, a disdain for and contemptuous rejection of the press's role in a democratic society.

In addition, there was the use of grand juries as an instrument to gather political information about radical movements; the indictments of newsmen for refusing to disclose confidential sources; the executive order seeking to expand the powers of the Subversive Activities Control Board (happily now defunct) to enable the attorney general more easily to add names to the "subversive" list (also now formally abolished); the infiltration of political groups by informers who deliberately provoked others to commit crimes; the use of harsh, retaliatory police tactics, all violative of constitutional rights, against those who sought a confrontation with government over Vietnam war policies; government surveillance of political dissidents by means of dossiers and other privacy-invading devices; the creation of a "secret police" unit within the White House to carry out bugging and invasion of private citizens' premises; the czar-like refusal to inform the public of the bombing of Cambodia—the breadth and depth of the administration's assault explain why so many civil libertarians in the 1970s felt that certain of the abuses were so gross that impeachment of the president and his removal from office were essential to the preservation of civil liberties.

Many of these libertarians also fear that this period matches and even exceeds the wrongs of the McCarthyite fifties. This fear is understandable, but there are marked differences between the two eras. Opposition in the fifties to civil liberties violations had to be built in the face of an anti-Communist hysteria that swept the country. As soon as the Nixon administration's attacks were initiated, strong opposition developed, and it is continuing. Group demands for rights, little heard in the fifties, are now loudly voiced, against a better background of public understanding of what civil liberties consist of. Widescale loss of employment because of an individual's political beliefs and associations is not part of the current scene. Nor, unlike the fifties, have government prosecutions of dissenters been successful. This does not mean that the people caught in the net today are unaffected and do not suffer, but that they have a larger degree of public support and can often win vindication.

The current assault on the Bill of Rights is not all Washington-directed, although the mood created by the administration certainly filtered down to lower levels. The tough law-and-order posture in Washington set the tone for restrictive state laws aimed at the drug culture [32] and for drives to reinstitute capital punishment, already successful in twenty-nine states. Attacks on "overpermissiveness," a handy slogan in defense of punitive authoritarianism, fuel campaigns to circumvent the Supreme Court's decision on abortion laws. Crackdowns mount on "freeloading" welfare recipients, including coerced sterilization of young girls and ruthless pruning of welfare rolls based on arbitrary financial criteria rather than standards of human need.

The principle of equal opportunity is scoffed at by new forms of local discrimination, such as the many land zoning arrangements which effectively bar minorities from housing and employment in suburbs to which white industry is fleeing, and the refusal to recognize the responsibility of states to provide equal funds to all school districts so as to redress the imbalance between tax-rich and tax-poor areas.

A new quiet envelops the campus as educational institutions no longer are the site of dramatic social protest, one partial reflection of the repressive political climate. With the Vietnam war regarded as over and the draft ended, and with attacks on racial discrimination focusing more on economics than political action, the student activism previously expressed in speeches and demonstrations is taking on new forms. Com-

---

[32] There is growing agreement that laws punishing use, possession, and even sale of marijuana are overly harsh, and some states have reduced criminal sanctions in this area. However, criminal penalties concerning other drugs have been made much more severe. These penalties raise several questions about violations of due process: plea bargaining, which denies a defendant a chance to disprove guilt; mandatory lengthy sentences (which, among other faults, eliminates a judge's consideration of individual circumstances in a particular case); applying unequal sentences to persons guilty of the same offense; and imposing cruel and unusual punishment for the "crime" of drug addiction, which, in the 1962 *Robinson* case, the Supreme Court said is an illness.

munity projects with tangible goals attract more personal involvement and interest than national political movements which seem removed from the local scene. Progress and growth are measured in terms of immediate personal satisfactions, as general distrust of government and political leadership swells. Moreover, with fewer job opportunities available, the hard economic facts of life have heightened concern with careers and academic performance.

The quietus may not, however, be permanent. The lesson of organized student power was learned in the crucible of the sixties, and this strength could be expressed again when issues crop up that affect students' and teachers' lives directly. One acid test for civil liberties action is being demonstrated now in both higher and lower education, where the financial strains affecting all institutions jeopardize teachers' rights in hiring, firing, and non-renewal of contracts. These exigencies have placed the hallowed principle of tenure under fresh scrutiny, especially in the light of charges that younger, more reform-oriented teachers are being dropped in favor of older teachers less likely to disturb the peace of educational institutions.

The financial crisis also has accelerated demands for unionization of faculties, a unique civil liberties conundrum: how can the right of teachers to organize (freedom of association) be matched with the equally important right of teachers to be free of any imposed restraint or discipline that interferes with intellectual independence (freedom of thought and speech)?

Like that of earlier decades, the civil liberties scene of the seventies is stamped with assaults and challenging questions. But to declare that liberty is under special siege would not be totally accurate. For even before the Watergate period threw new light on the growing repression, there was a rising chorus of dissent and insistence upon rights, and it continues today.

Learning well what civil rights, students, and anti-war protestors realized in the sixties, that each encumbered group must vigorously make its needs known to society, other segments are now asserting demands which include the right to enjoy free speech, due process, and equal treatment. Women, military personnel, prisoners, persons regarded as mentally ill, schoolchildren and juveniles, homosexuals and lesbians have all progressed by forcing society and its institutions to recognize them as just as deserving of rights as others.

Here, as in past civil liberties victories, each forward step is being hacked out of a forest of bias and bitter resistance. As difficult as the present battle is, however, the new protestors attacking ingrained prejudices are also the beneficiaries of prior struggles, including the revival of social conscience in the sixties. This revival brought America face-to-face with the fact that its cherished principles of democracy were not being applied, that large numbers of citizens were denied fundamental rights. This awakening, even if grudgingly accepted, was codified in court decisions and legislation that helped the public to accept some change. It was this broadening of the application of rights to new groups that made today's advances possible and that will shape the direction of future efforts.

Speculation and crystal-ball gazing are not the civil libertarian's occupation. As events force the Bill of Rights barometer up or down, no one can accurately predict how freedom will fare in the years ahead. Even the portents of contemporary events themselves are not that sharply delineated.

In spite of Congress's reassertion of its legitimate function in balancing the power between the executive and the legislative branches, the lines are still to be clearly marked out. Will Congress's insistence on an equal role, springing from dissatisfaction with the Vietnam war and reinforced by the Watergate revelations, result in a permanent shift? Or will some renewed international threat more real than the Vietnam fiasco, or a domestic economic crisis, call for such a strong executive hand that Congress's involvement will once again be downplayed? And even if Congress achieves parity with the executive, will this necessarily improve the state of civil liberties?

Has the full reaction to the Vietnam war's ending been felt yet, with its impact on the economy, the disillusionment of unemployed veterans, and the refusal to consider seriously the amnesty appeal of thousands of Americans whose conscientious dissent subjected them to serious penalties?

Will military influence and preparation for war, now seemingly on the wane, continue to be deemphasized? Or will the threat to liberty inherent in the military-industrial complex be reinforced? And though the draft is ended, will the volunteer military forces breed new problems of equality and justice?

Has the complete impact of Watergate been measured, in terms of its actual effects on the future operations of government and on citizens' faith and participation in the political system?

These questions, and many more, have consequences for the future state of liberty which now are not distinctly defined. But we can be sure of one thing, that problems which have always beset libertarians will remain. Efforts to censor books, magazines, and films will continue. Academic freedom will be strained by drives to remove troublesome teachers who defy the community norms. Religious bodies will devise new ways to finance parochial education with government help. The mass media will need aid in defending themselves against governmental pressure, but also will require non-governmental prodding to achieve higher levels of information service to the public. To make real and more meaningful the rights of equality won through legislation and court decisions,[33] the quality of criminal justice must be improved, especially by curbing police mistreatment and changing the callousness of lower courts.

And, as has been true for all other decades, new issues will arise in the seventies requiring those concerned about defense of liberty to reexamine and reinterpret their definition of personal rights.[34]

[33] Implementation should focus on attacking those disabilities which flow from discriminatory treatment—non-employment, for example, merely because of arrest records, less-than-honorable discharges from the armed forces, or inadequate job training.

[34] It was comparatively simple to define issues fifty years ago, when civil liberties problems took the form of police interference in peaceful meetings, censorship of library books, the firing of a teacher because of a political belief. Such problems still exist. However, there are questions today, reflecting the rapid pace of social change and the kinds of social pressures confronting society, which are more complex. For example, should a nation committed to the principle of equal treatment for

How to apply the new zone of civil liberty, the right of privacy, by reining in technology's power to surveil, record, and disseminate the details of a person's life, accentuated by the large size of modern society; yet unloosening that power for positive purposes, such as creating new channels of communication on cable television that could increase and diversify the flow of information and opinion to the public?

Whether civil liberties can be exercised if such vital conditions of life as adequate education, employment opportunity, and health care are not enjoyed by every person; and as a concomitant, whether control of the environment, with its obvious connection to the humanitarian concept of the quality of life, comes within the orbit of the Bill of Rights?

Will the idea of individual rights and personal merit, the core of the libertarian's constitutional faith, be submerged by the need to provide equality for groups of people victimized by racial and ethnic discrimination?

Does the power exercised by private corporations over the lives and liberty of millions of people, often paralleling the power of government itself, make such private organizations a proper target for libertarian attack?

Will science, which promises such great human benefits, ride roughshod over individual rights in research and treatment and thus dehumanize those it seeks to serve?

Can rights in the United States survive, and thrive, if the same rights are not enjoyed by people in other nations?

These are only a few of the frontier questions which will be posed in the decade of the seventies. And, as in each decade, those who cherish liberty will have to find their own answers, answers which are illuminated by the struggles of the past but whose contours must always be shaped anew by men and women of courage and conviction who love liberty and freedom and will strive to defend them.

The dips and rises of the half-century struggle to defend and widen the bounds of civil liberties, more fully described

everyone allow groups like the American Indians, which undeniably have been victimized by whites, to opt out of the white society and follow their own tribal standards of justice, when those standards are less protective of rights than the United States Constitution?

in the preceding chapters, leave unanswered this question: how can today's challenges, more formidable than ever, be met? Do those who value both the letter and the spirit of the Bill of Rights possess the capacity and know-how to throw back the new attacks and to carve out still another niche of progress?

At first glance there are grounds for optimism. The civil liberties movement is no longer the handful of intellectuals and social reformers who organized the American Civil Liberties Union five decades ago. With more than 275,000 current members, and an annual growth of 20,000; with organized groups in 400 communities in all 50 states; with 5,000 cooperating attorneys and an additional 3,000 persons involved in the daily operations of a large national organization, there is good basis for the claim of the ACLU that "eternal vigilance is the price of liberty," and that it will be maintained.

Of equal significance is the fact that the ACLU no longer possesses a near-monopoly in the civil liberties business. Other organizations, with a less comprehensive view of civil liberties than the ACLU and a concentration on special group problems, vigorously press their interpretations of liberty before courts, legislatures, and the public. Many national social and professional organizations, now sensing the tight connection between their objectives and preservation of the open society, are showing a keener awareness of civil liberties and are willing to join coalitions on particular issues.

Young people see in the securing of specific rights one way of beginning to deal with government's and society's refusal to make basic changes. "Client groups" of all kinds—the poor, women, students, military personnel—by their insistence that society pay heed to their grievances are articulate exponents of the proposition that civil liberties standards be observed for everyone. Abuses of individual rights in highly publicized controversies, such as the Watergate revelations, pinpoint for the public the nature of civil liberties and their importance. Even government itself, while always the chief source of civil liberties infringement, displays an understanding of, if not respect for, individual rights in particular situations.[35]

[35] In the earliest stages of the Watergate investigation, the Nixon administration endorsed the ACLU's letter to the Senate committee urging

The technique of legal challenge, honed over fifty years, has evolved into a fine art, and court calendars are clogged with cases raising both traditional and frontier issues. The social activism of the sixties has generated intense interest in the use of law as a mechanism for change, as reflected in the revision of law schools' curricula and the desire of many graduates to eschew higher-paying corporate law positions for a more personally satisfying community-service practice.[36] One of the most interesting litigational developments has been the shift in emphasis from (though not abandonment of) planned, key test cases which seek to vindicate a civil liberties principle via a Supreme Court decision, to a multiplicity of cases at lower court levels aimed at forcing police, prosecutors, and other government officials to adhere to the high court's rulings.

These positive signposts should not leave libertarians with the notion that they can rest on past laurels or rely on the interest and energy of new advocates of the Bill of Rights. The ebb and flow of civil liberties over fifty years belies any relaxation of vigilance. Moreover, vigorous effort is needed in two vital spheres which have not always received the same attention as the legal arena—the relatively untouched areas of legislative lobbying and public education.

The change in the composition of the Supreme Court makes plain that, at least for the foreseeable future, the high court cannot be relied upon, as in past decades, to be the paladin of civil liberties. Legal challenges, of course, should continue and undoubtedly will form a large part of civil liberties defense. But it no longer is advisable to wait and then try to reverse the inroads made by Congress, state legislatures, and even city councils by turning to the nine justices in Washington. A more

that a code of fair procedures be adopted for witnesses. The late FBI director, J. Edgar Hoover, a favorite target of libertarians, was quoted as being concerned that the White House plan to plug so-called security leaks by secret surveillance and disruptive tactics would draw fire from the "civil liberties people."

[36] A quasi-legal development which shows promise for the strengthening of rights is the creative idea of lay advocates before administrative bodies of government. Although not lawyers, such advocates are trained in laws and regulations affecting housing, consumer rights, and schools, and may prove to be an effective tool in speeding up and improving the quality of defense of rights.

organized and sophisticated effort is necessary to deal with violations of individual rights at the legislative point of origin.

Such activity requires attorneys whose training makes them skilled in the interstices of legislative language and parliamentary stratagems. It also calls for civil liberties practitioners to develop a better informed citizenry, committed to the principles of liberty, knowledgeable about current issues, and willing to translate conviction and information into social action—be it letters to legislators, governors, and mayors; personal at-home lobbying; organizational resolutions; rallies, marches, or other active but peaceful demonstrations of concern for rights.

The technique of citizens' lobbies must be kept free of political partisanship, both in tone and substance, which is not always easy in the heat of political combat. Those who organize such lobbies much understand that while they are political in the best sense of the word, by working with the government process, their effectiveness can be blunted if legislators, press, and public come to believe that their client is not the Bill of Rights but a particular political figure or the substantive cause of the group whose rights are being championed. It will take skill, shrewdness, and maturity to organize legislative campaigns casting a positive civil liberties image, without the political hyperbole and "wheeling and dealing" that jeopardize libertarians' bona fides.

These lobbies cannot succeed unless more heed is paid to ways and means of educating Americans about civil liberties and their contemporary significance. In the flush of legal and legislative action, admittedly an excellent educational method of dramatizing real-life examples of denied freedoms, insufficient time, money, and energy have been devoted to educational ventures.

The need for such increased effort has been shown by polls and special studies over the years which illustrated Americans' ignorance of their freedoms, be it the refusal of July 4 picnickers to sign a newspaper reporter's petition (actually a statement supporting the Bill of Rights) or high school students' rejection of fundamental precepts of the Constitution.[37]

---

[37] In 1957, H. H. Remmers and D. H. Radler published in *The American Teenager* (Indianapolis, Ind.: Bobbs-Merrill) the results of their

Happily, more recent attitudinal polls covering the general population show a definite upward turn, as more people become educated and aware of authentic violation of rights, such as occurred in the McCarthy era and the stormy protests of the sixties.

But still young people are insufficiently informed about what freedom really is. As late as December, 1973, in a report on young Americans' attitudes toward social affairs, the National Assessment of Educational Progress, a project of the Education Commission of the States, declared that while youth generally support the concepts of freedom of speech, religion, and assembly, a large number qualify their support in specific instances. The findings show that nearly 25 percent of young adults in the nation are unaware that the U.S. Constitution contains a statement protecting an individual's civil rights; that 25 percent of thirteen-year-olds would support the idea that citizens under the voting age should not be allowed to write to government officials or express their political views publicly; that about 40 percent of seventeen-year-olds contend that a person who does not believe in God should not hold public office; and that a similar number are also opposed to picketing both of rock festivals and police stations.

Are formal institutions which, despite their reduced influence, still touch the lives of millions of Americans, trying to fill the gap? With rare exceptions, their leaders do little to explain why it is so important for citizens to join in defense of liberty, or to have their organizations affirmatively act in situations which involve the essence of free speech, due process, and equality. Most culpable is the institution of education, the target of student activism precisely because it has so miserably failed to let students enjoy the liberties proclaimed in civics and social studies textbooks as the precious heritage of the nation. Until recently awakened by student demands for seventeen-year Purdue University polls of high school students' social attitudes. As reported in 1958 in *Scientific American*, "more than half believed that censorship of books, magazines, newspapers, radio, and TV is all right. More than half believed that the FBI and local police should be allowed to use wiretapping at will, that police should be permitted to use 'the third degree,' that people who refuse to testify against themselves should be forced to do so."

recognition of rights, elementary and most secondary schools, fearful of stirring local controversy, skirted the reality of current civil liberties conflict. Instead, the lessons of liberty were taught mainly through backward-looking references to hoary historical episodes.

The bankruptcy of the educational system in this key area of citizen education may in large measure explain the results of a Harris Poll conducted in the early seventies which parallels the NAEP report. As reported by Louis Harris in his book *The Anguish of Change*,[38] there are "some enormous gaps between the protestations of freedom in principle among our people, and their patent willingness to scrap freedom in specific instances. Out of eighteen basic guarantees laid down in the Bill of Rights, the public would willingly violate a majority of eleven. . . ." Harris cited these results: although by a 91 percent to 5 percent margin Americans believed "every citizen has the right to express any opinion he wants to," a majority of 67 percent to 22 percent favored outlawing "organizations which preach the violent overthrow of the government." Similarly, by 86 percent to 7 percent, most people backed the right of the accused "to question witnesses against him," but by 50 percent to 32 percent the public also supported allowing "FBI agents to testify in criminal cases without cross-examinations." A sizable majority, 79 percent to 11 percent, supported the right to reasonable and not excessive bail, but by 57 percent to 31 percent a majority favored the idea that "criminals rearrested a second time be held without bail."

There are a few signs of welcome change on the educational horizon. The American Bar Association's Special Committee on Youth Education for Citizenship, organized in the wake of student violence in the sixties to develop a better understanding of the legal process, is working with educators to develop curricula and teaching projects which stress human rights under law. The California-based Constitutional Rights Foundation is now broadening its structure and fashioning a national program for teachers and students, weaving major civil liberties conflict situations into the regular educational process.

[38] Louis Harris, *The Anguish of Change* (New York: Norton, 1973), pp. 278–79.

Approximately 175 other local projects bearing on a deeper understanding of the rule of law are now underway.

High school debate competitions across the country include civil liberties topics. Some educational films on civil liberties, but still far too few, are available for schools.[39] Here and there, in-service teacher training courses in civil liberties are conducted. The ACLU and other civil liberties groups circulate "know your rights" handbooks and other literature, and provide speakers for college and high school clubs.

But all of these formal efforts barely scratch the surface and will not succeed unless students have personal experience with the specifics of liberty, real student self-government, freedom of debate and publication, and respect for due process in school governance.

The fact that many Americans still lack real knowledge and understanding of civil liberties, and seem willing to forego their freedoms when governmental authority conjures up the specter of peril, proves how little these threads of liberty have been woven into our educational fabric. It also clearly illuminates the challenge of increased educational labors which faces the civil liberties movement as the nation approaches its bicentennial anniversary in 1976.

Special programs in schools, religious institutions, the mass media, and professional societies, devoted to improving public comprehension of civil liberties, would be an obvious gain. This affirmation of libertarian values would strengthen public adherence to the Bill of Rights, especially if such programs focused on the universality of rights, that civil liberties belong to all people—rich and poor, black, brown, and white—regardless of their station in life.

But such programs are no substitute for the lessons of lib-

---

[39] But television at home is a far greater educational force for young people. Educational TV programs for the young have dealt with brotherhood and equality concepts, but rarely touch on First Amendment and due process values. Even more could be accomplished if these values were woven into the commercial TV programs which attract young audiences. Some programs are beginning to treat civil liberties problems, but more is needed to offset the harm done on other programs such as "Dragnet," or "The FBI," which, in their idolatry of police, frequently ignore the rights of suspects.

erty taught by the everyday reality of people striving to achieve freedom. Citizens will be reminded of liberty's content and meaning by new episodes of social controversy involving free speech, due process, and equal treatment, even if the sparks thrown off by confrontation politics result.[40] The success of powerless groups to weld alliances could also bring the issue of rights back into the mainstream of political thinking, not an easy task given the conservative pressures of the day.

All these factors will bring to the fore those ingredients of civil liberties struggle which have marked the scene over five decades: personal courage, commitment to liberty, and perseverance. The triumphs of great personal courage occur not too frequently in our history, but they do happen, as witness the success of Martin Luther King, Jr., and his followers in moving the heart of a nation.[41] If citizens, looking for fuller life meaning and clear values in the midst of confusion, mistrust, and alienation can, in a maturing experience, release the inner springs of courage; if they can act on the words of a wise journalist, Elmer Davis, who asserted, in the despairing fifties, "But we were born free"; or the advice of a respected jurist, Learned Hand, who said that "liberty lies in the hearts

[40] It is ironic that such confrontations, which frequently involve denial of rights, can pave the way for increased respect or rights, as was illustrated in the contest between young people and governmental authority in the sixties. This is true not only of conflict between groups and the government, but conflict caused by disastrous events involving individuals. The emotions discharged by the assassinations of the Kennedys and of Martin Luther King, Jr., undoubtedly helped to propel new civil rights legislation through the Congress. This public reaction to the killings raises the question of whether the legislative victories would have been scored in the absence of such shocking violence, and whether the public really wanted the legislation or approved it as a guilt reaction to the murders.

[41] The existence of other reasons compelling social change cannot be discounted. The civil rights advances were aided enormously by previous court decisions, World War II's end of the colonial era, and the emerging demand for independence and freedom by subjugated peoples abroad. Yet all these evidences of "an idea whose time had come" would have been insufficient if the personal courage of Dr. King had not been exercised in the face of tremendous opposition.

of men and women; when it dies there, no constitution, no law, no court can save it"; then our practices can match our pledges, civil liberties can be preserved, and the further quest for freedom continued.

INDEX

343